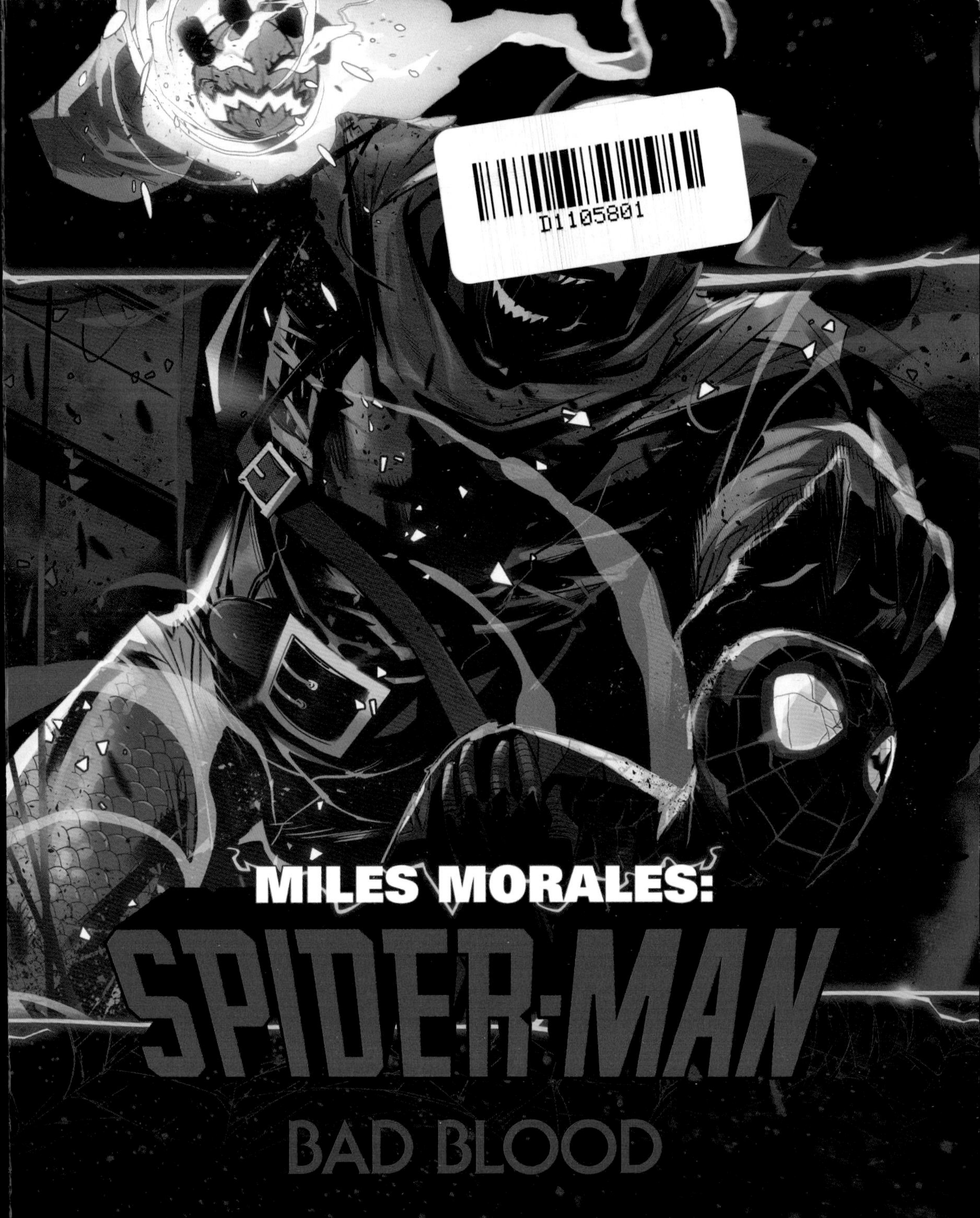

MILES MORALES: SPIDER-MAN

BAD BLOOD

Years ago, high school student MILES MORALES was bitten by a genetically altered spider and gained incredible arachnid-like abilities: the proportional speed, strength, and agility of a spider, adhesive fingers and toes, the power to direct a bioelectric charge like a sting, to camouflage himself to the point of invisibility, and to detect approaching danger using his precognitive "Spider-Sense." He hid these abilities at first, until a hero inspired him to use them to try to make the world more just. HE IS…

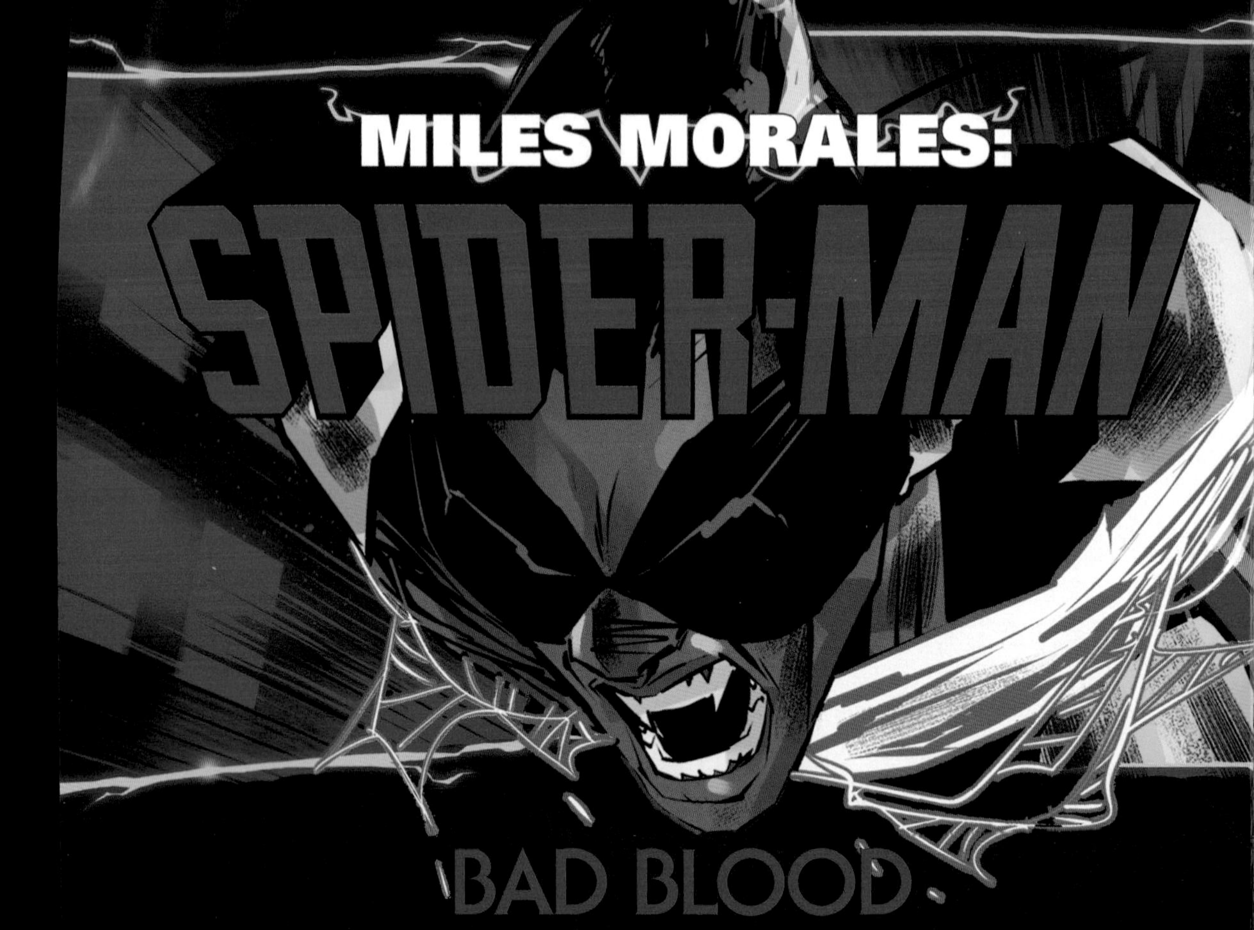
MILES MORALES:
SPIDER-MAN
BAD BLOOD

Miles has had a heck of a time lately. After super villain RABBLE learned Spidey's secret identity and destroyed the Morales family home, Miles, Jeff, Rio and Billie moved to an apartment in a new neighborhood. Before they could even get settled, Spider-Man battled CARNAGE when CLETUS KASADY returned to threaten all of NYC.

Though Carnage was defeated and Miles' powers are growing, Spider-Man still faces grave threats — like the city's anti-super-hero task force, the CAPE KILLERS, led by AGENT GAO — who's put a target on Miles' back. It's only a matter of time before Gao tries to bring Spidey in.

And there's always another errant power-hungry, hyper-violent super villain Spider-Man needs to deal with.

MILES MORALES: SPIDER-MAN BY CODY ZIGLAR VOL. 2 — BAD BLOOD. Contains material originally published in magazine form as MILES MORALES: SPIDER-MAN (2022) #8-12. First printing 2023. ISBN 978-1-302-94853-5. Published by MARVEL WORLDWIDE, INC., a subsidiary of MARVEL ENTERTAINMENT, LLC. OFFICE OF PUBLICATION: 1290 Avenue of the Americas, New York, NY 10104. **Printed in the U.S.A.** KEVIN FEIGE, Chief Creative Officer; DAN BUCKLEY, President, Marvel Entertainment; DAVID BOGART, Associate Publisher & SVP of Talent Affairs; TOM BREVOORT, VP, Executive Editor; NICK LOWE, Executive Editor, VP of Content, Digital Publishing; DAVID GABRIEL, VP of Print & Digital Publishing; SVEN LARSEN, VP of Licensed Publishing; MARK ANNUNZIATO, VP of Planning & Forecasting; JEFF YOUNGQUIST, VP of Production & Special Projects; ALEX MORALES, Director of Publishing Operations; DAN EDINGTON, Director of Editorial Operations; RICKEY PURDIN, Director of Talent Relations; JENNIFER GRÜNWALD, Director of Production & Special Projects; SUSAN CRESPI, Production Manager; STAN LEE, Chairman Emeritus. For information regarding advertising in Marvel Comics or on Marvel.com, please contact Vit DeBellis, Custom Solutions & Integrated Advertising Manager, at vdebellis@marvel.com. For Marvel subscription inquiries, please call 888-511-5480. **Manufactured between 12/8/2023 and 1/16/2024 by SEAWAY PRINTING, GREEN BAY, WI, USA.**

10 9 8 7 6 5 4 3 2 1

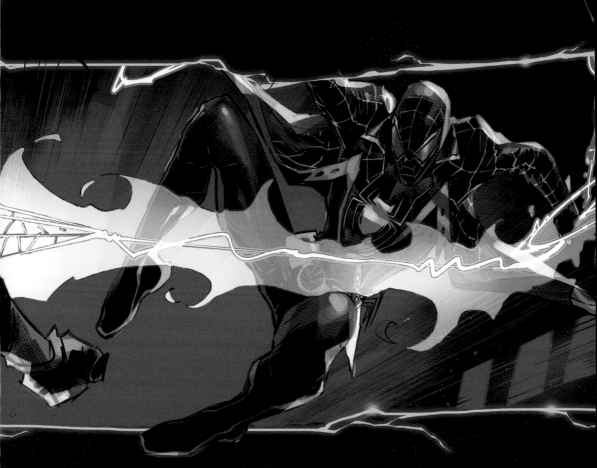

CODY ZIGLAR WRITER

FEDERICO VICENTINI (#8-9), **FEDERICO SABBATINI** (#9-10),
PARTHA PRATIM (#10, #12) & **FEDERICA MANCIN** (#11) ARTISTS

BRYAN VALENZA COLOR ARTIST

VC's **CLAYTON COWLES** (#8), VC's **CORY PETIT** (#9-10, #12) &
VC's **JOE CARAMAGNA** (#11) LETTERERS

DIKE RUAN & **ALEJANDRO SÁNCHEZ** (#9-10),
FEDERICO VICENTINI & **ALEJANDRO SÁNCHEZ** (#11) AND
FEDERICO VICENTINI & **RICHARD ISANOVE** (#12) COVER ARTISTS

KAEDEN McGAHEY ASSISTANT EDITOR   **TOM GRONEMAN** EDITOR

NICK LOWE EXECUTIVE EDITOR

SPIDER-MAN CREATED BY STAN LEE AND STEVE DITKO

DANIEL KIRCHHOFFER COLLECTION EDITOR ◈ LISA MONTALBANO ASSOCIATE MANAGER, TALENT RELATIONS
JENNIFER GRÜNWALD DIRECTOR, PRODUCTION & SPECIAL PROJECTS ◈ JEFF YOUNGQUIST VP PRODUCTION & SPECIAL PROJECTS
STACIE ZUCKER BOOK DESIGNER ◈ ADAM DEL RE MANAGER & SENIOR DESIGNER ◈ JAY BOWEN LEAD DESIGNER
DAVID GABRIEL SVP PRINT, SALES & MARKETING ◈ C.B. CEBULSKI EDITOR IN CHIEF

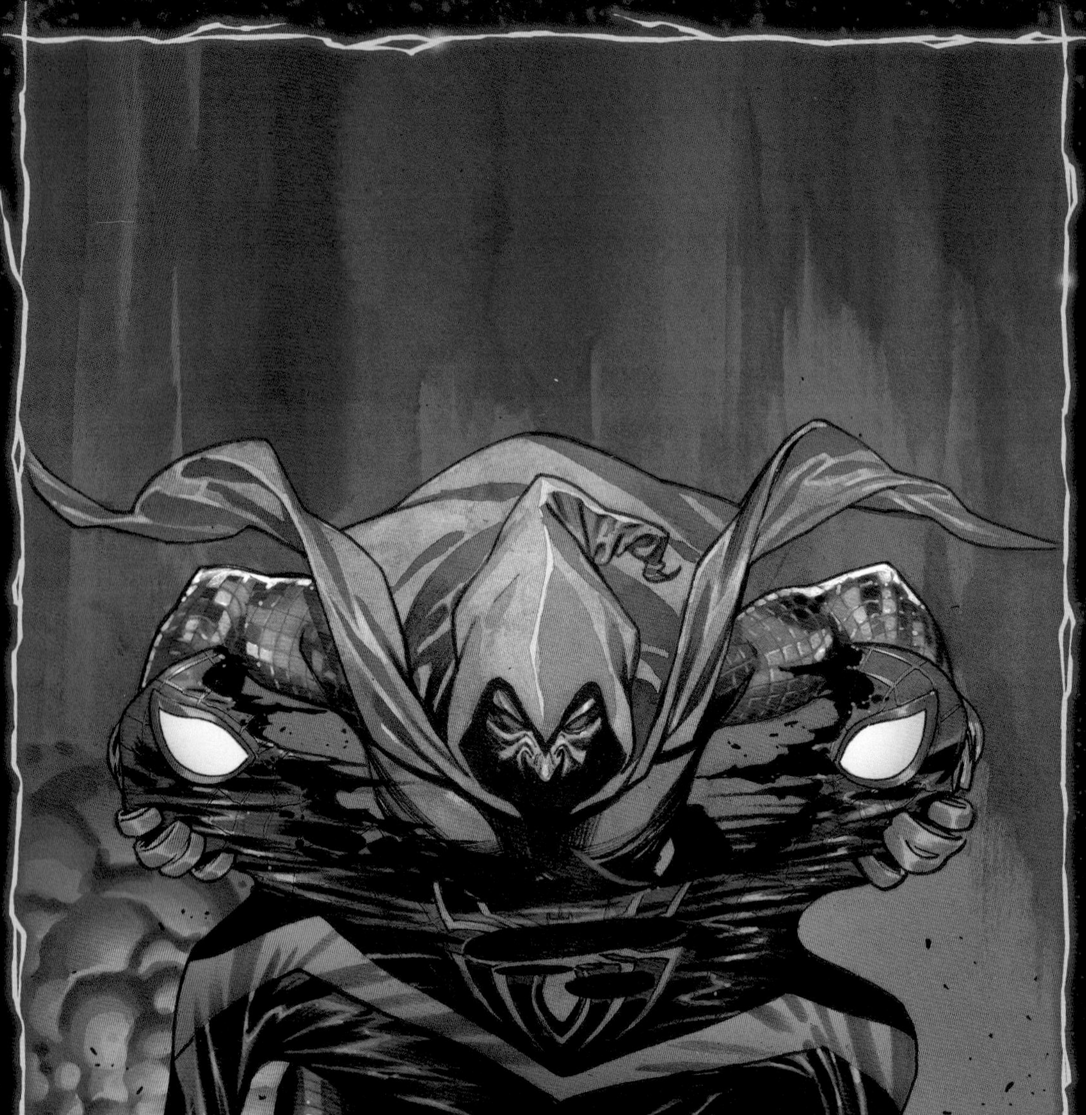

8

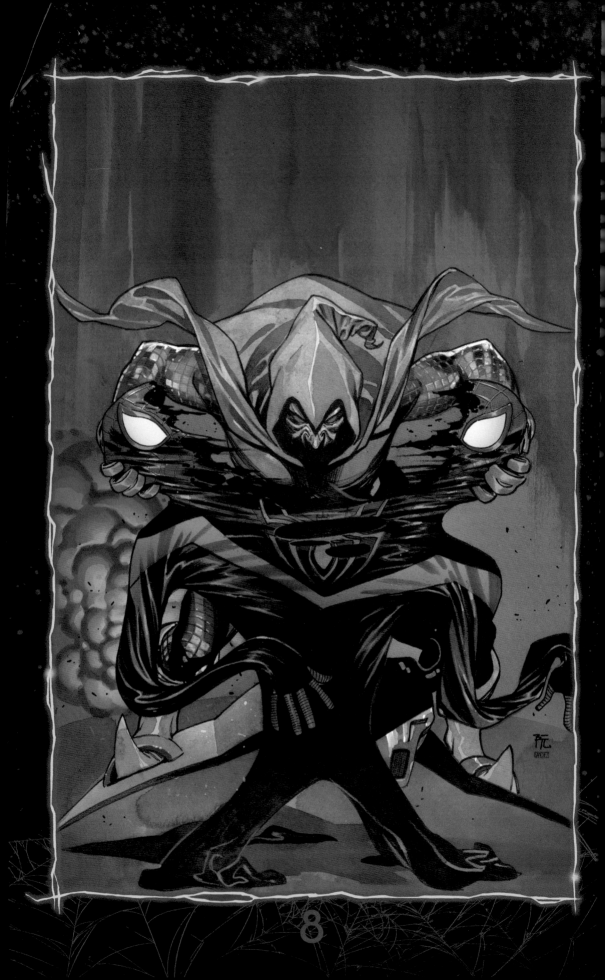

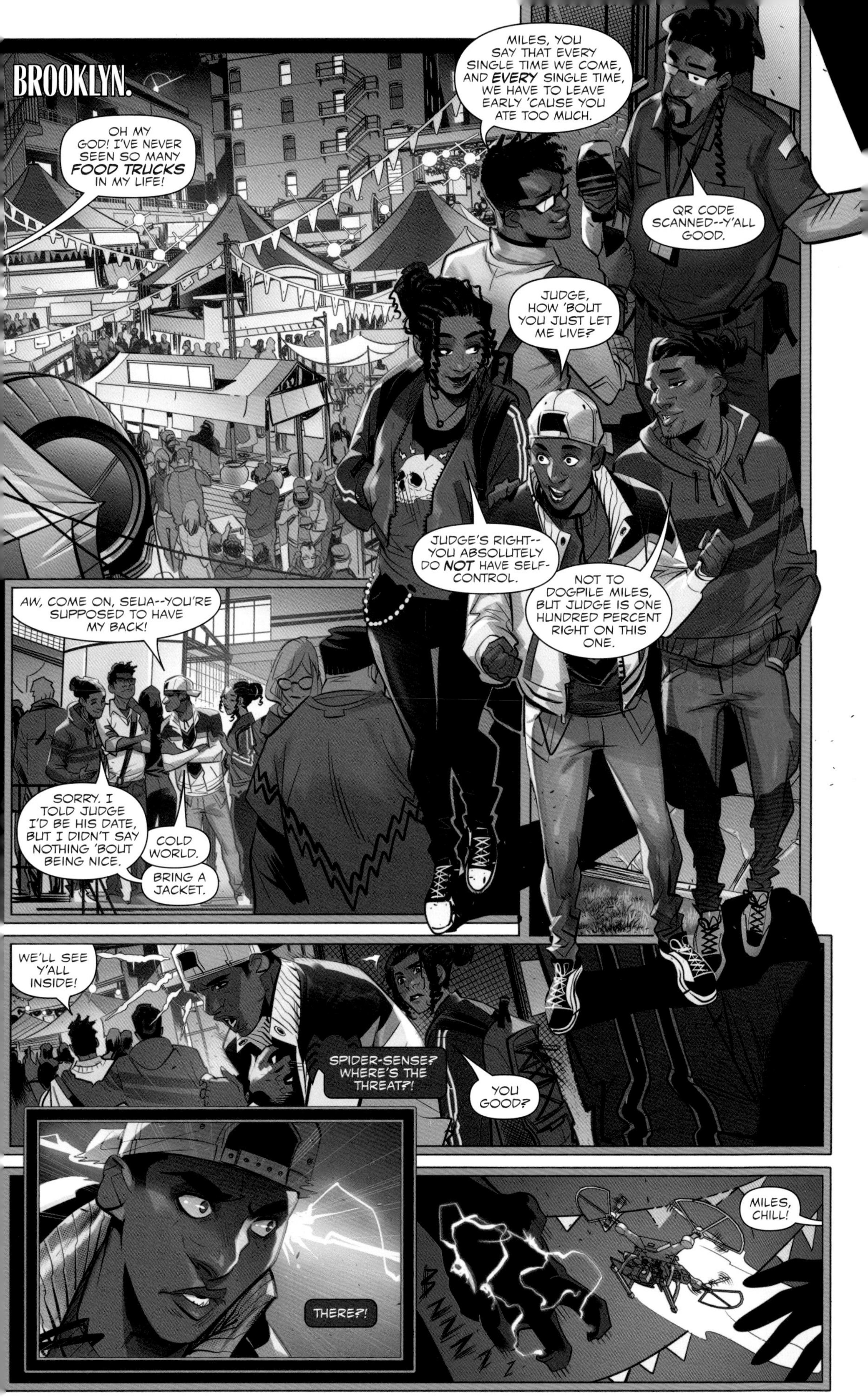
BROOKLYN.
OH MY GOD! I'VE NEVER SEEN SO MANY FOOD TRUCKS IN MY LIFE!
MILES, YOU SAY THAT EVERY SINGLE TIME WE COME, AND EVERY SINGLE TIME, WE HAVE TO LEAVE EARLY 'CAUSE YOU ATE TOO MUCH.
QR CODE SCANNED--Y'ALL GOOD.
JUDGE, HOW 'BOUT YOU JUST LET ME LIVE?
JUDGE'S RIGHT--YOU ABSOLUTELY DO NOT HAVE SELF-CONTROL.
NOT TO DOGPILE MILES, BUT JUDGE IS ONE HUNDRED PERCENT RIGHT ON THIS ONE.
AW, COME ON, SELIA--YOU'RE SUPPOSED TO HAVE MY BACK!
SORRY. I TOLD JUDGE I'D BE HIS DATE, BUT I DIDN'T SAY NOTHING 'BOUT BEING NICE.
COLD WORLD.
BRING A JACKET.
WE'LL SEE Y'ALL INSIDE!
SPIDER-SENSE? WHERE'S THE THREAT?!
YOU GOOD?
THERE?!
MILES, CHILL!

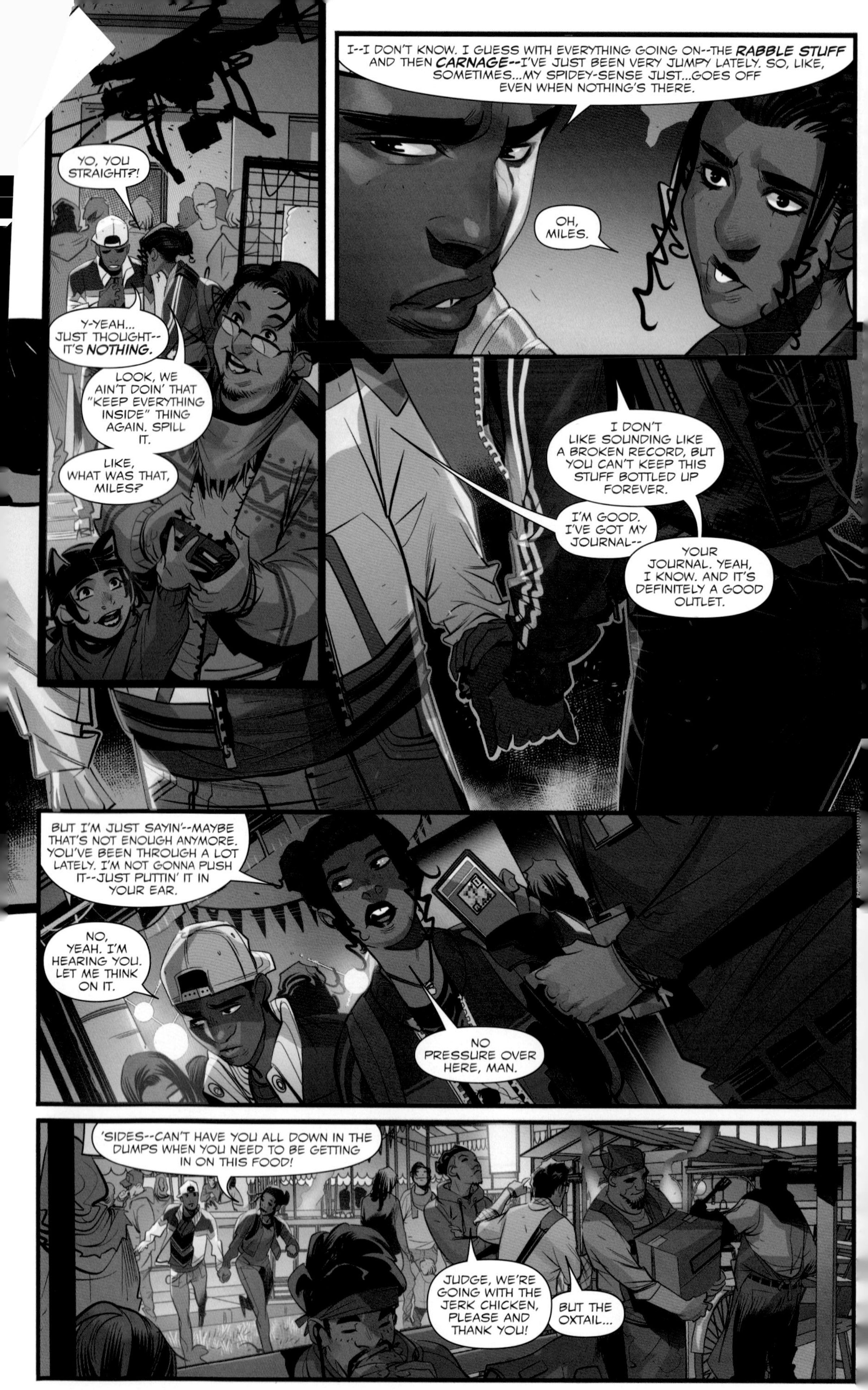
YO, YOU STRAIGHT?!
Y-YEAH... JUST THOUGHT-- IT'S **NOTHING.**
LOOK, WE AIN'T DOIN' THAT "KEEP EVERYTHING INSIDE" THING AGAIN. SPILL IT.
LIKE, WHAT WAS THAT, MILES?
I--I DON'T KNOW. I GUESS WITH EVERYTHING GOING ON--THE ***RABBLE STUFF*** AND THEN ***CARNAGE***--I'VE JUST BEEN VERY JUMPY LATELY. SO, LIKE, SOMETIMES...MY SPIDEY-SENSE JUST...GOES OFF EVEN WHEN NOTHING'S THERE.
OH, MILES.
I DON'T LIKE SOUNDING LIKE A BROKEN RECORD, BUT YOU CAN'T KEEP THIS STUFF BOTTLED UP FOREVER.
I'M GOOD. I'VE GOT MY JOURNAL--
YOUR JOURNAL. YEAH, I KNOW. AND IT'S DEFINITELY A GOOD OUTLET.
BUT I'M JUST SAYIN'--MAYBE THAT'S NOT ENOUGH ANYMORE. YOU'VE BEEN THROUGH A LOT LATELY. I'M NOT GONNA PUSH IT--JUST PUTTIN' IT IN YOUR EAR.
NO, YEAH. I'M HEARING YOU. LET ME THINK ON IT.
NO PRESSURE OVER HERE, MAN.
'SIDES--CAN'T HAVE YOU ALL DOWN IN THE DUMPS WHEN YOU NEED TO BE GETTING IN ON THIS FOOD!
JUDGE, WE'RE GOING WITH THE JERK CHICKEN, PLEASE AND THANK YOU!
BUT THE OXTAIL...

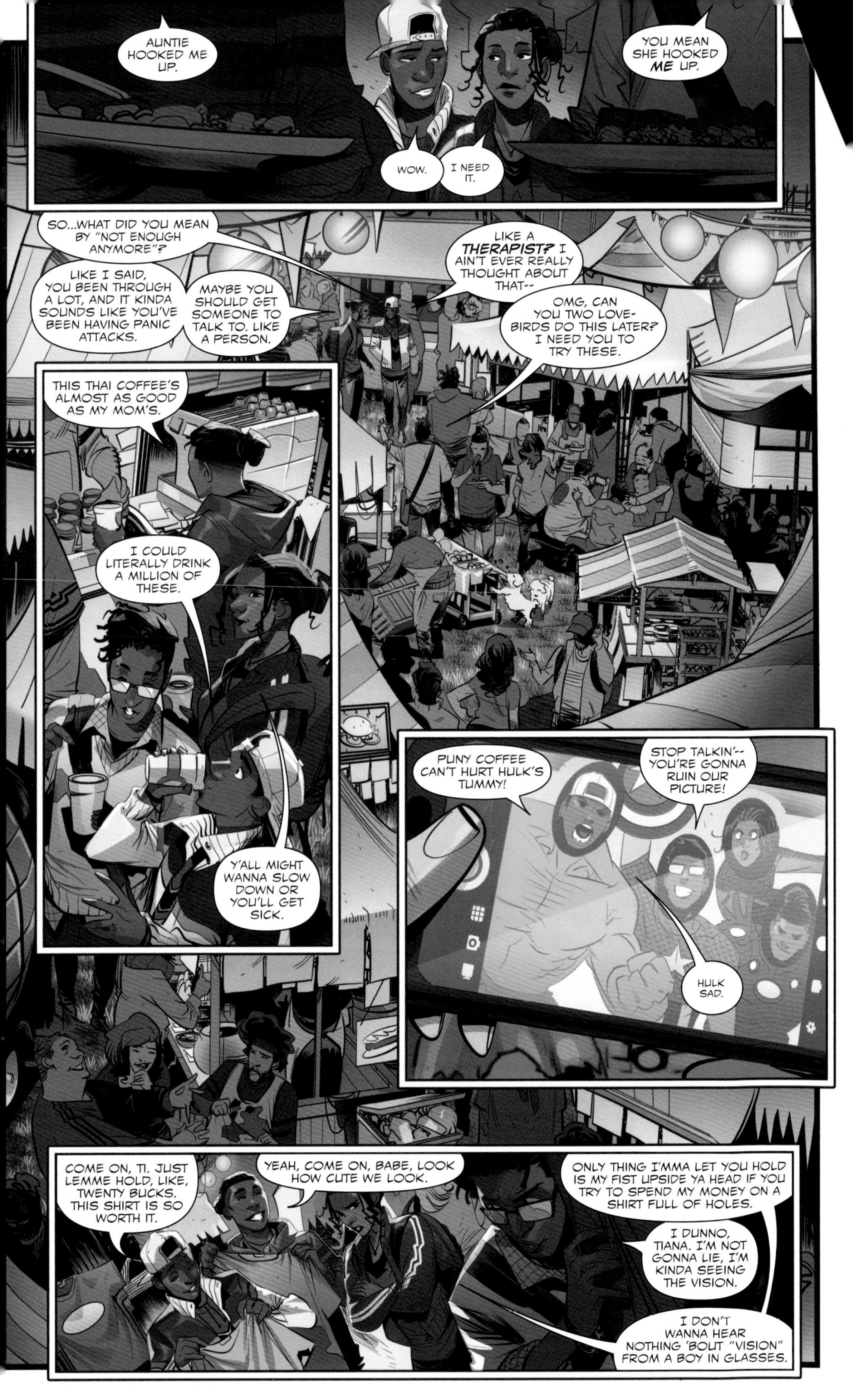
AUNTIE HOOKED ME UP.
YOU MEAN SHE HOOKED ME UP.
WOW.
I NEED IT.
SO...WHAT DID YOU MEAN BY "NOT ENOUGH ANYMORE"?
LIKE I SAID, YOU BEEN THROUGH A LOT, AND IT KINDA SOUNDS LIKE YOU'VE BEEN HAVING PANIC ATTACKS.
MAYBE YOU SHOULD GET SOMEONE TO TALK TO. LIKE A PERSON.
LIKE A THERAPIST? I AIN'T EVER REALLY THOUGHT ABOUT THAT--
OMG, CAN YOU TWO LOVE-BIRDS DO THIS LATER? I NEED YOU TO TRY THESE.
THIS THAI COFFEE'S ALMOST AS GOOD AS MY MOM'S.
I COULD LITERALLY DRINK A MILLION OF THESE.
Y'ALL MIGHT WANNA SLOW DOWN OR YOU'LL GET SICK.
PUNY COFFEE CAN'T HURT HULK'S TUMMY!
STOP TALKIN'-- YOU'RE GONNA RUIN OUR PICTURE!
HULK SAD.
COME ON, TI. JUST LEMME HOLD, LIKE, TWENTY BUCKS. THIS SHIRT IS SO WORTH IT.
YEAH, COME ON, BABE, LOOK HOW CUTE WE LOOK.
ONLY THING I'MMA LET YOU HOLD IS MY FIST UPSIDE YA HEAD IF YOU TRY TO SPEND MY MONEY ON A SHIRT FULL OF HOLES.
I DUNNO, TIANA. I'M NOT GONNA LIE, I'M KINDA SEEING THE VISION.
I DON'T WANNA HEAR NOTHING 'BOUT "VISION" FROM A BOY IN GLASSES.

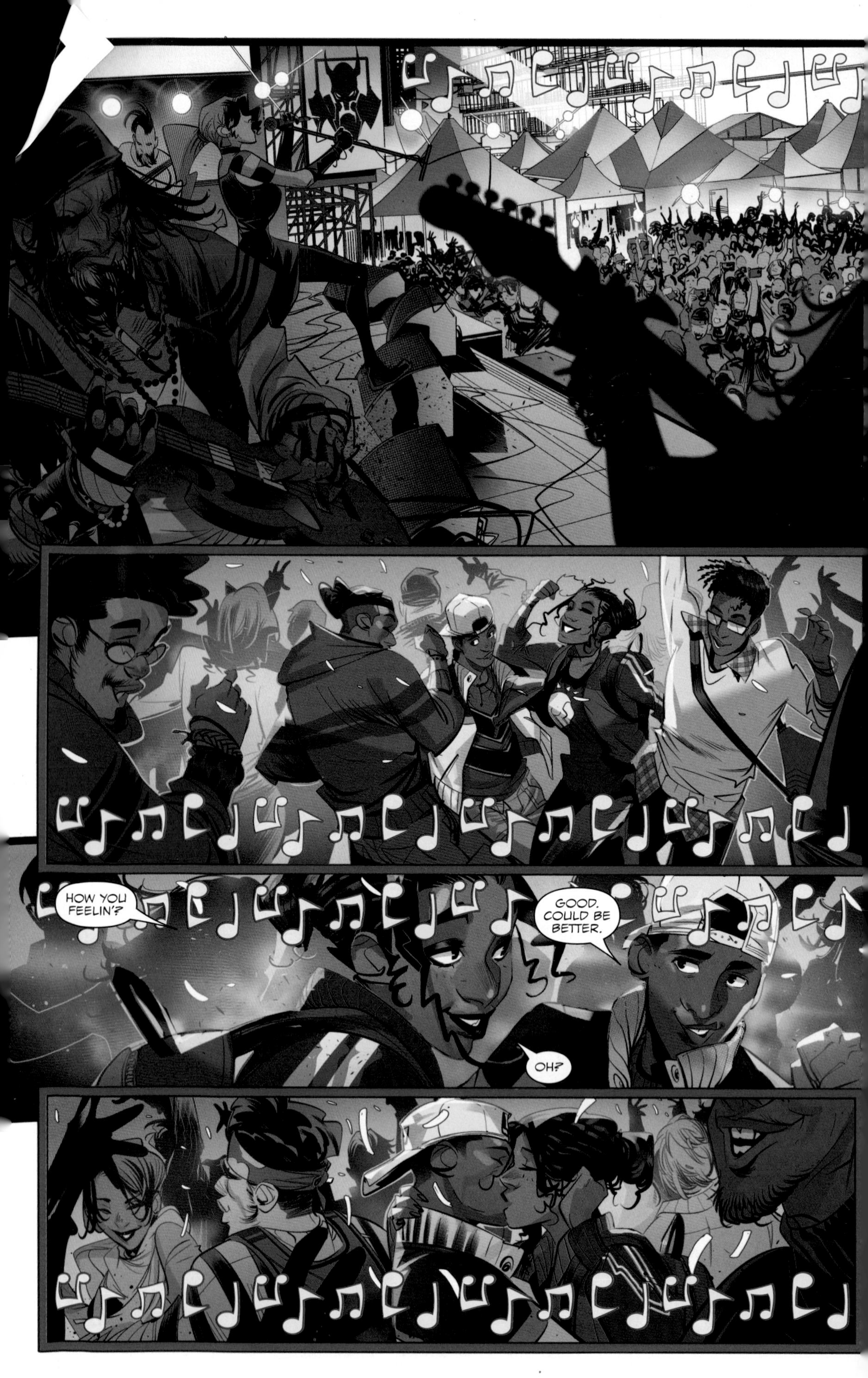

HOW YOU FEELIN'?
GOOD. COULD BE BETTER.
OH?

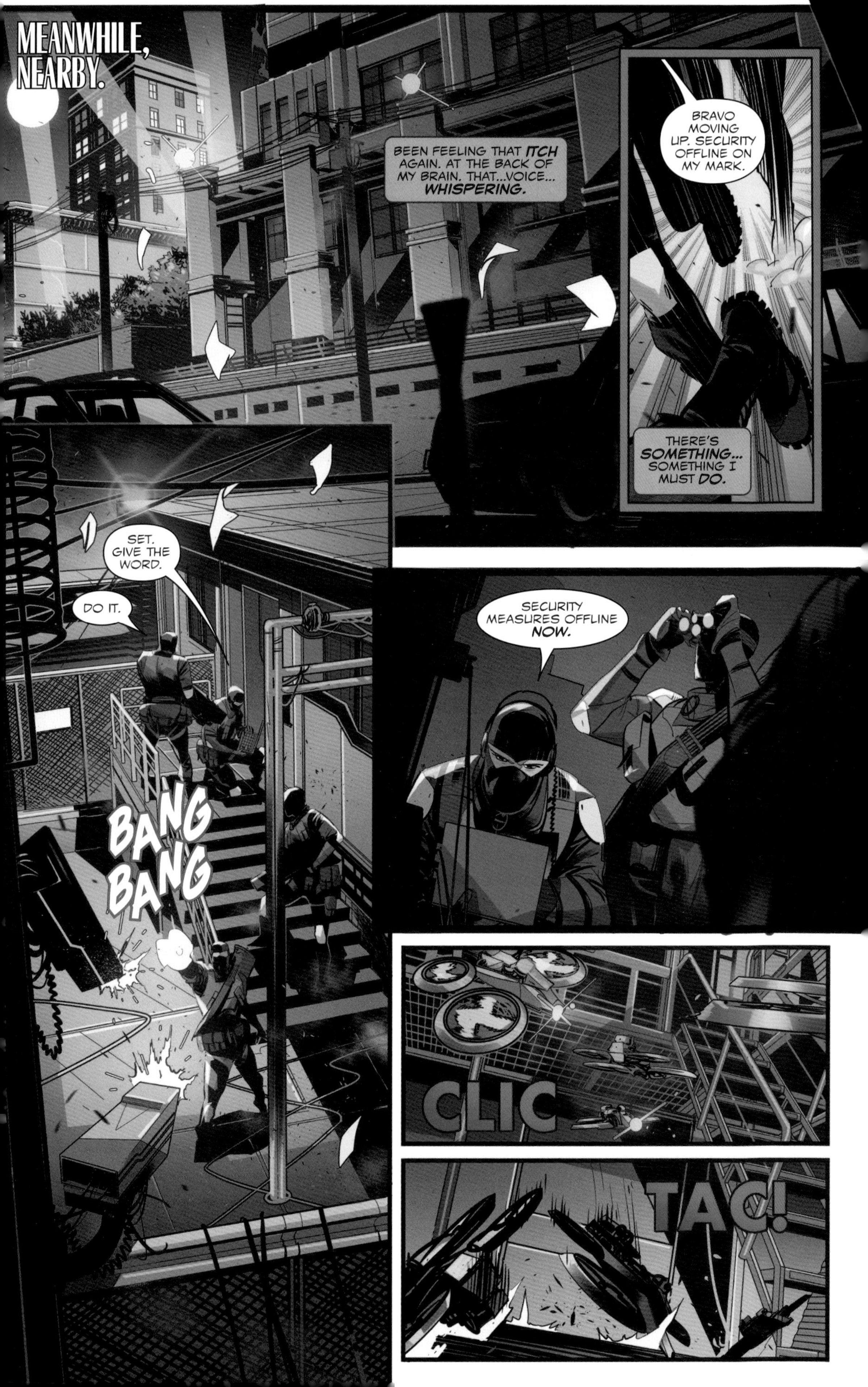
MEANWHILE, NEARBY.
BEEN FEELING THAT ITCH AGAIN. AT THE BACK OF MY BRAIN. THAT...VOICE... WHISPERING.
BRAVO MOVING UP. SECURITY OFFLINE ON MY MARK.
THERE'S SOMETHING... SOMETHING I MUST DO.
SET. GIVE THE WORD.
DO IT.
BANG BANG
SECURITY MEASURES OFFLINE NOW.
CLIC
TAC!

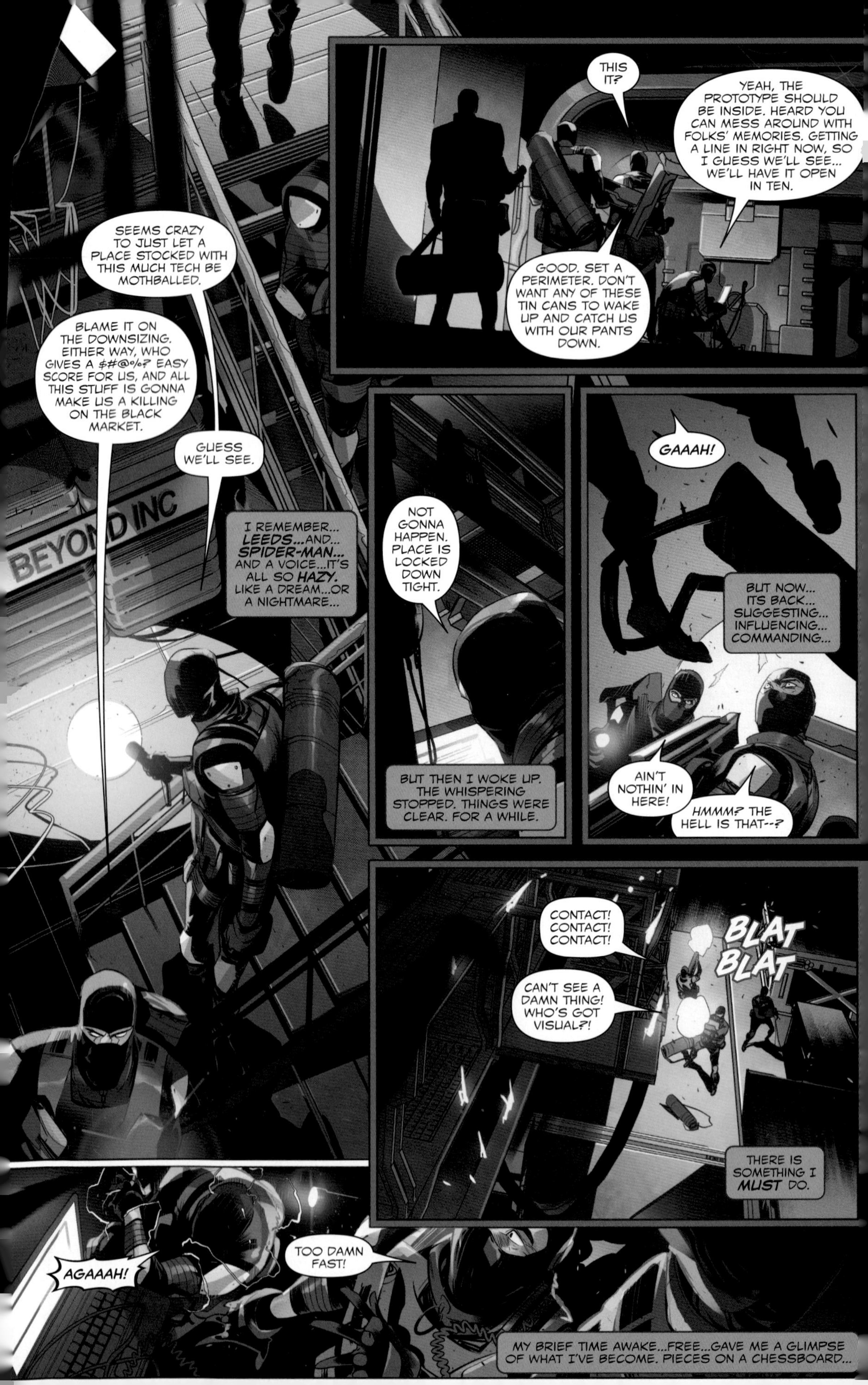
SEEMS CRAZY TO JUST LET A PLACE STOCKED WITH THIS MUCH TECH BE MOTHBALLED.
BLAME IT ON THE DOWNSIZING. EITHER WAY, WHO GIVES A $#@%? EASY SCORE FOR US, AND ALL THIS STUFF IS GONNA MAKE US A KILLING ON THE BLACK MARKET.
GUESS WE'LL SEE.
BEYOND INC
I REMEMBER... LEEDS...AND... SPIDER-MAN... AND A VOICE...IT'S ALL SO HAZY. LIKE A DREAM...OR A NIGHTMARE...
THIS IT?
YEAH, THE PROTOTYPE SHOULD BE INSIDE. HEARD YOU CAN MESS AROUND WITH FOLKS' MEMORIES. GETTING A LINE IN RIGHT NOW, SO I GUESS WE'LL SEE... WE'LL HAVE IT OPEN IN TEN.
GOOD. SET A PERIMETER. DON'T WANT ANY OF THESE TIN CANS TO WAKE UP AND CATCH US WITH OUR PANTS DOWN.
NOT GONNA HAPPEN. PLACE IS LOCKED DOWN TIGHT.
BUT THEN I WOKE UP. THE WHISPERING STOPPED. THINGS WERE CLEAR. FOR A WHILE.
GAAAH!
BUT NOW... ITS BACK... SUGGESTING... INFLUENCING... COMMANDING...
AIN'T NOTHIN' IN HERE!
HMMM? THE HELL IS THAT--?
CONTACT! CONTACT! CONTACT!
CAN'T SEE A DAMN THING! WHO'S GOT VISUAL?!
BLAT BLAT
THERE IS SOMETHING I MUST DO.
AGAAAH!
TOO DAMN FAST!
MY BRIEF TIME AWAKE...FREE...GAVE ME A GLIMPSE OF WHAT I'VE BECOME. PIECES ON A CHESSBOARD...

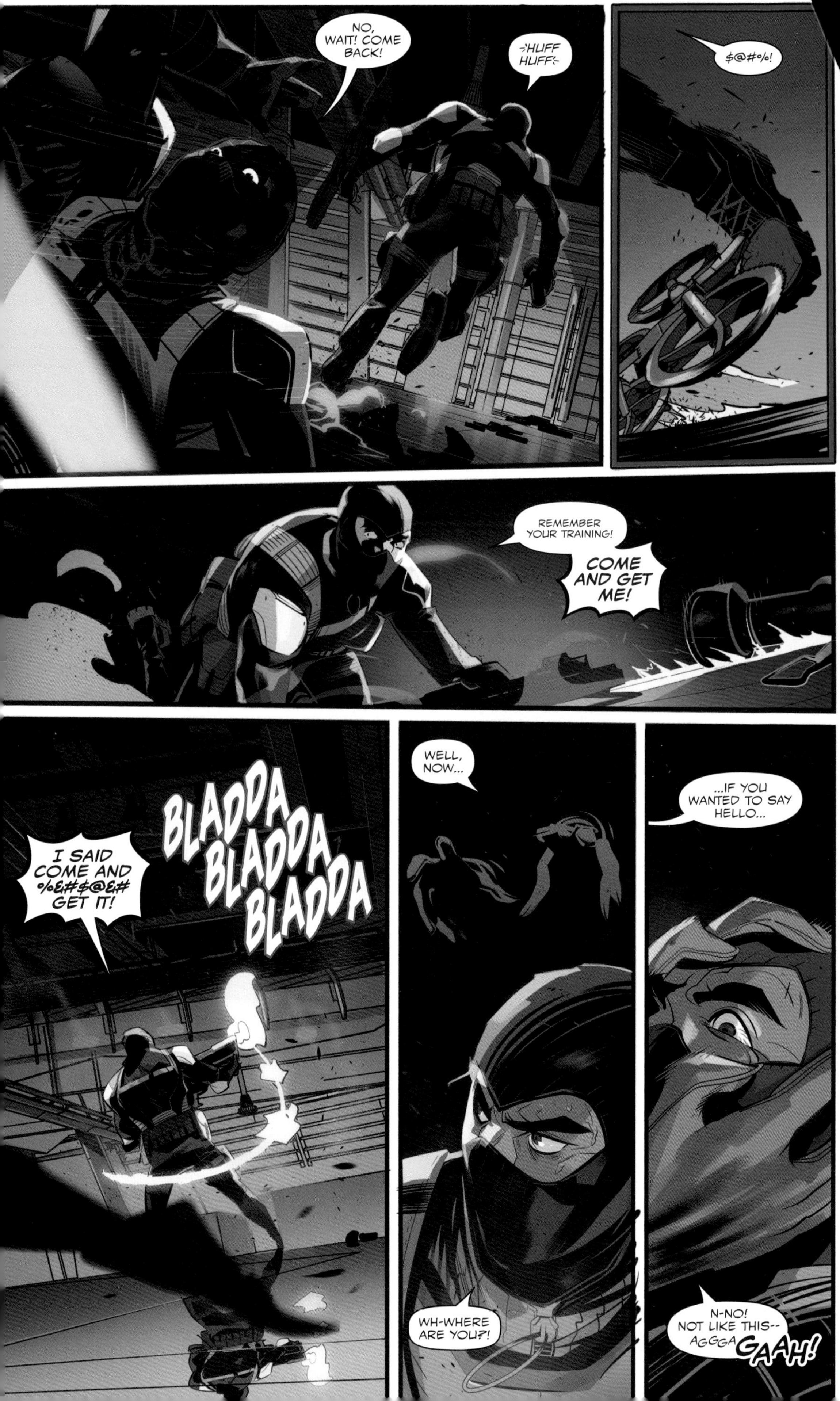
NO, WAIT! COME BACK!
HUFF HUFF
$@#%!
REMEMBER YOUR TRAINING!
COME AND GET ME!
BLADDA BLADDA BLADDA
I SAID COME AND %&#$@&# GET IT!
WELL, NOW...
WH-WHERE ARE YOU?!
...IF YOU WANTED TO SAY HELLO...
N-NO! NOT LIKE THIS-- AGGGA GAAH!

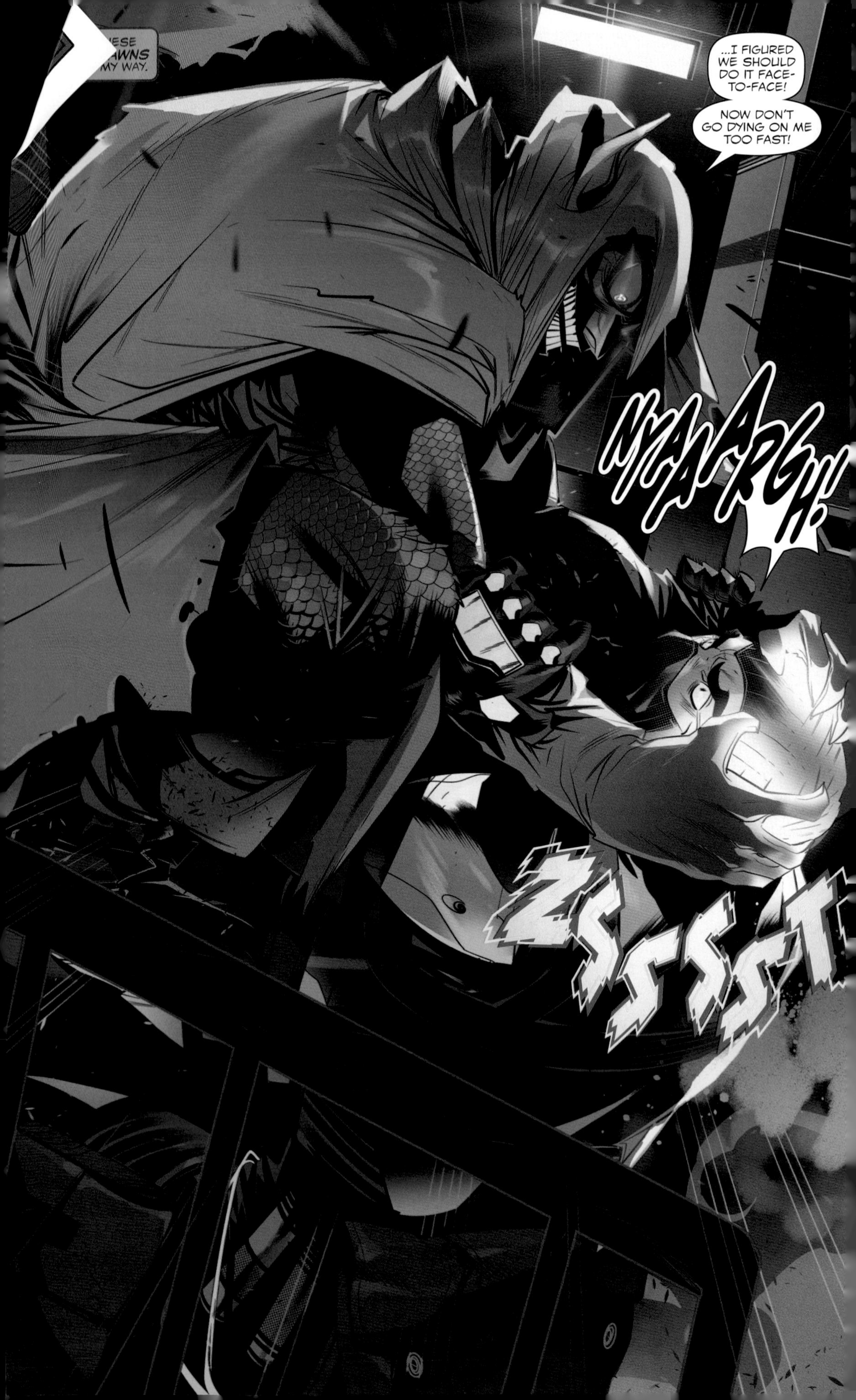
ESE AWNS MY WAY.
...I FIGURED WE SHOULD DO IT FACE-TO-FACE!
NOW DON'T GO DYING ON ME TOO FAST!
NYAAARGH!
ZSSST

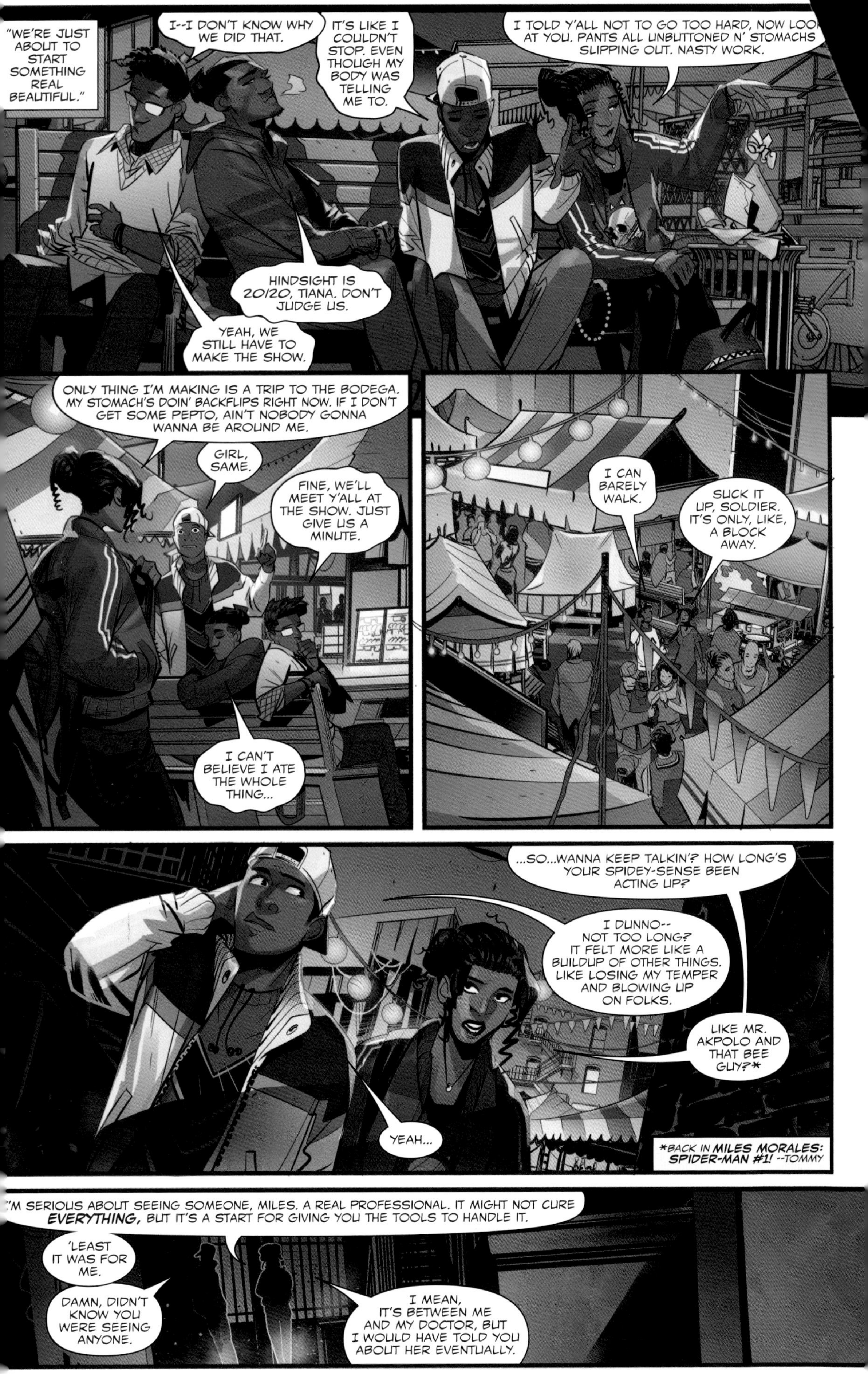
"WE'RE JUST ABOUT TO START SOMETHING REAL BEAUTIFUL."
I--I DON'T KNOW WHY WE DID THAT.
IT'S LIKE I COULDN'T STOP. EVEN THOUGH MY BODY WAS TELLING ME TO.
I TOLD Y'ALL NOT TO GO TOO HARD, NOW LOOK AT YOU. PANTS ALL UNBUTTONED N' STOMACHS SLIPPING OUT. NASTY WORK.
HINDSIGHT IS 20/20, TIANA. DON'T JUDGE US.
YEAH, WE STILL HAVE TO MAKE THE SHOW.
ONLY THING I'M MAKING IS A TRIP TO THE BODEGA. MY STOMACH'S DOIN' BACKFLIPS RIGHT NOW. IF I DON'T GET SOME PEPTO, AIN'T NOBODY GONNA WANNA BE AROUND ME.
GIRL, SAME.
FINE, WE'LL MEET Y'ALL AT THE SHOW. JUST GIVE US A MINUTE.
I CAN'T BELIEVE I ATE THE WHOLE THING...
I CAN BARELY WALK.
SUCK IT UP, SOLDIER. IT'S ONLY, LIKE, A BLOCK AWAY.
...SO...WANNA KEEP TALKIN'? HOW LONG'S YOUR SPIDEY-SENSE BEEN ACTING UP?
I DUNNO-- NOT TOO LONG? IT FELT MORE LIKE A BUILDUP OF OTHER THINGS. LIKE LOSING MY TEMPER AND BLOWING UP ON FOLKS.
LIKE MR. AKPOLO AND THAT BEE GUY?*
YEAH...
*BACK IN MILES MORALES: SPIDER-MAN #1! --TOMMY
I'M SERIOUS ABOUT SEEING SOMEONE, MILES. A REAL PROFESSIONAL. IT MIGHT NOT CURE EVERYTHING, BUT IT'S A START FOR GIVING YOU THE TOOLS TO HANDLE IT.
'LEAST IT WAS FOR ME.
DAMN, DIDN'T KNOW YOU WERE SEEING ANYONE.
I MEAN, IT'S BETWEEN ME AND MY DOCTOR, BUT I WOULD HAVE TOLD YOU ABOUT HER EVENTUALLY.

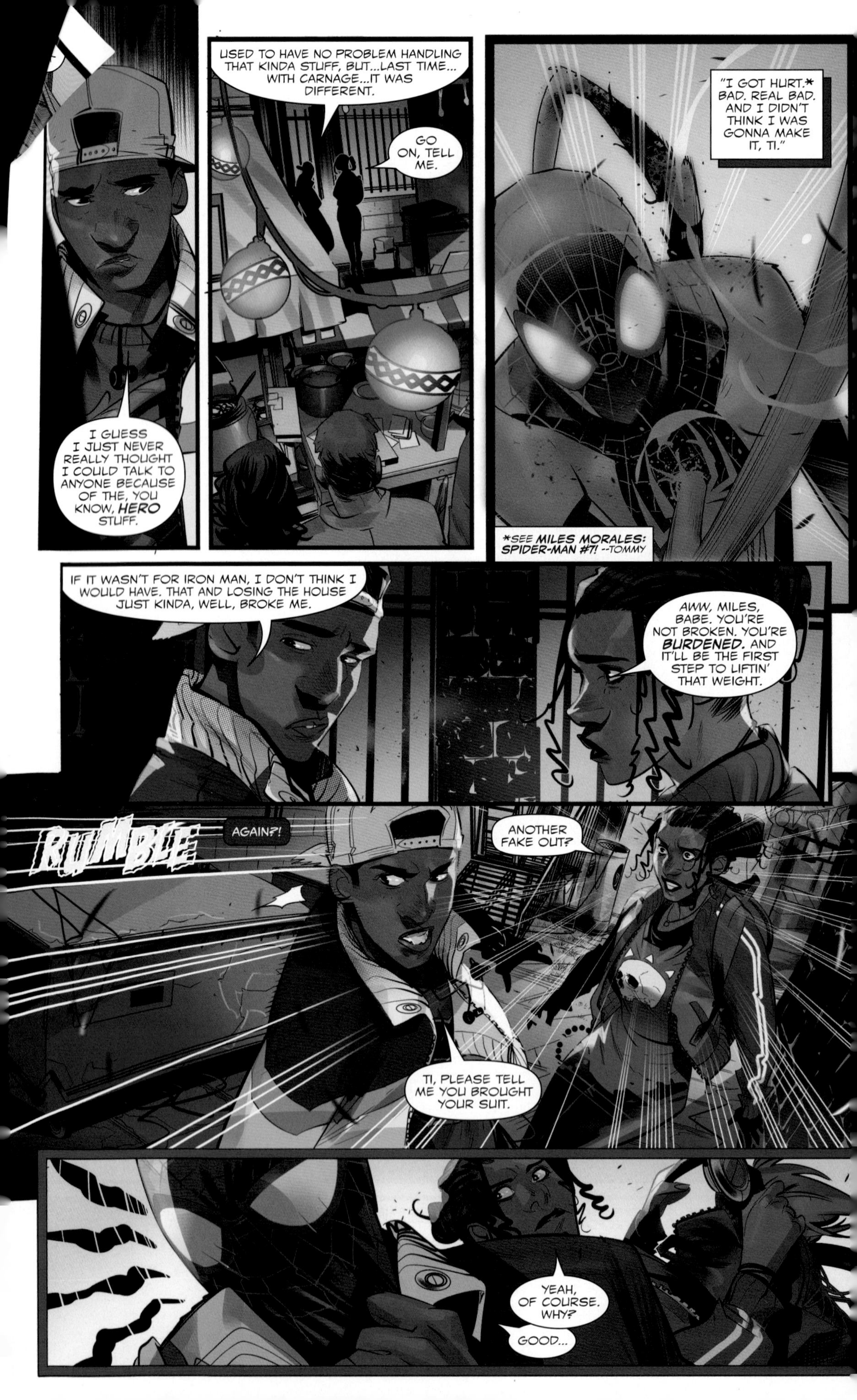
I GUESS I JUST NEVER REALLY THOUGHT I COULD TALK TO ANYONE BECAUSE OF THE, YOU KNOW, HERO STUFF.
USED TO HAVE NO PROBLEM HANDLING THAT KINDA STUFF, BUT...LAST TIME... WITH CARNAGE...IT WAS DIFFERENT.
GO ON, TELL ME.
"I GOT HURT.* BAD. REAL BAD. AND I DIDN'T THINK I WAS GONNA MAKE IT, TI."
*SEE MILES MORALES: SPIDER-MAN #7! --TOMMY
IF IT WASN'T FOR IRON MAN, I DON'T THINK I WOULD HAVE. THAT AND LOSING THE HOUSE JUST KINDA, WELL, BROKE ME.
AWW, MILES, BABE. YOU'RE NOT BROKEN. YOU'RE BURDENED. AND IT'LL BE THE FIRST STEP TO LIFTIN' THAT WEIGHT.
RUMBLE
AGAIN?!
ANOTHER FAKE OUT?
TI, PLEASE TELL ME YOU BROUGHT YOUR SUIT.
YEAH, OF COURSE. WHY?
GOOD...

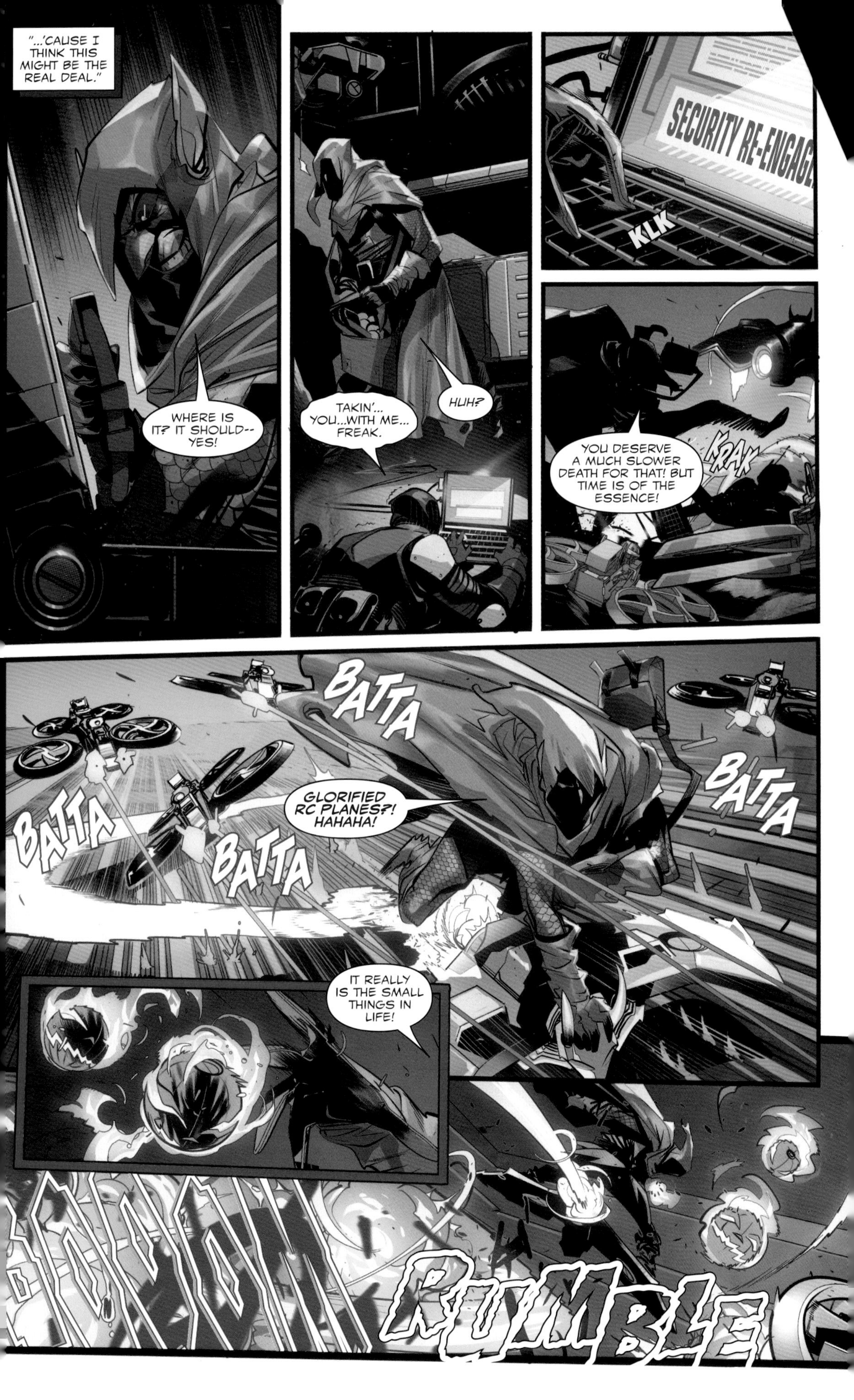
"...'CAUSE I THINK THIS MIGHT BE THE REAL DEAL."
WHERE IS IT? IT SHOULD-- YES!
TAKIN'... YOU...WITH ME... FREAK.
HUH?
SECURITY RE-ENGAGE
KLK
YOU DESERVE A MUCH SLOWER DEATH FOR THAT! BUT TIME IS OF THE ESSENCE!
KRAK
BATTA
GLORIFIED RC PLANES?! HAHAHA!
BATTA
BATTA
BATTA
IT REALLY IS THE SMALL THINGS IN LIFE!
RUMBLE

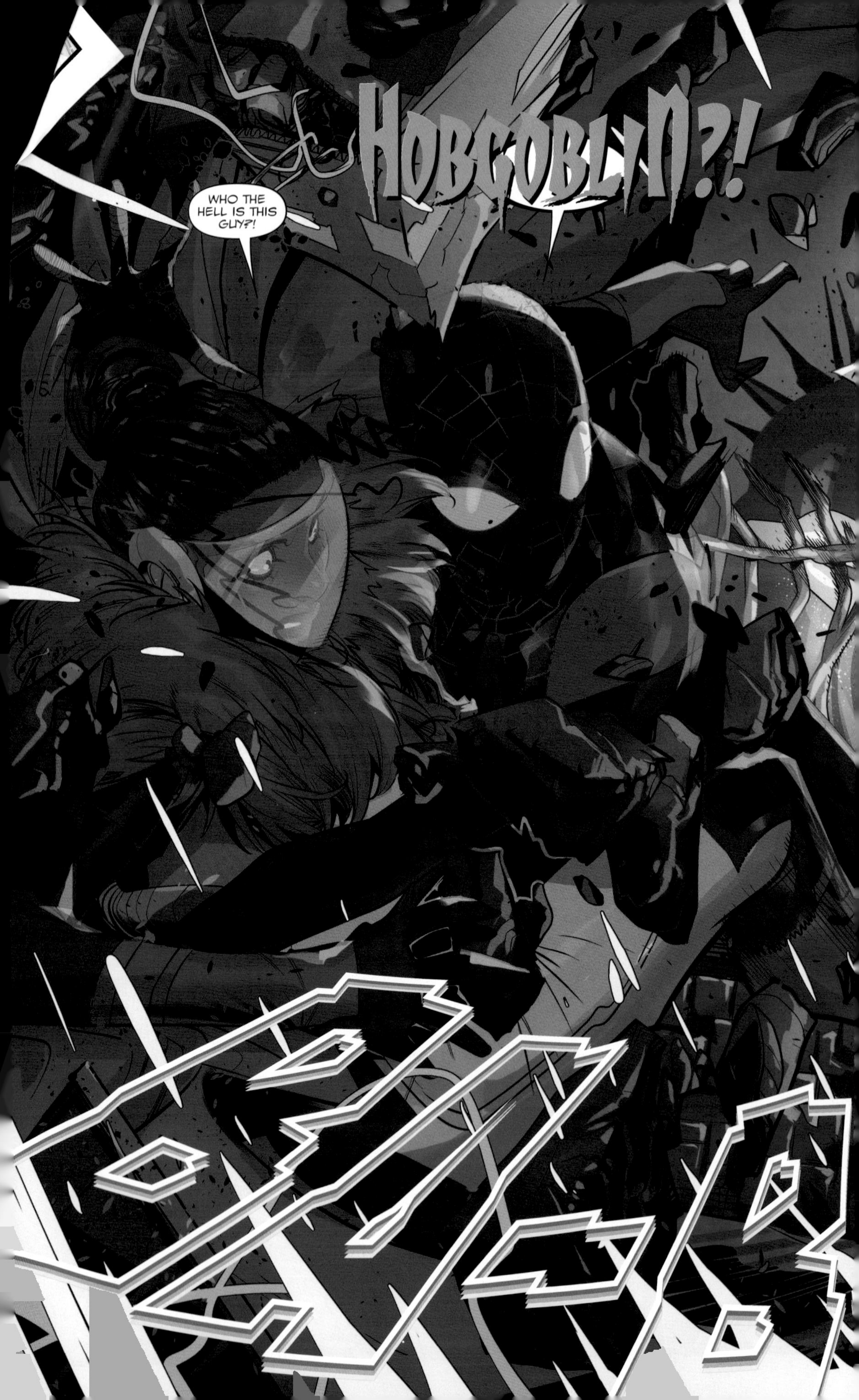
HOBGOBLIN?!
WHO THE HELL IS THIS GUY?!

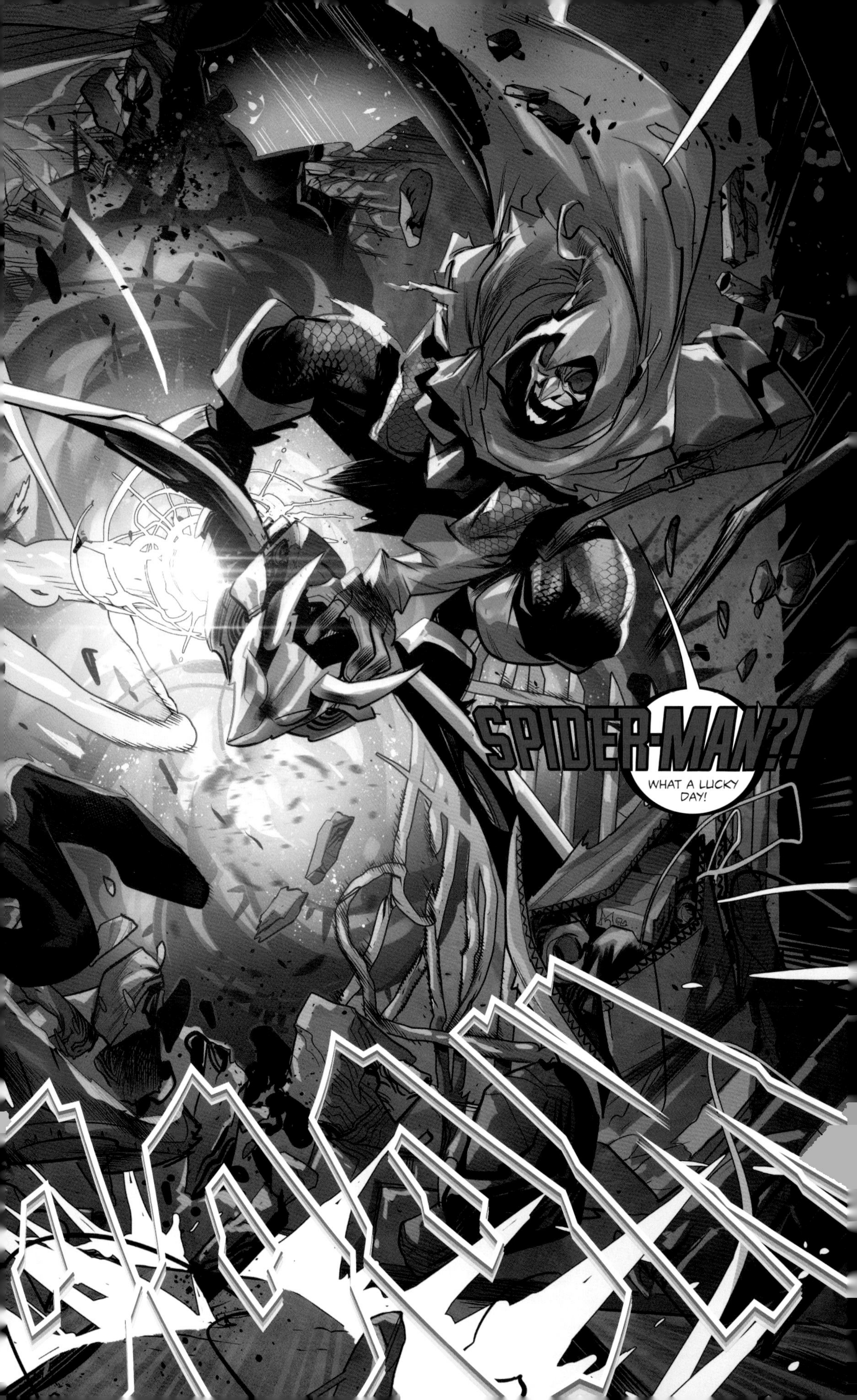
SPIDER-MAN?!
WHAT A LUCKY DAY!

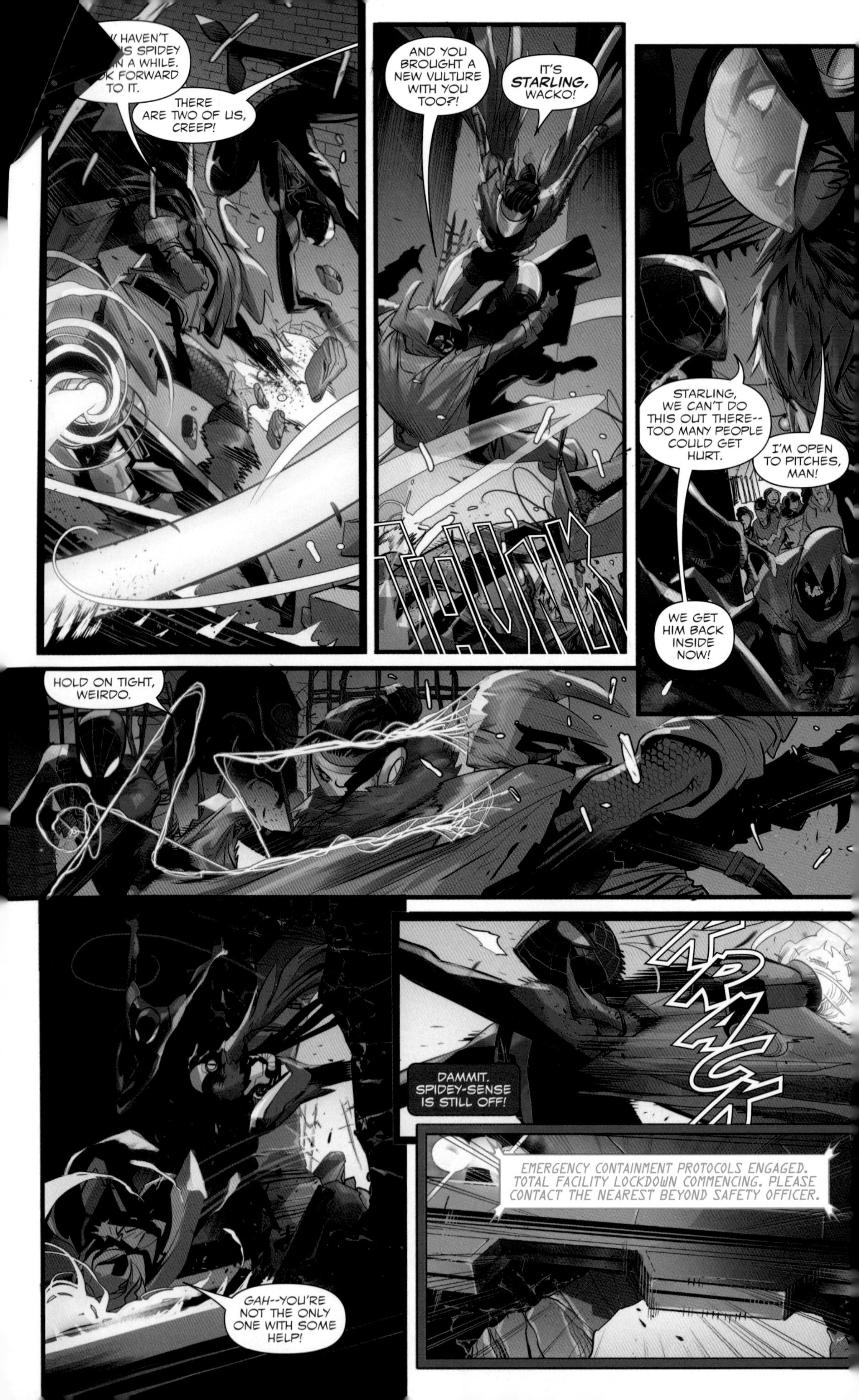
W HAVEN'T IS SPIDEY N A WHILE. OK FORWARD TO IT.
THERE ARE TWO OF US, CREEP!
AND YOU BROUGHT A NEW VULTURE WITH YOU TOO?!
IT'S STARLING, WACKO!
STARLING, WE CAN'T DO THIS OUT THERE-- TOO MANY PEOPLE COULD GET HURT.
I'M OPEN TO PITCHES, MAN!
WE GET HIM BACK INSIDE NOW!
HOLD ON TIGHT, WEIRDO.
GAH--YOU'RE NOT THE ONLY ONE WITH SOME HELP!
DAMMIT. SPIDEY-SENSE IS STILL OFF!
EMERGENCY CONTAINMENT PROTOCOLS ENGAGED. TOTAL FACILITY LOCKDOWN COMMENCING. PLEASE CONTACT THE NEAREST BEYOND SAFETY OFFICER.

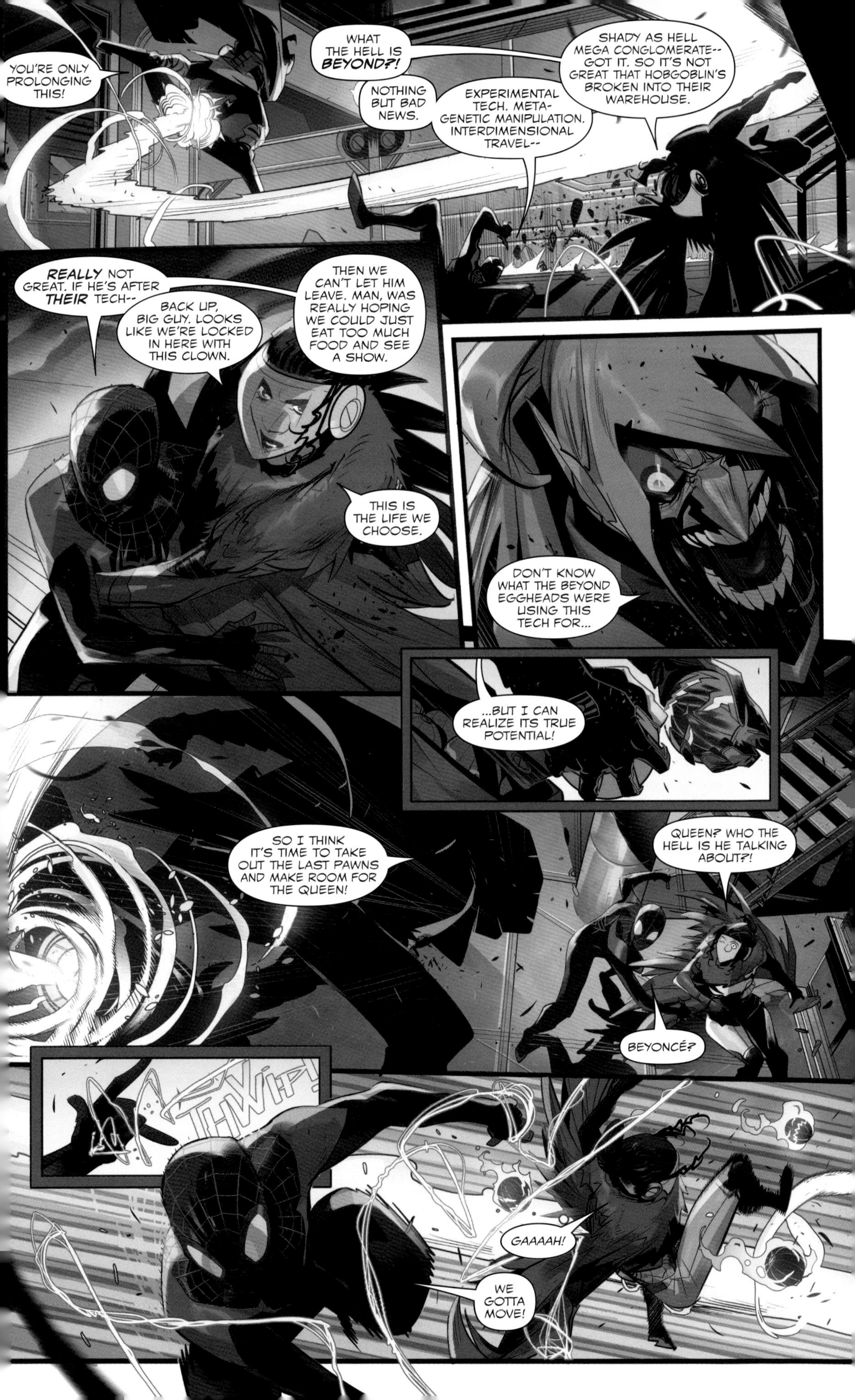
YOU'RE ONLY PROLONGING THIS!
WHAT THE HELL IS BEYOND?!
NOTHING BUT BAD NEWS.
EXPERIMENTAL TECH. META-GENETIC MANIPULATION. INTERDIMENSIONAL TRAVEL--
SHADY AS HELL MEGA CONGLOMERATE-- GOT IT. SO IT'S NOT GREAT THAT HOBGOBLIN'S BROKEN INTO THEIR WAREHOUSE.
REALLY NOT GREAT. IF HE'S AFTER THEIR TECH--
THEN WE CAN'T LET HIM LEAVE. MAN, WAS REALLY HOPING WE COULD JUST EAT TOO MUCH FOOD AND SEE A SHOW.
BACK UP, BIG GUY. LOOKS LIKE WE'RE LOCKED IN HERE WITH THIS CLOWN.
THIS IS THE LIFE WE CHOOSE.
DON'T KNOW WHAT THE BEYOND EGGHEADS WERE USING THIS TECH FOR...
...BUT I CAN REALIZE ITS TRUE POTENTIAL!
SO I THINK IT'S TIME TO TAKE OUT THE LAST PAWNS AND MAKE ROOM FOR THE QUEEN!
QUEEN? WHO THE HELL IS HE TALKING ABOUT?!
BEYONCÉ?
THWIP!
GAAAAH!
WE GOTTA MOVE!

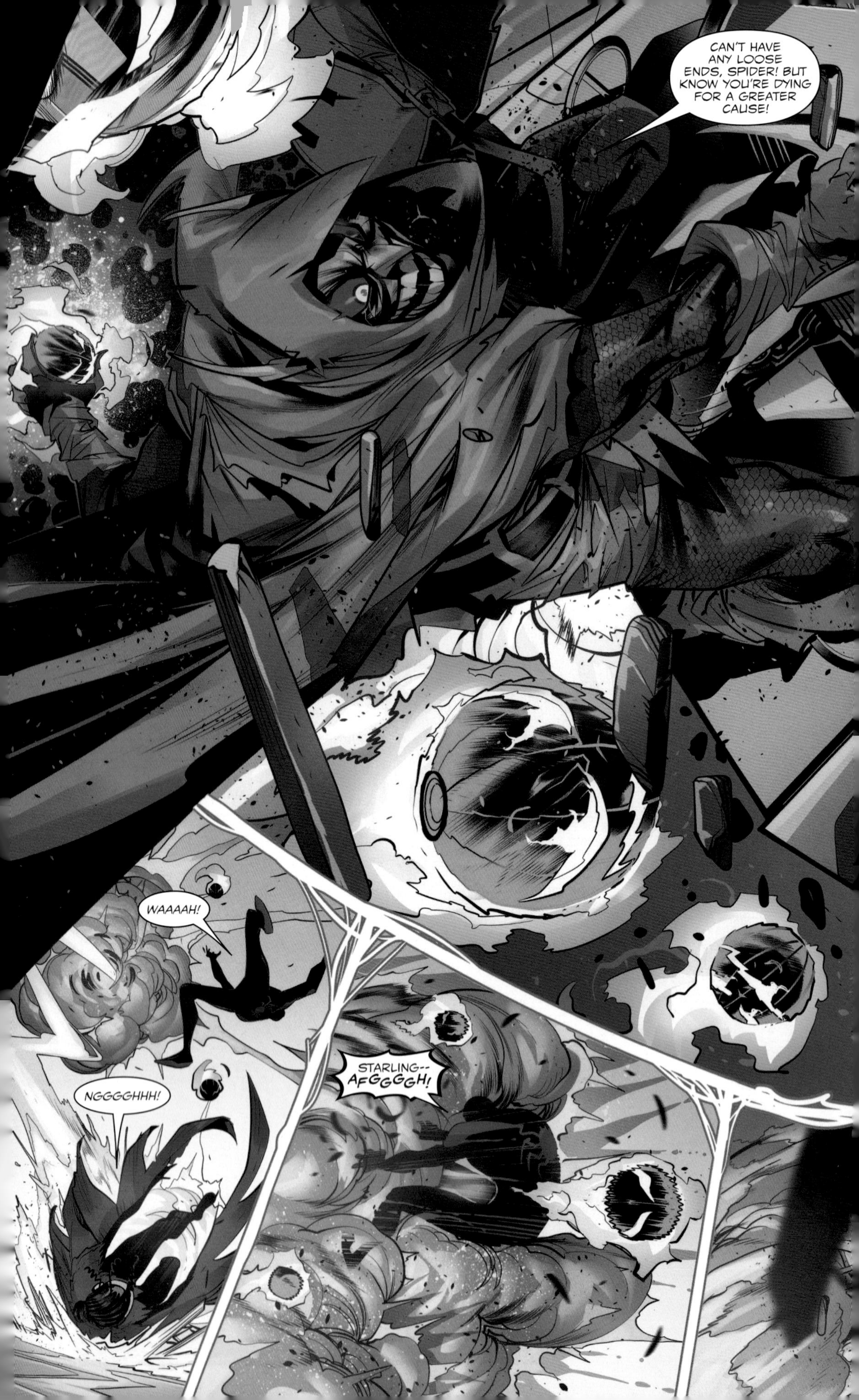
CAN'T HAVE ANY LOOSE ENDS, SPIDER! BUT KNOW YOU'RE DYING FOR A GREATER CAUSE!
WAAAAH!
STARLING-- AFGGGGH!
NGGGGHHH!

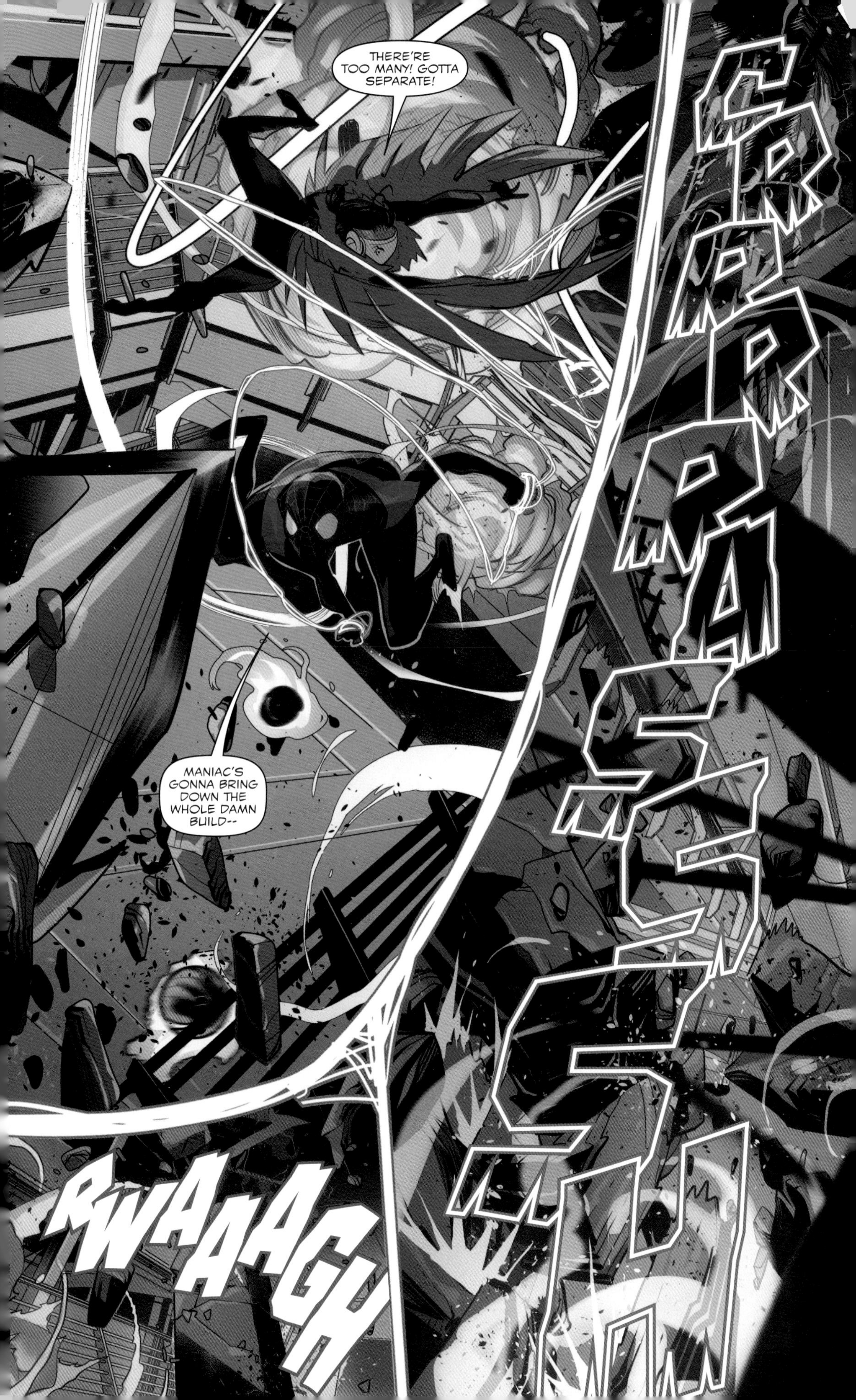
THERE'RE TOO MANY! GOTTA SEPARATE!
MANIAC'S GONNA BRING DOWN THE WHOLE DAMN BUILD--
CRRRRAAASSSHHH
RWAAAAGH

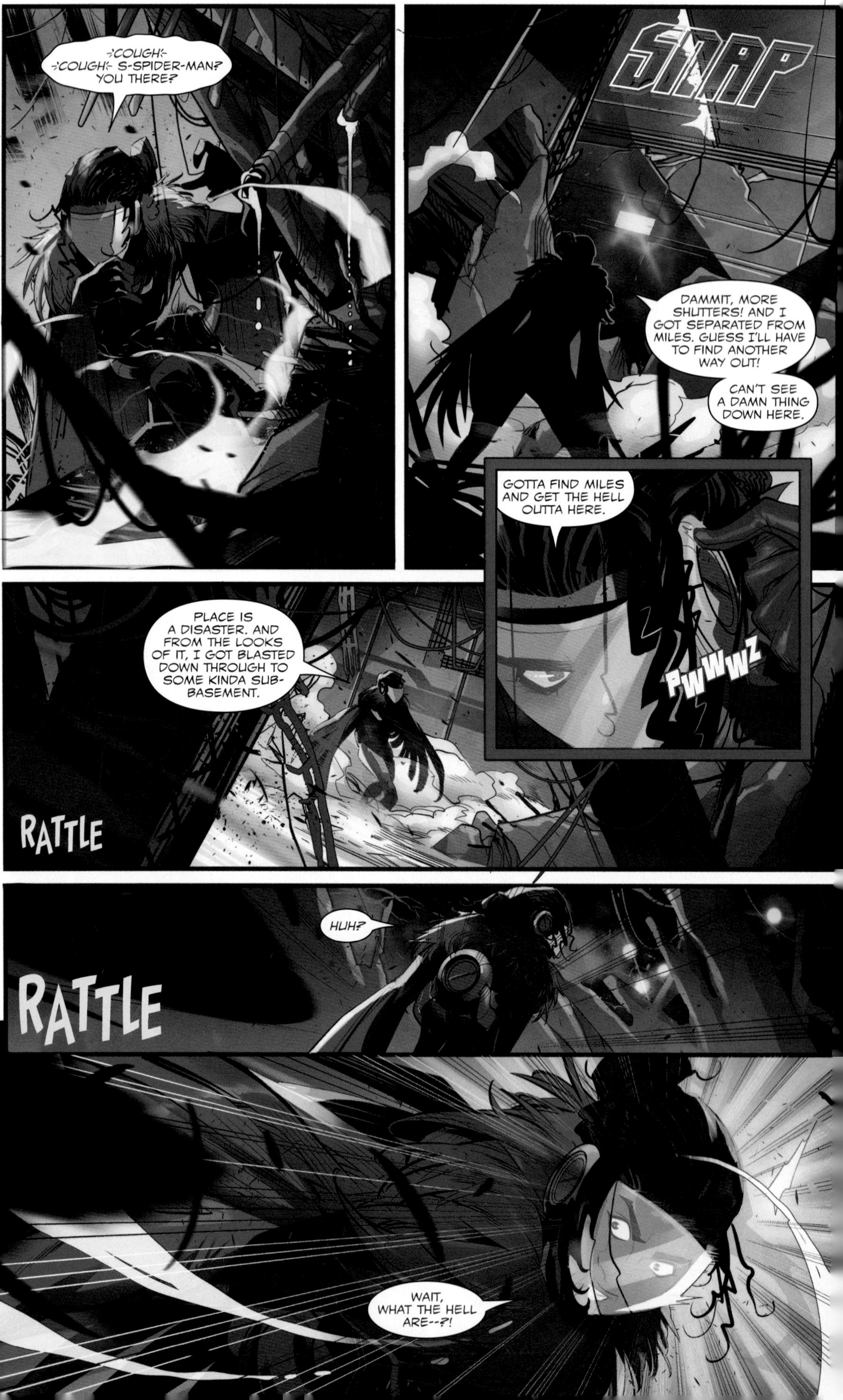
-COUGH-
-COUGH- S-SPIDER-MAN? YOU THERE?
SNAP
DAMMIT, MORE SHUTTERS! AND I GOT SEPARATED FROM MILES. GUESS I'LL HAVE TO FIND ANOTHER WAY OUT!
CAN'T SEE A DAMN THING DOWN HERE.
GOTTA FIND MILES AND GET THE HELL OUTTA HERE.
PWWWZ
PLACE IS A DISASTER. AND FROM THE LOOKS OF IT, I GOT BLASTED DOWN THROUGH TO SOME KINDA SUB-BASEMENT.
RATTLE
HUH?
RATTLE
WAIT, WHAT THE HELL ARE--?!

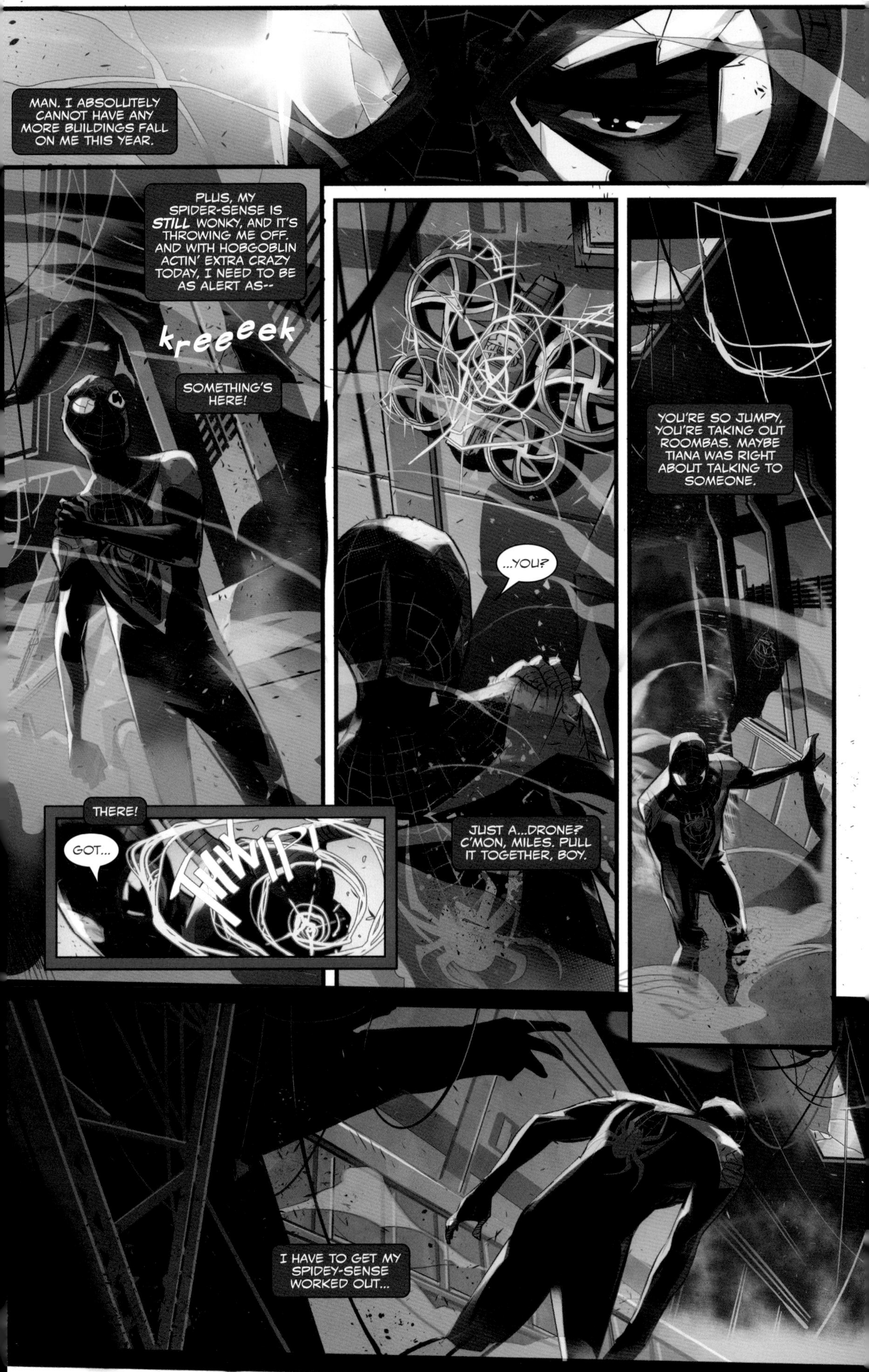
MAN. I ABSOLUTELY CANNOT HAVE ANY MORE BUILDINGS FALL ON ME THIS YEAR.
PLUS, MY SPIDER-SENSE IS STILL WONKY, AND IT'S THROWING ME OFF. AND WITH HOBGOBLIN ACTIN' EXTRA CRAZY TODAY, I NEED TO BE AS ALERT AS--
kreeeek
SOMETHING'S HERE!
THERE!
GOT...
THWIP!
...YOU?
JUST A...DRONE? C'MON, MILES. PULL IT TOGETHER, BOY.
YOU'RE SO JUMPY, YOU'RE TAKING OUT ROOMBAS. MAYBE TIANA WAS RIGHT ABOUT TALKING TO SOMEONE.
I HAVE TO GET MY SPIDEY-SENSE WORKED OUT...

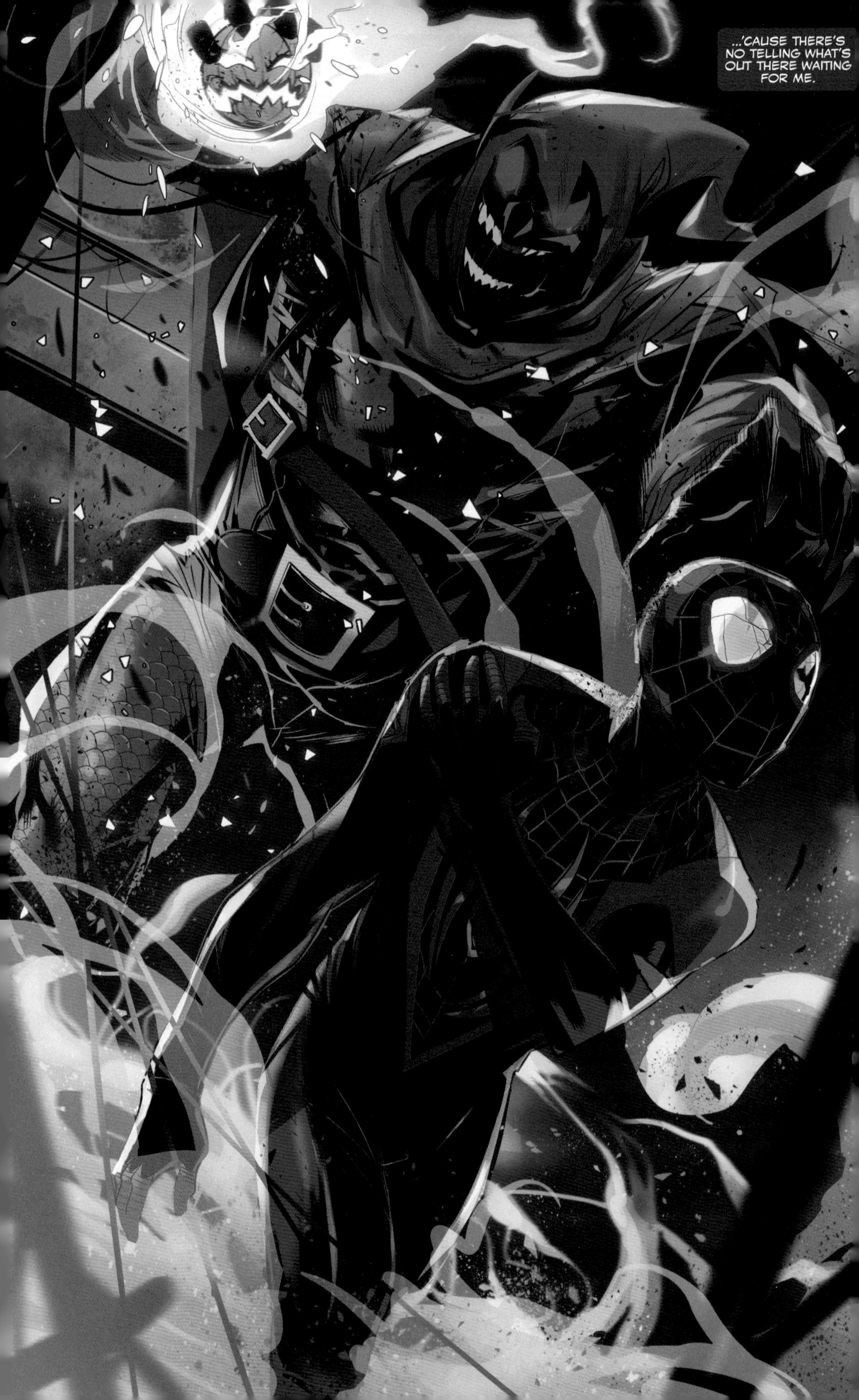
...'CAUSE THERE'S NO TELLING WHAT'S OUT THERE WAITING FOR ME.

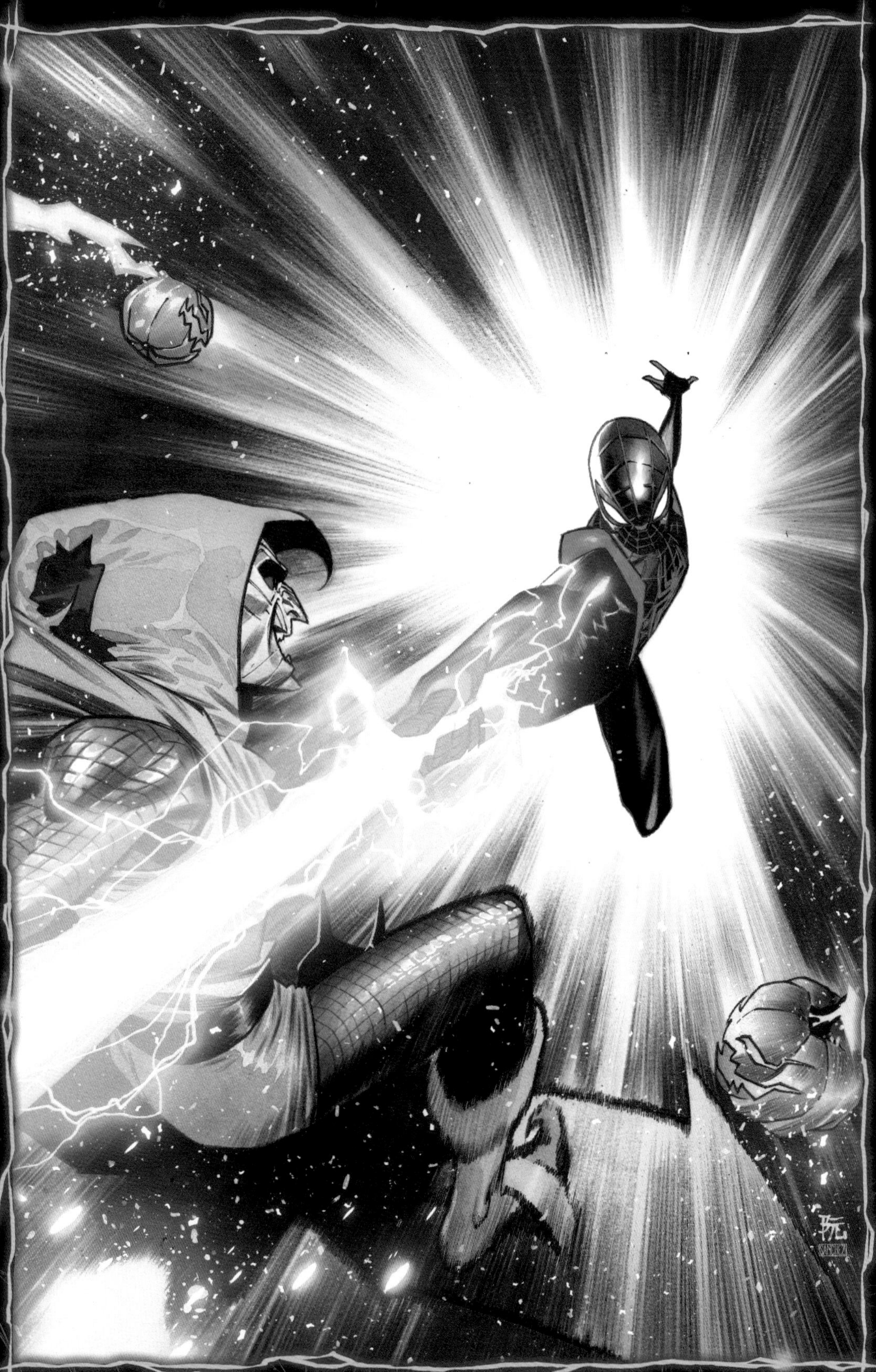

9

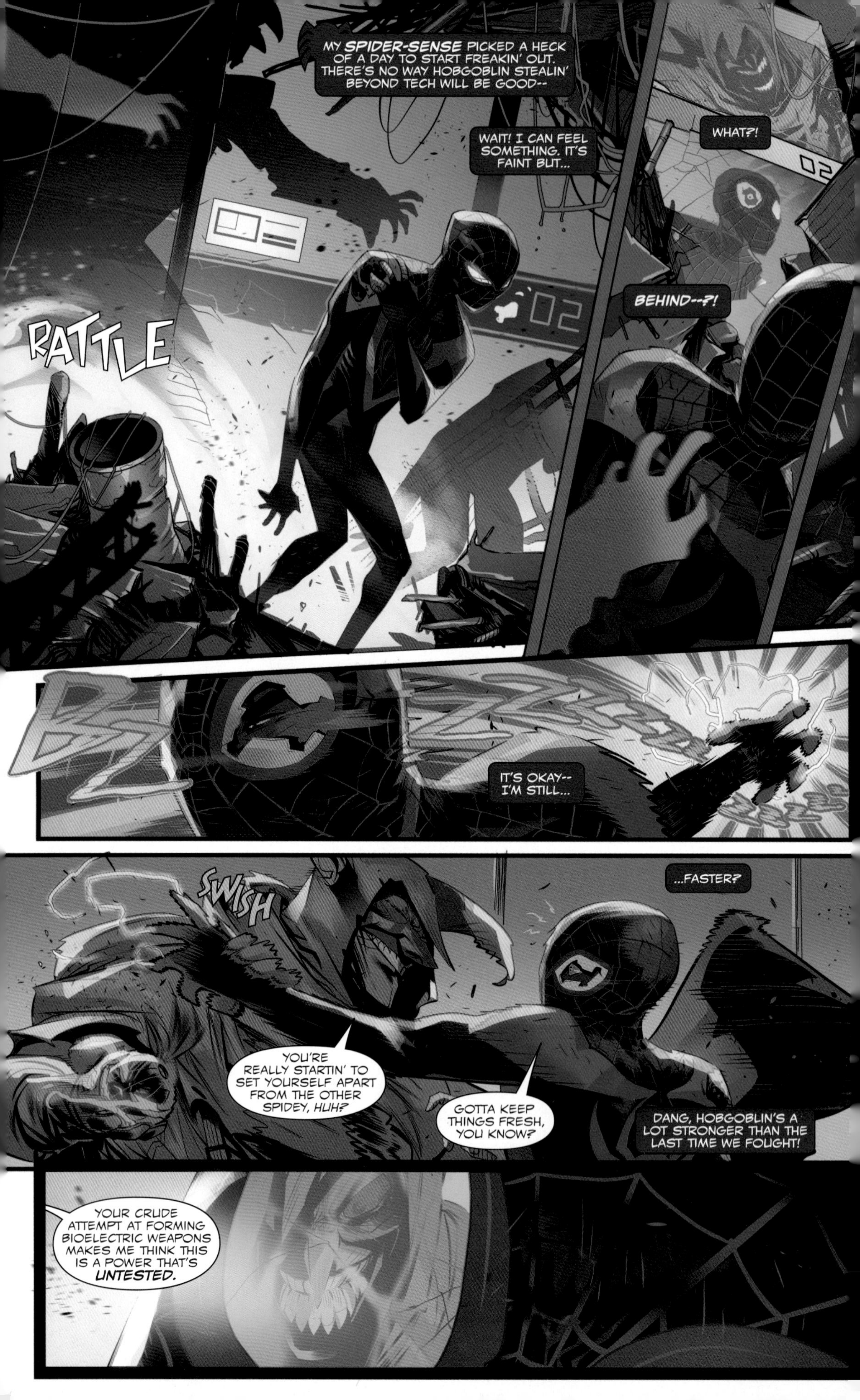
MY SPIDER-SENSE PICKED A HECK OF A DAY TO START FREAKIN' OUT. THERE'S NO WAY HOBGOBLIN STEALIN' BEYOND TECH WILL BE GOOD--
WAIT! I CAN FEEL SOMETHING. IT'S FAINT BUT...
RATTLE
WHAT?!
BEHIND--?!
IT'S OKAY-- I'M STILL...
...FASTER?
SWISH
YOU'RE REALLY STARTIN' TO SET YOURSELF APART FROM THE OTHER SPIDEY, HUH?
GOTTA KEEP THINGS FRESH, YOU KNOW?
DANG, HOBGOBLIN'S A LOT STRONGER THAN THE LAST TIME WE FOUGHT!
YOUR CRUDE ATTEMPT AT FORMING BIOELECTRIC WEAPONS MAKES ME THINK THIS IS A POWER THAT'S UNTESTED.

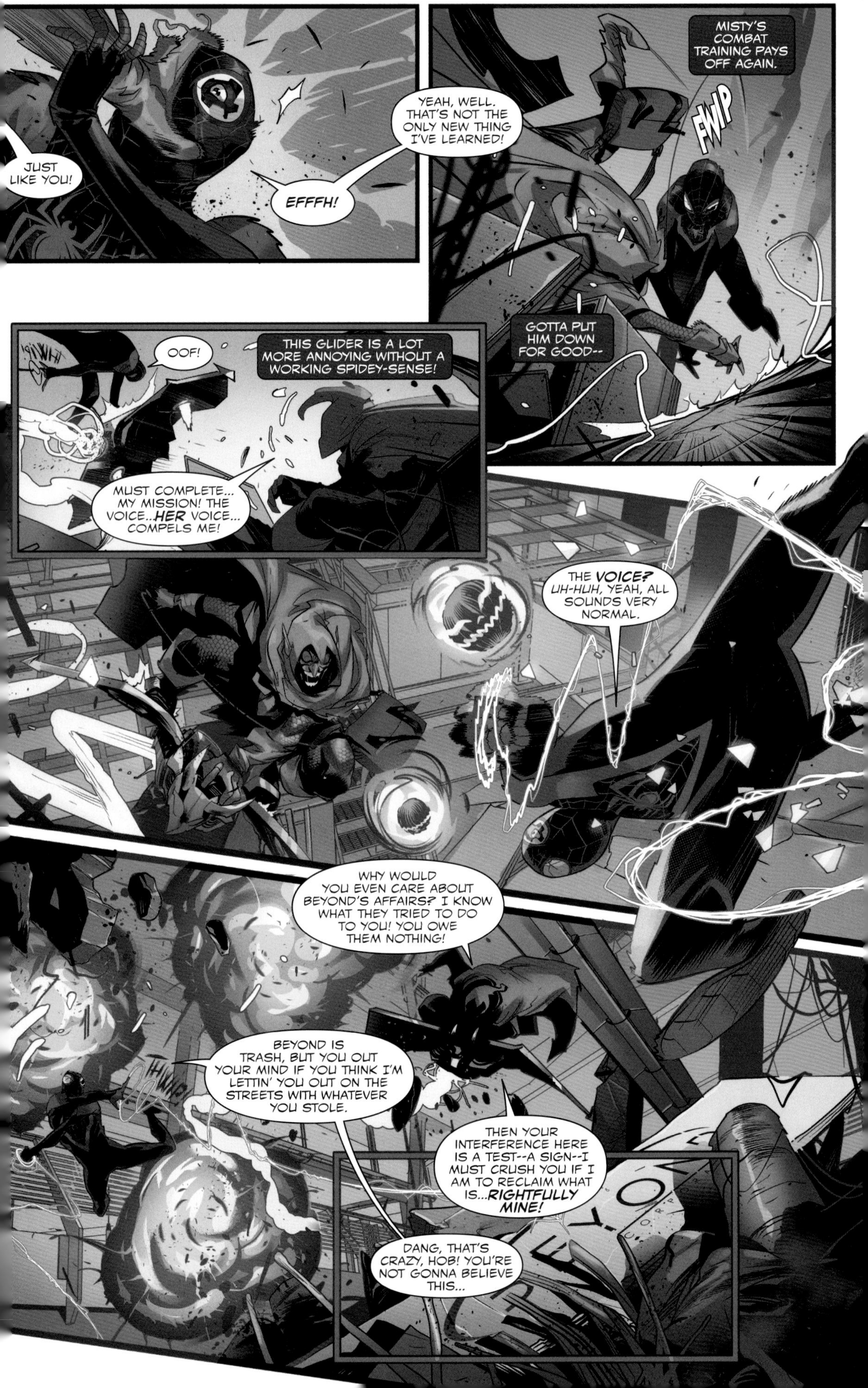
JUST LIKE YOU!
EFFFH!
YEAH, WELL. THAT'S NOT THE ONLY NEW THING I'VE LEARNED!
MISTY'S COMBAT TRAINING PAYS OFF AGAIN.
FWIP
GOTTA PUT HIM DOWN FOR GOOD--
OOF!
THIS GLIDER IS A LOT MORE ANNOYING WITHOUT A WORKING SPIDEY-SENSE!
MUST COMPLETE... MY MISSION! THE VOICE...HER VOICE... COMPELS ME!
THE VOICE? UH-HUH, YEAH, ALL SOUNDS VERY NORMAL.
WHY WOULD YOU EVEN CARE ABOUT BEYOND'S AFFAIRS? I KNOW WHAT THEY TRIED TO DO TO YOU! YOU OWE THEM NOTHING!
BEYOND IS TRASH, BUT YOU OUT YOUR MIND IF YOU THINK I'M LETTIN' YOU OUT ON THE STREETS WITH WHATEVER YOU STOLE.
THWIP
THEN YOUR INTERFERENCE HERE IS A TEST--A SIGN--I MUST CRUSH YOU IF I AM TO RECLAIM WHAT IS...RIGHTFULLY MINE!
DANG, THAT'S CRAZY, HOB! YOU'RE NOT GONNA BELIEVE THIS...

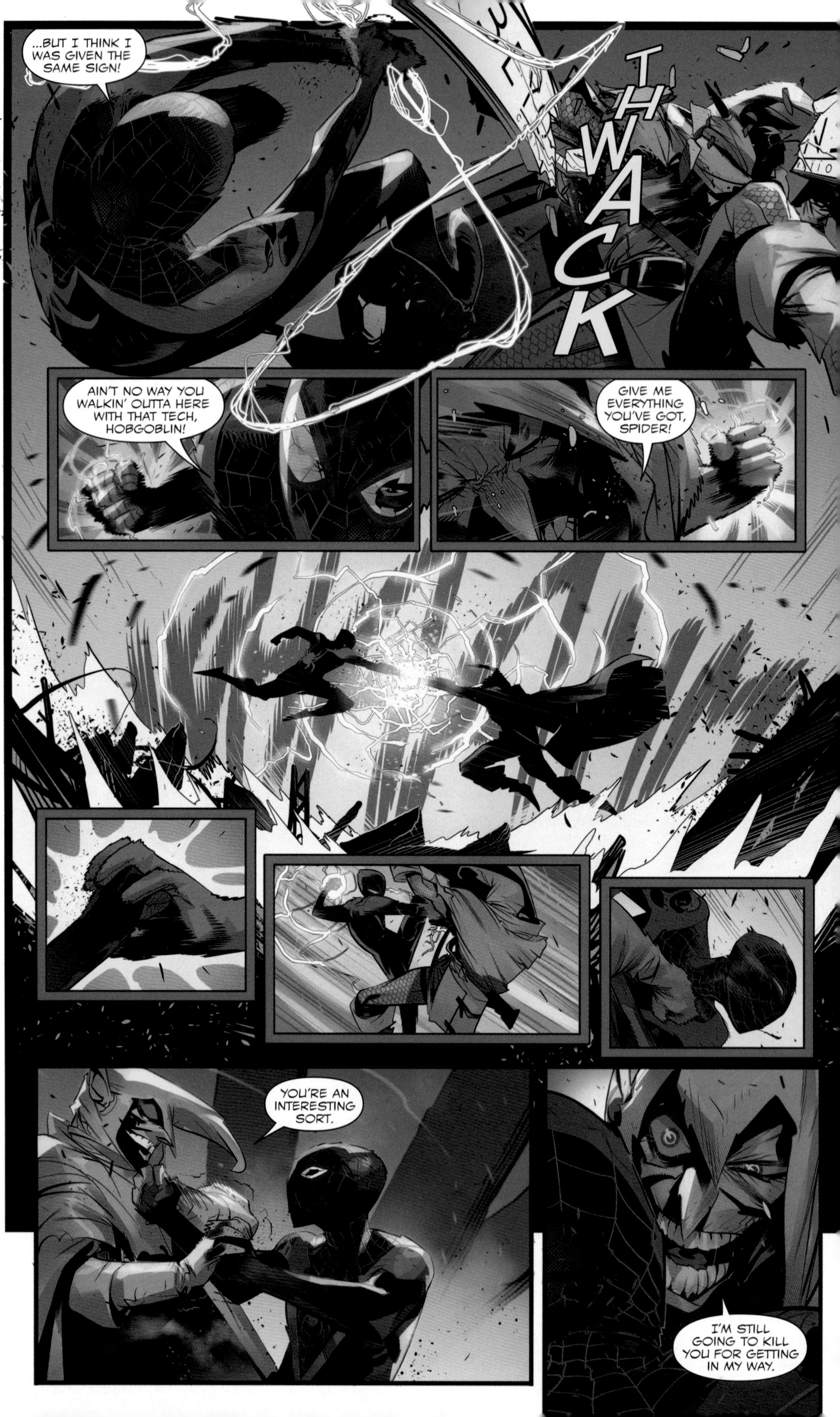
...BUT I THINK I WAS GIVEN THE SAME SIGN!
THWACK
AIN'T NO WAY YOU WALKIN' OUTTA HERE WITH THAT TECH, HOBGOBLIN!
GIVE ME EVERYTHING YOU'VE GOT, SPIDER!
YOU'RE AN INTERESTING SORT.
I'M STILL GOING TO KILL YOU FOR GETTING IN MY WAY.

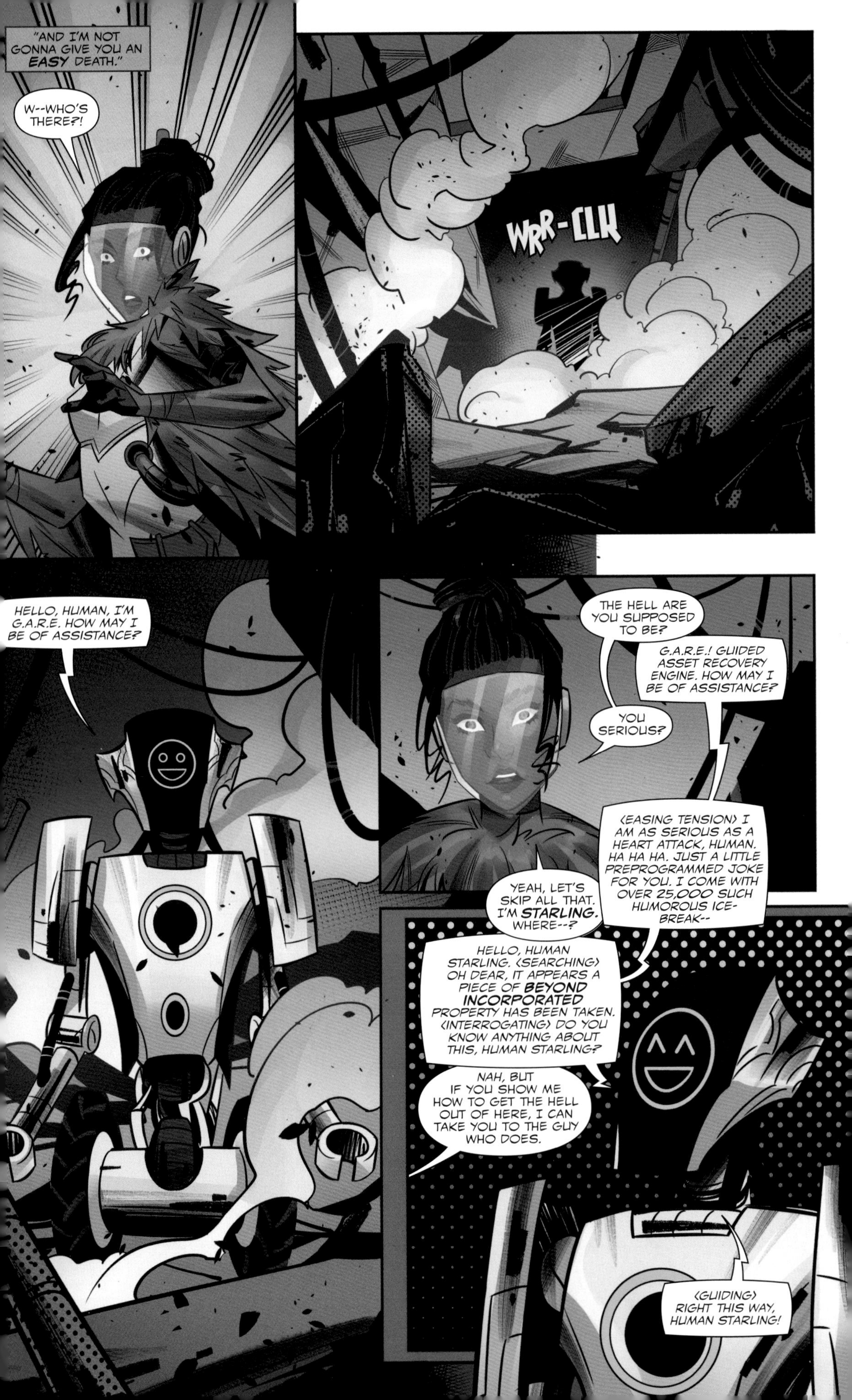
"AND I'M NOT GONNA GIVE YOU AN EASY DEATH."
W--WHO'S THERE?!
WRR-CLK
HELLO, HUMAN, I'M G.A.R.E. HOW MAY I BE OF ASSISTANCE?
THE HELL ARE YOU SUPPOSED TO BE?
G.A.R.E.! GUIDED ASSET RECOVERY ENGINE. HOW MAY I BE OF ASSISTANCE?
YOU SERIOUS?
<EASING TENSION> I AM AS SERIOUS AS A HEART ATTACK, HUMAN. HA HA HA. JUST A LITTLE PREPROGRAMMED JOKE FOR YOU. I COME WITH OVER 25,000 SUCH HUMOROUS ICE-BREAK--
YEAH, LET'S SKIP ALL THAT. I'M STARLING. WHERE--?
HELLO, HUMAN STARLING. <SEARCHING> OH DEAR, IT APPEARS A PIECE OF BEYOND INCORPORATED PROPERTY HAS BEEN TAKEN. <INTERROGATING> DO YOU KNOW ANYTHING ABOUT THIS, HUMAN STARLING?
NAH, BUT IF YOU SHOW ME HOW TO GET THE HELL OUT OF HERE, I CAN TAKE YOU TO THE GUY WHO DOES.
<GUIDING> RIGHT THIS WAY, HUMAN STARLING!

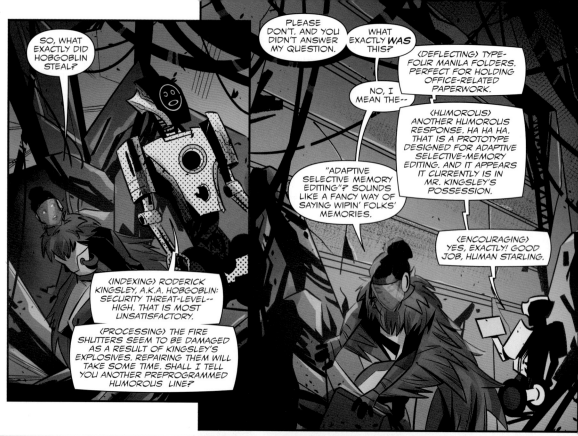

SO, WHAT EXACTLY DID HOBGOBLIN STEAL?

(INDEXING) RODERICK KINGSLEY, A.K.A. HOBGOBLIN: SECURITY THREAT-LEVEL-- HIGH. THAT IS MOST UNSATISFACTORY.

(PROCESSING) THE FIRE SHUTTERS SEEM TO BE DAMAGED AS A RESULT OF KINGSLEY'S EXPLOSIVES. REPAIRING THEM WILL TAKE SOME TIME. SHALL I TELL YOU ANOTHER PREPROGRAMMED HUMOROUS LINE?

PLEASE DON'T. AND YOU DIDN'T ANSWER MY QUESTION.

WHAT EXACTLY **WAS** THIS?

NO, I MEAN THE--

"ADAPTIVE SELECTIVE MEMORY EDITING"? SOUNDS LIKE A FANCY WAY OF SAYING WIPIN' FOLKS' MEMORIES.

(DEFLECTING) TYPE-FOUR MANILA FOLDERS. PERFECT FOR HOLDING OFFICE-RELATED PAPERWORK.

(HUMOROUS) ANOTHER HUMOROUS RESPONSE. HA HA HA. THAT IS A PROTOTYPE DESIGNED FOR ADAPTIVE SELECTIVE-MEMORY EDITING. AND IT APPEARS IT CURRENTLY IS IN MR. KINGSLEY'S POSSESSION.

(ENCOURAGING) YES, EXACTLY! GOOD JOB, HUMAN STARLING.

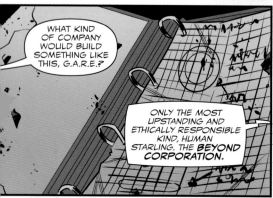

WHAT KIND OF COMPANY WOULD BUILD SOMETHING LIKE THIS, G.A.R.E.?

ONLY THE MOST UPSTANDING AND ETHICALLY RESPONSIBLE KIND, HUMAN STARLING. THE **BEYOND** CORPORATION.

THOOM

AIN'T GOT TIME FOR THIS.

SORRY, BUT WE'RE ON A TIME CRUNCH HERE.

HUMAN STARLING, THAT COULD DAMAGE THE FIRE SHUTTERS IF YOU'RE NOT CAREFUL--

GOOD.

CLANG

WE NEED TO GET OUT OF HERE.

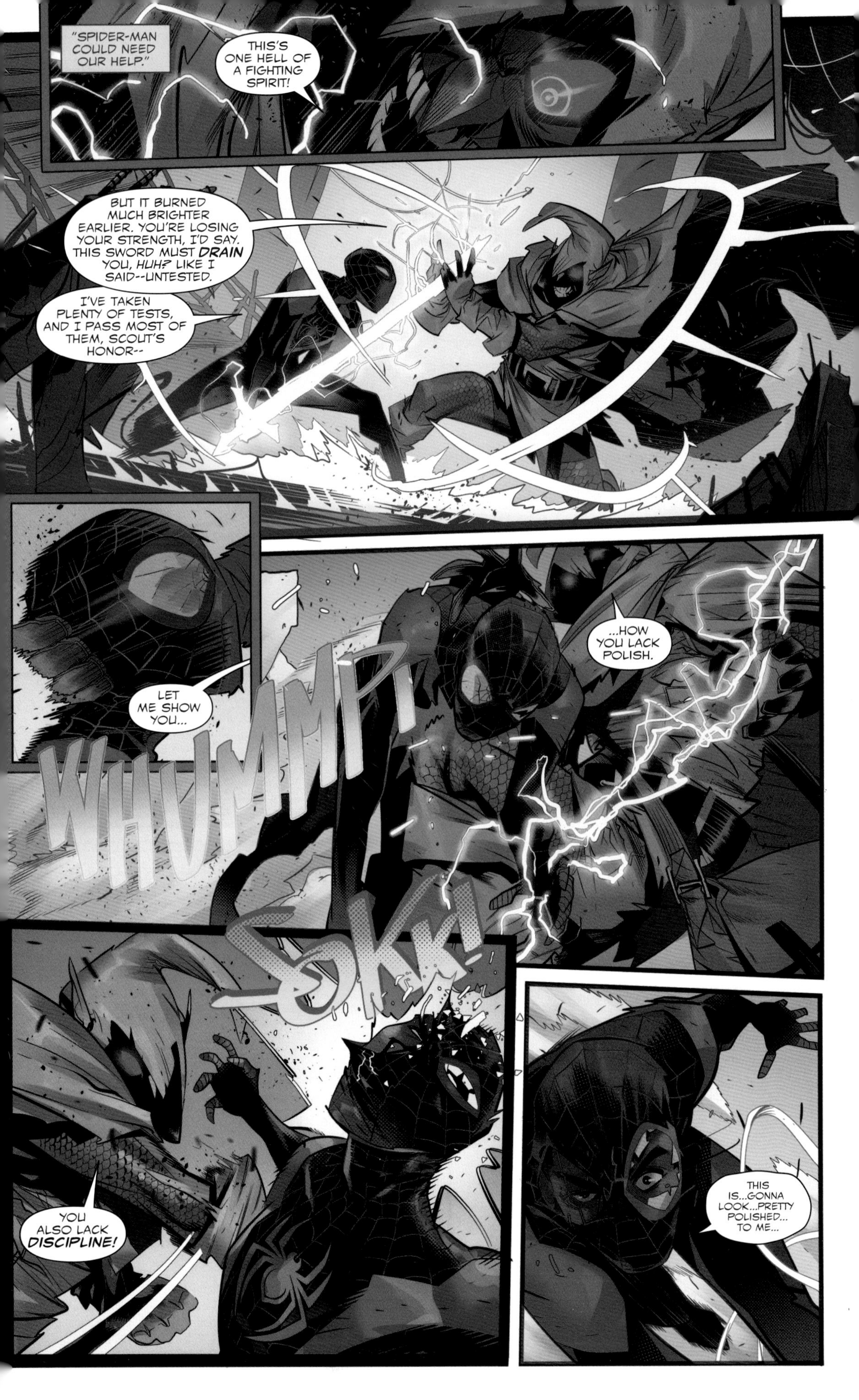

"SPIDER-MAN COULD NEED OUR HELP."
THIS'S ONE HELL OF A FIGHTING SPIRIT!
BUT IT BURNED MUCH BRIGHTER EARLIER. YOU'RE LOSING YOUR STRENGTH, I'D SAY. THIS SWORD MUST **DRAIN** YOU, *HUH?* LIKE I SAID--UNTESTED.
I'VE TAKEN PLENTY OF TESTS, AND I PASS MOST OF THEM, SCOUT'S HONOR--
LET ME SHOW YOU...
WHUMMP!
...HOW YOU LACK POLISH.
SKK!
YOU ALSO LACK **DISCIPLINE!**
THIS IS...GONNA LOOK...PRETTY POLISHED... TO ME...

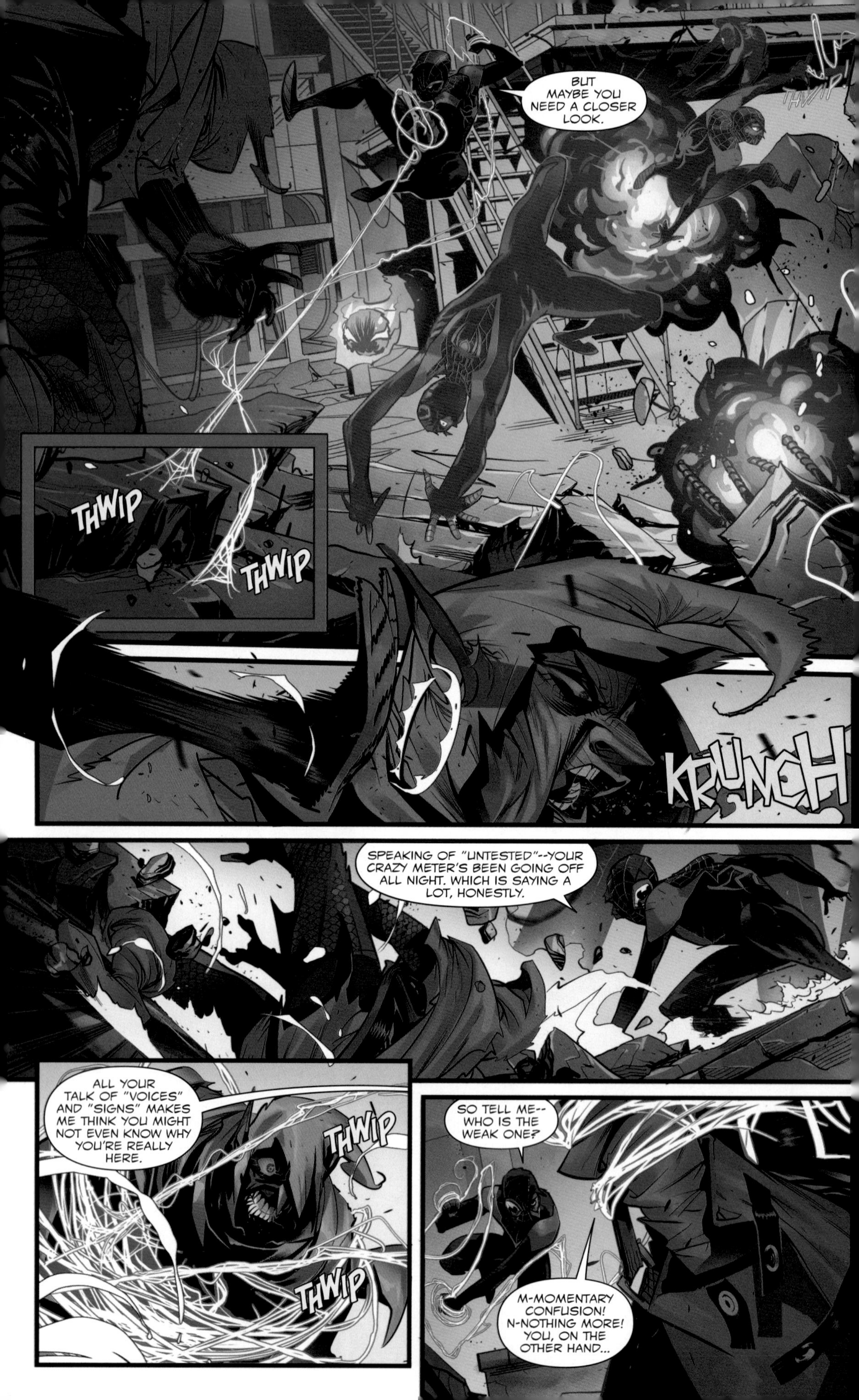
BUT MAYBE YOU NEED A CLOSER LOOK.
THWIP
THWIP
THWIP
KRUNCH
SPEAKING OF "UNTESTED"--YOUR CRAZY METER'S BEEN GOING OFF ALL NIGHT. WHICH IS SAYING A LOT, HONESTLY.
ALL YOUR TALK OF "VOICES" AND "SIGNS" MAKES ME THINK YOU MIGHT NOT EVEN KNOW WHY YOU'RE REALLY HERE.
THWIP
THWIP
SO TELL ME-- WHO IS THE WEAK ONE?
M-MOMENTARY CONFUSION! N-NOTHING MORE! YOU, ON THE OTHER HAND...

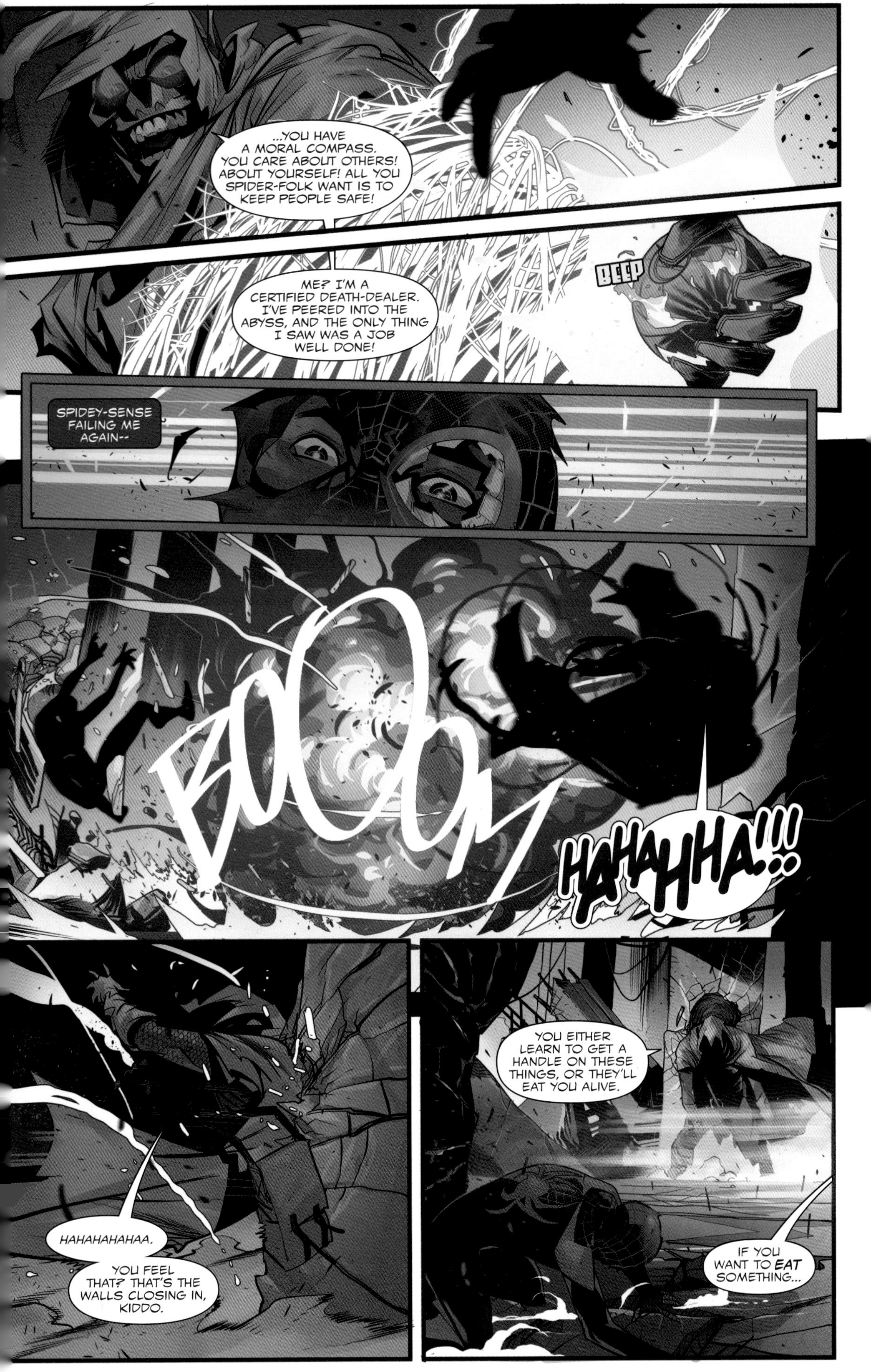
...YOU HAVE A MORAL COMPASS. YOU CARE ABOUT OTHERS! ABOUT YOURSELF! ALL YOU SPIDER-FOLK WANT IS TO KEEP PEOPLE SAFE!
ME? I'M A CERTIFIED DEATH-DEALER. I'VE PEERED INTO THE ABYSS, AND THE ONLY THING I SAW WAS A JOB WELL DONE!
BEEP
SPIDEY-SENSE FAILING ME AGAIN--
BOOOM
HAHAHHA!!!
HAHAHAHAHAA.
YOU FEEL THAT? THAT'S THE WALLS CLOSING IN, KIDDO.
YOU EITHER LEARN TO GET A HANDLE ON THESE THINGS, OR THEY'LL EAT YOU ALIVE.
IF YOU WANT TO EAT SOMETHING...

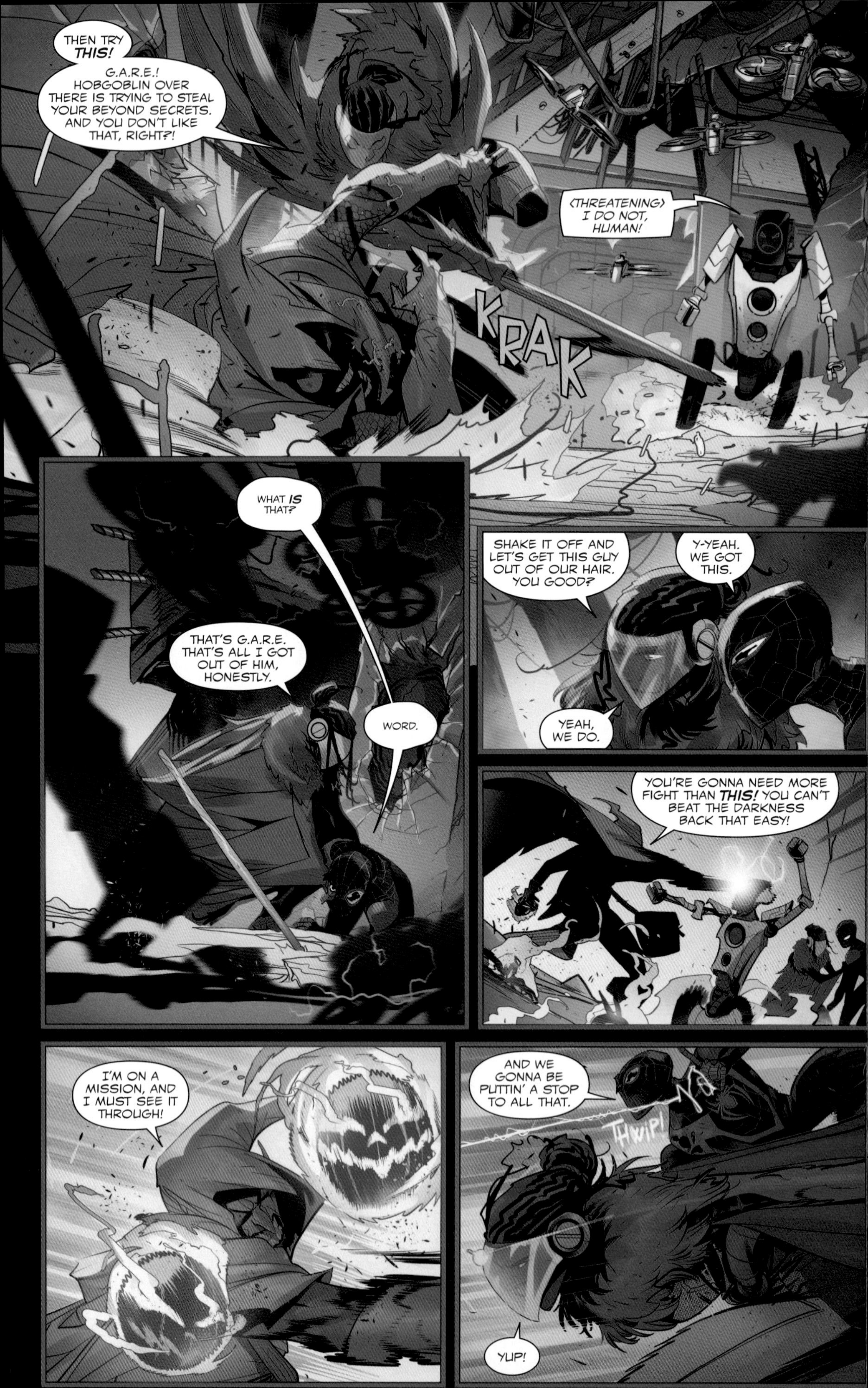
THEN TRY THIS!
G.A.R.E.! HOBGOBLIN OVER THERE IS TRYING TO STEAL YOUR BEYOND SECRETS. AND YOU DON'T LIKE THAT, RIGHT?!
<THREATENING> I DO NOT, HUMAN!
KRAK
WHAT IS THAT?
THAT'S G.A.R.E. THAT'S ALL I GOT OUT OF HIM, HONESTLY.
WORD.
SHAKE IT OFF AND LET'S GET THIS GUY OUT OF OUR HAIR. YOU GOOD?
Y-YEAH. WE GOT THIS.
YEAH, WE DO.
YOU'RE GONNA NEED MORE FIGHT THAN THIS! YOU CAN'T BEAT THE DARKNESS BACK THAT EASY!
I'M ON A MISSION, AND I MUST SEE IT THROUGH!
AND WE GONNA BE PUTTIN' A STOP TO ALL THAT.
THWIP!
YUP!

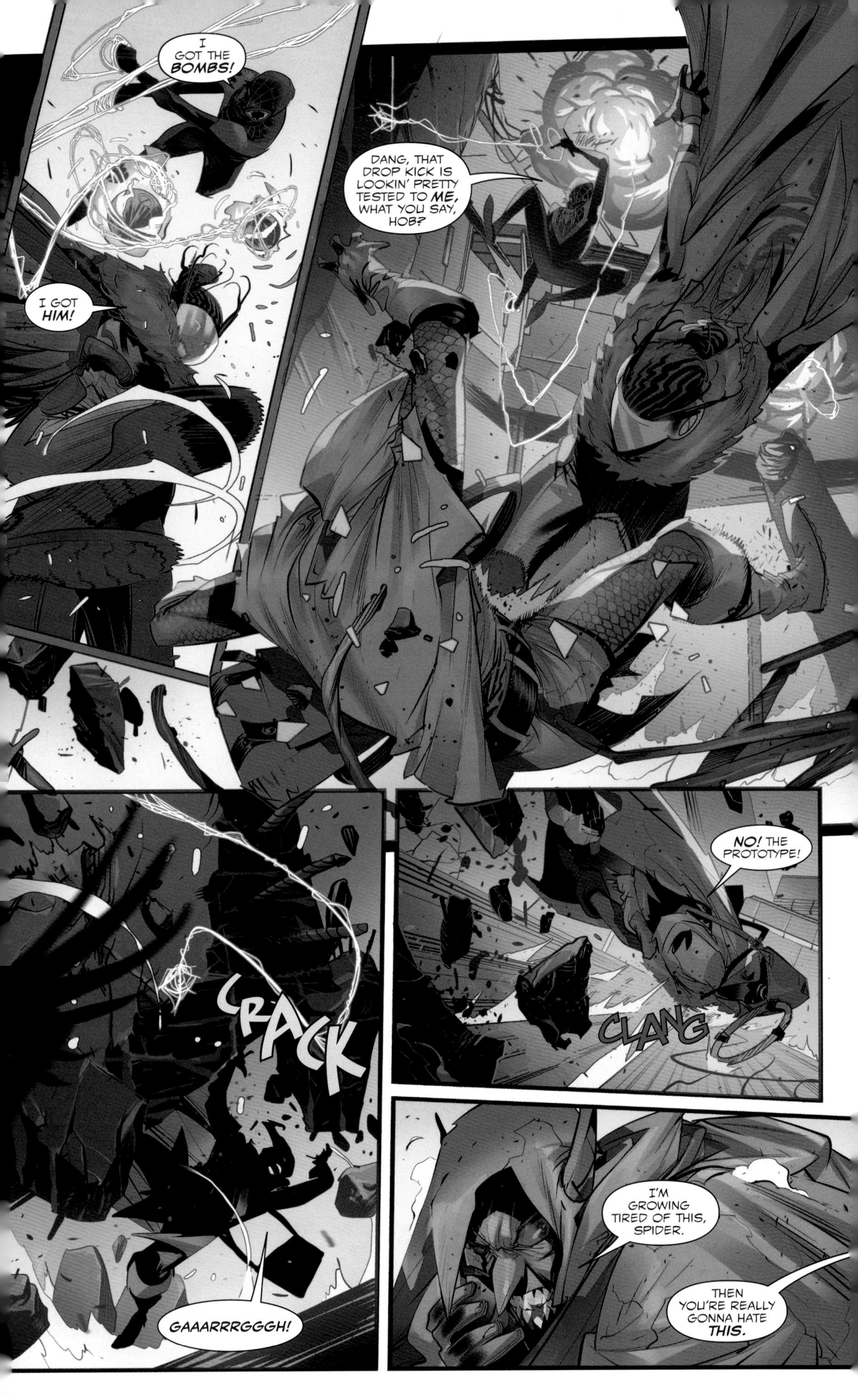
I GOT THE BOMBS!
I GOT HIM!
DANG, THAT DROP KICK IS LOOKIN' PRETTY TESTED TO ME, WHAT YOU SAY, HOB?
CRACK
GAAARRRGGGH!
NO! THE PROTOTYPE!
CLANG
I'M GROWING TIRED OF THIS, SPIDER.
THEN YOU'RE REALLY GONNA HATE THIS.

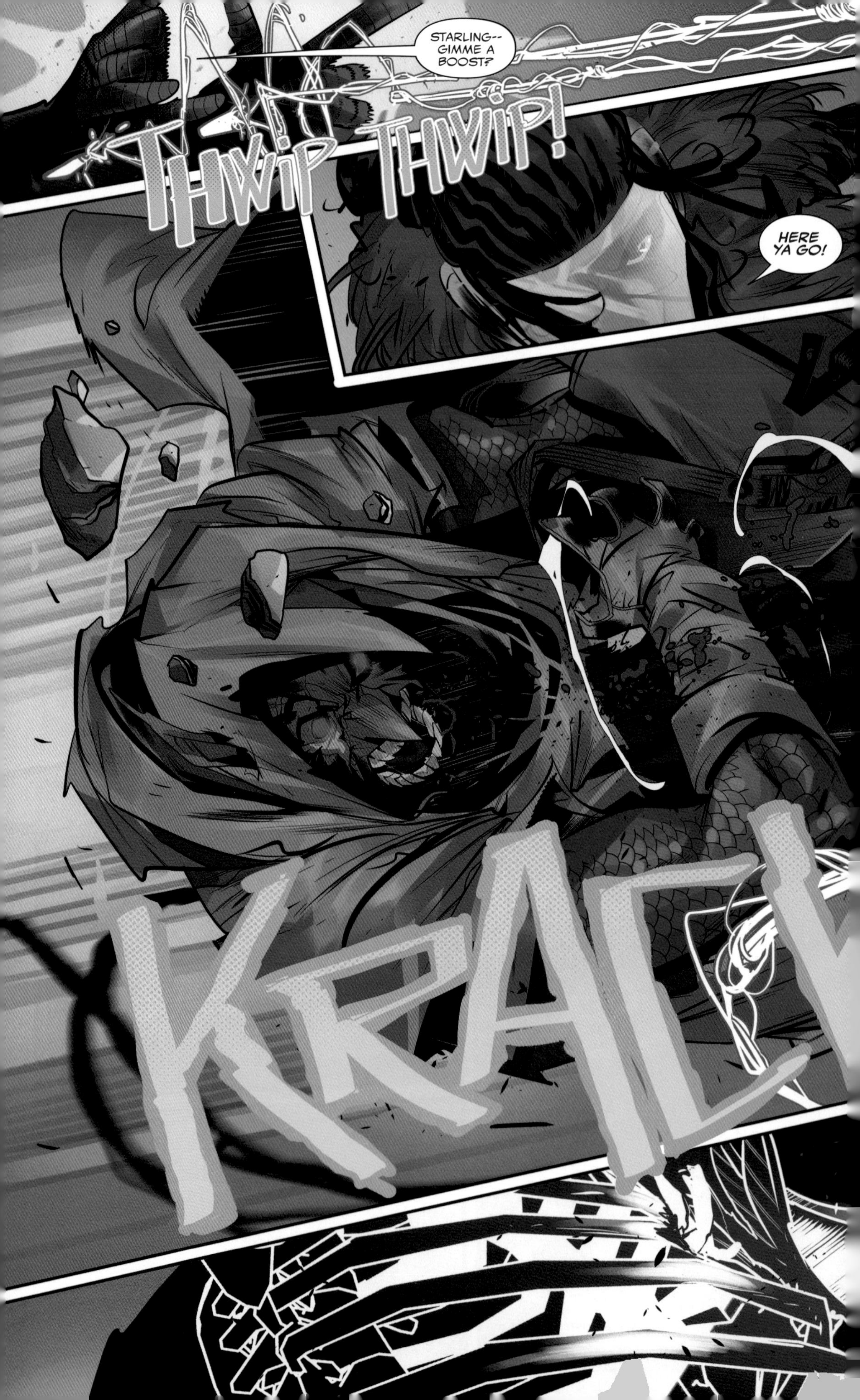
STARLING--
GIMME A
BOOST?
THWIP THWIP!
HERE
YA GO!
KRAC

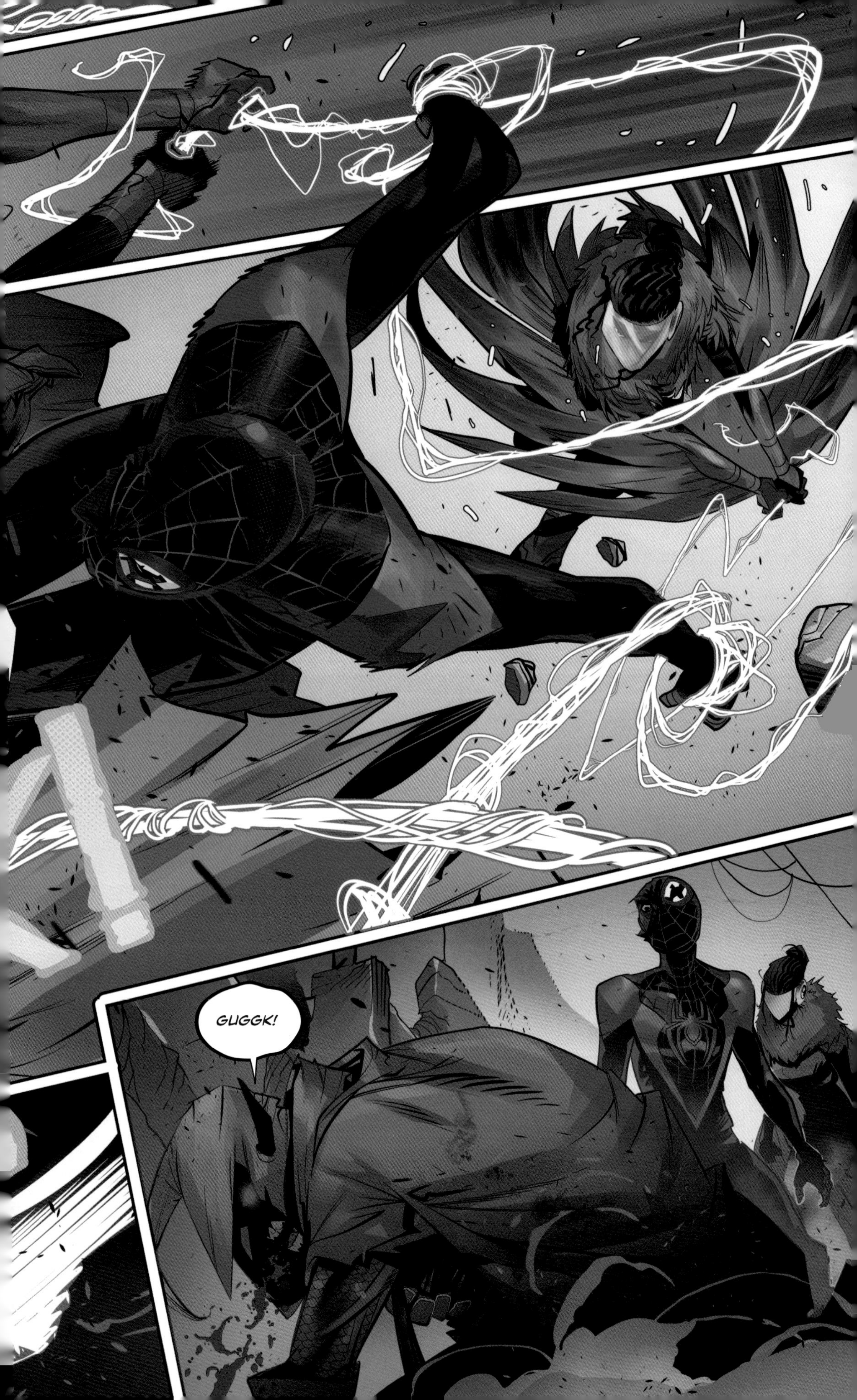
GUGGK!

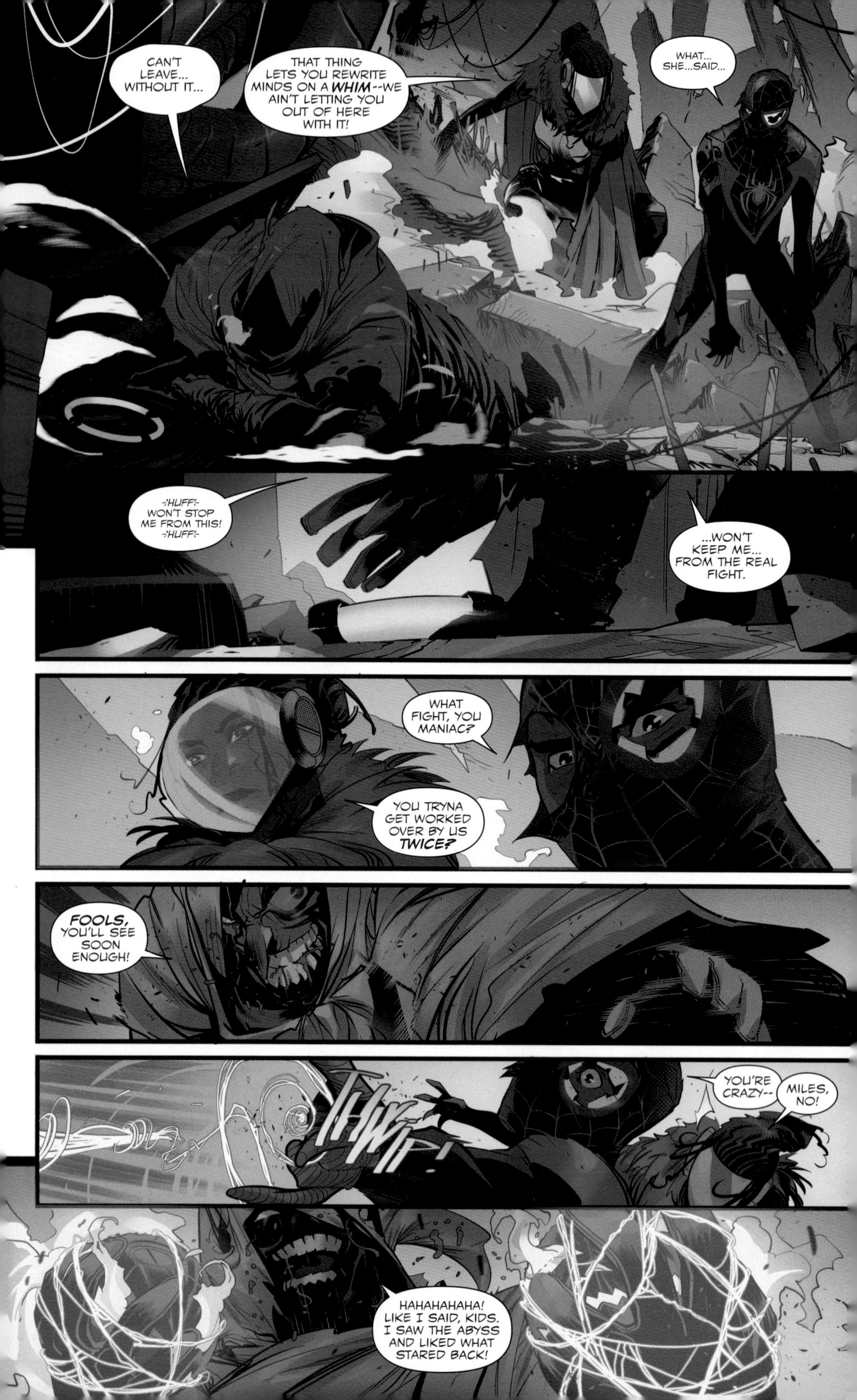
CAN'T LEAVE... WITHOUT IT...
THAT THING LETS YOU REWRITE MINDS ON A *WHIM*--WE AIN'T LETTING YOU OUT OF HERE WITH IT!
WHAT... SHE...SAID...
-HUFF- WON'T STOP ME FROM THIS! -HUFF-
...WON'T KEEP ME... FROM THE REAL FIGHT.
WHAT FIGHT, YOU MANIAC?
YOU TRYNA GET WORKED OVER BY US *TWICE?*
FOOLS, YOU'LL SEE SOON ENOUGH!
THWIP!
YOU'RE CRAZY--
MILES, NO!
HAHAHAHAHA! LIKE I SAID, KIDS. I SAW THE ABYSS AND LIKED WHAT STARED BACK!

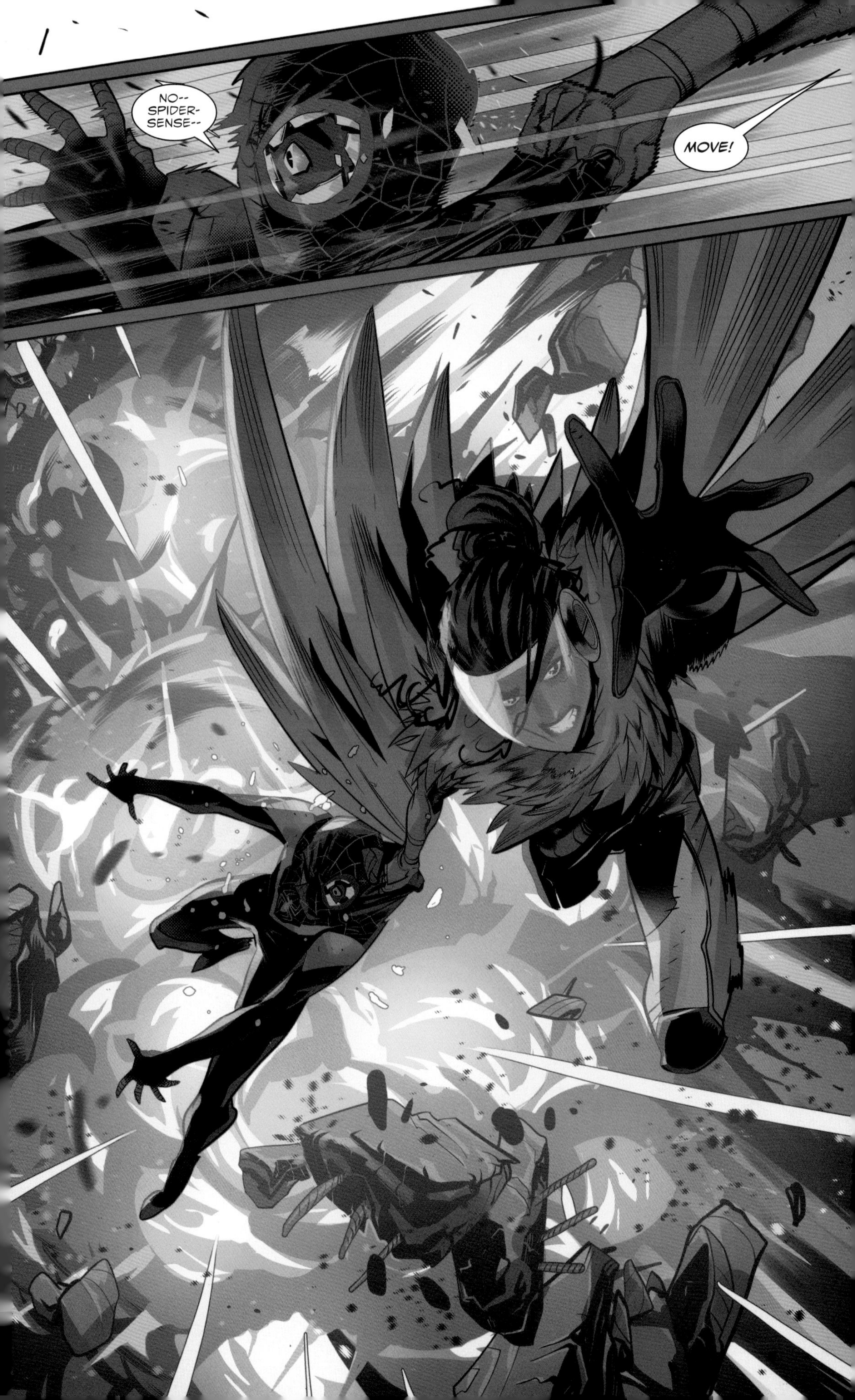
NO--
SPIDER-
SENSE--
MOVE!

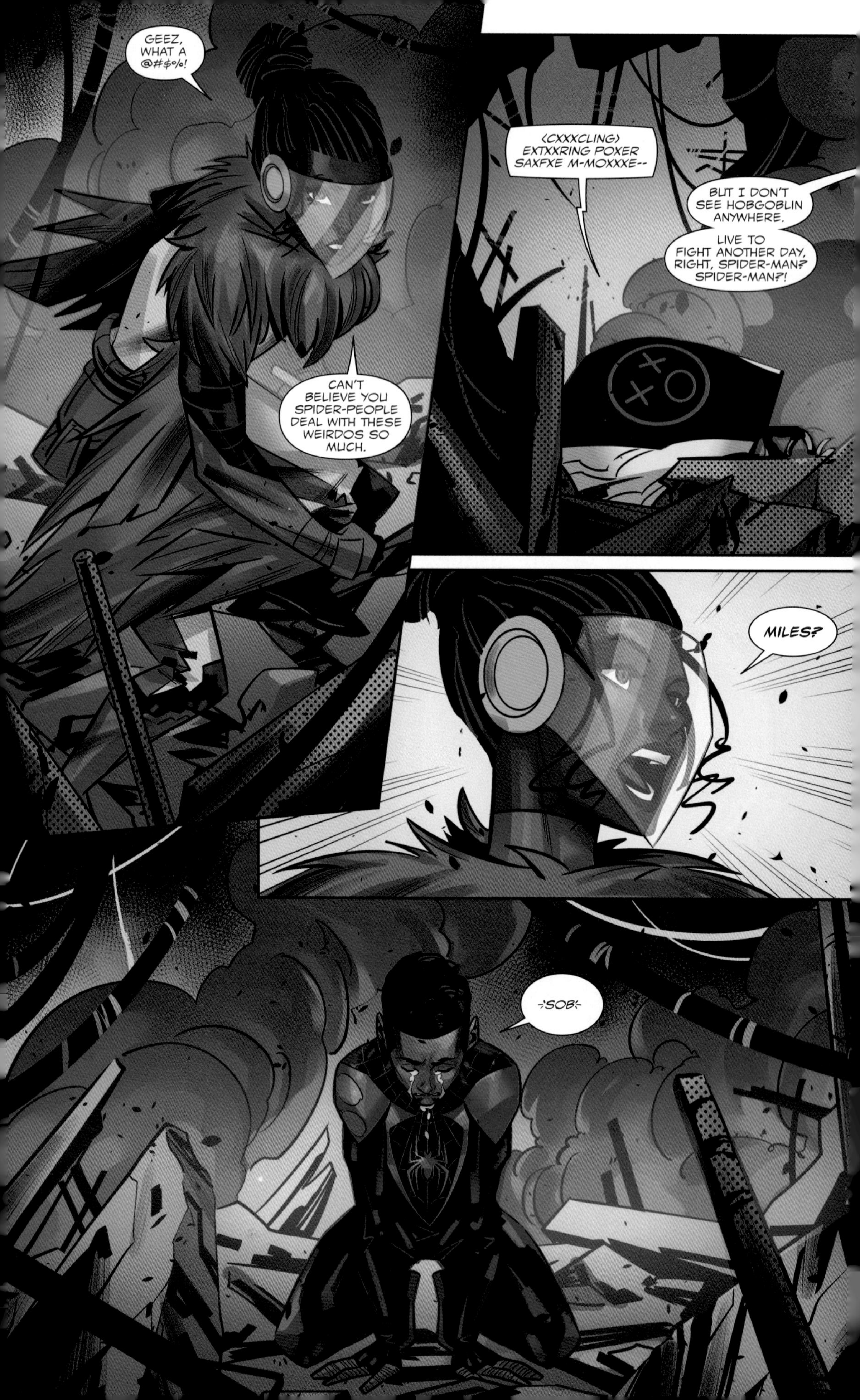
GEEZ, WHAT A @#$%!
CAN'T BELIEVE YOU SPIDER-PEOPLE DEAL WITH THESE WEIRDOS SO MUCH.
<CXXXCLING> EXTXXRING POXER SAXFXE M-MOXXXE--
BUT I DON'T SEE HOBGOBLIN ANYWHERE.
LIVE TO FIGHT ANOTHER DAY, RIGHT, SPIDER-MAN? SPIDER-MAN?!
MILES?
SOB

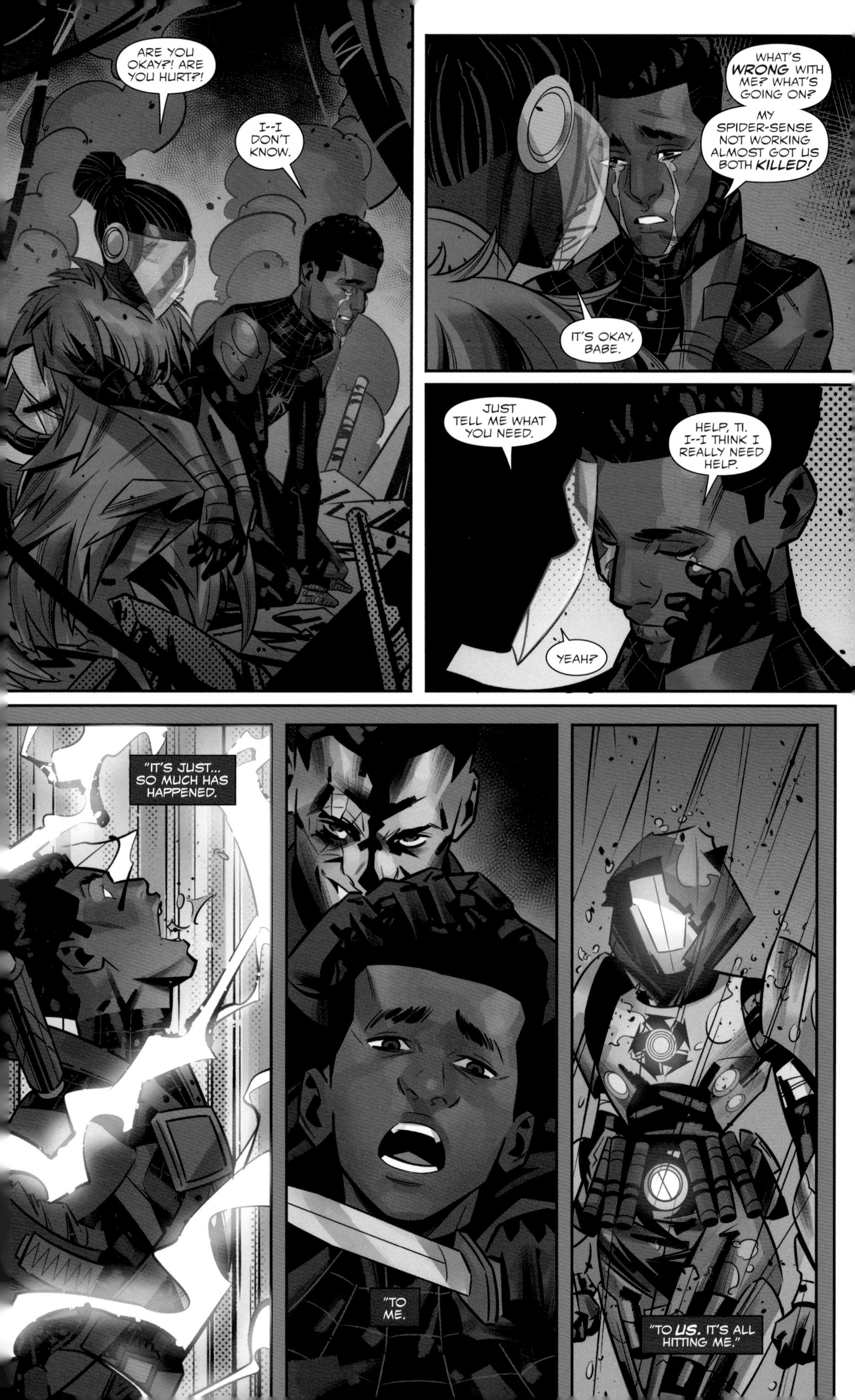
ARE YOU OKAY?! ARE YOU HURT?!
I--I DON'T KNOW.
WHAT'S WRONG WITH ME? WHAT'S GOING ON?
MY SPIDER-SENSE NOT WORKING ALMOST GOT US BOTH KILLED!
IT'S OKAY, BABE.
JUST TELL ME WHAT YOU NEED.
HELP, TI. I--I THINK I REALLY NEED HELP.
YEAH?
"IT'S JUST... SO MUCH HAS HAPPENED.
"TO ME.
"TO US. IT'S ALL HITTING ME."

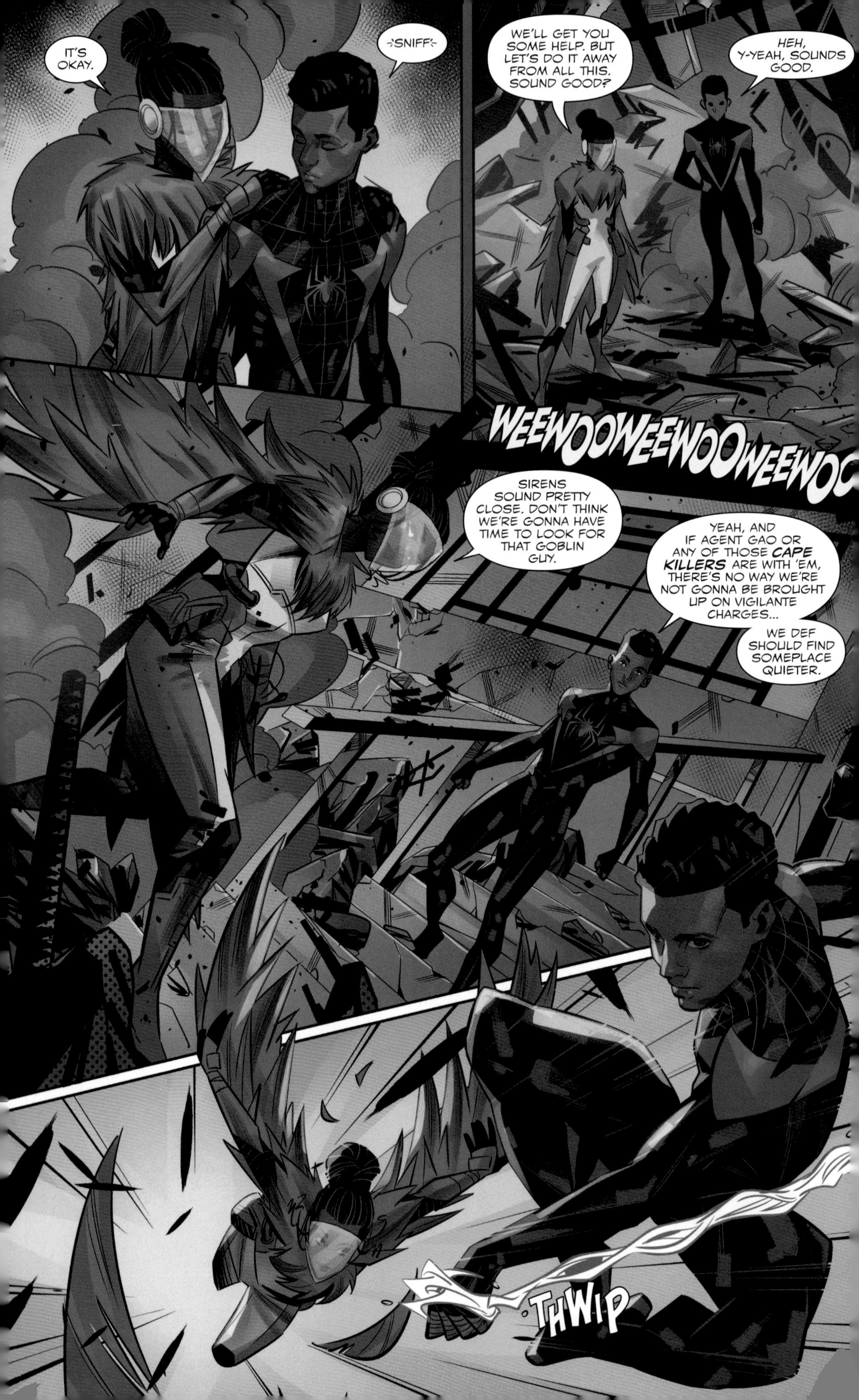
IT'S OKAY.
-SNIFF-
WE'LL GET YOU SOME HELP. BUT LET'S DO IT AWAY FROM ALL THIS. SOUND GOOD?
HEH, Y-YEAH, SOUNDS GOOD.
WEEWOOWEEWOOWEEWOO
SIRENS SOUND PRETTY CLOSE. DON'T THINK WE'RE GONNA HAVE TIME TO LOOK FOR THAT GOBLIN GUY.
YEAH, AND IF AGENT GAO OR ANY OF THOSE CAPE KILLERS ARE WITH 'EM, THERE'S NO WAY WE'RE NOT GONNA BE BROUGHT UP ON VIGILANTE CHARGES...
WE DEF SHOULD FIND SOMEPLACE QUIETER.
THWIP

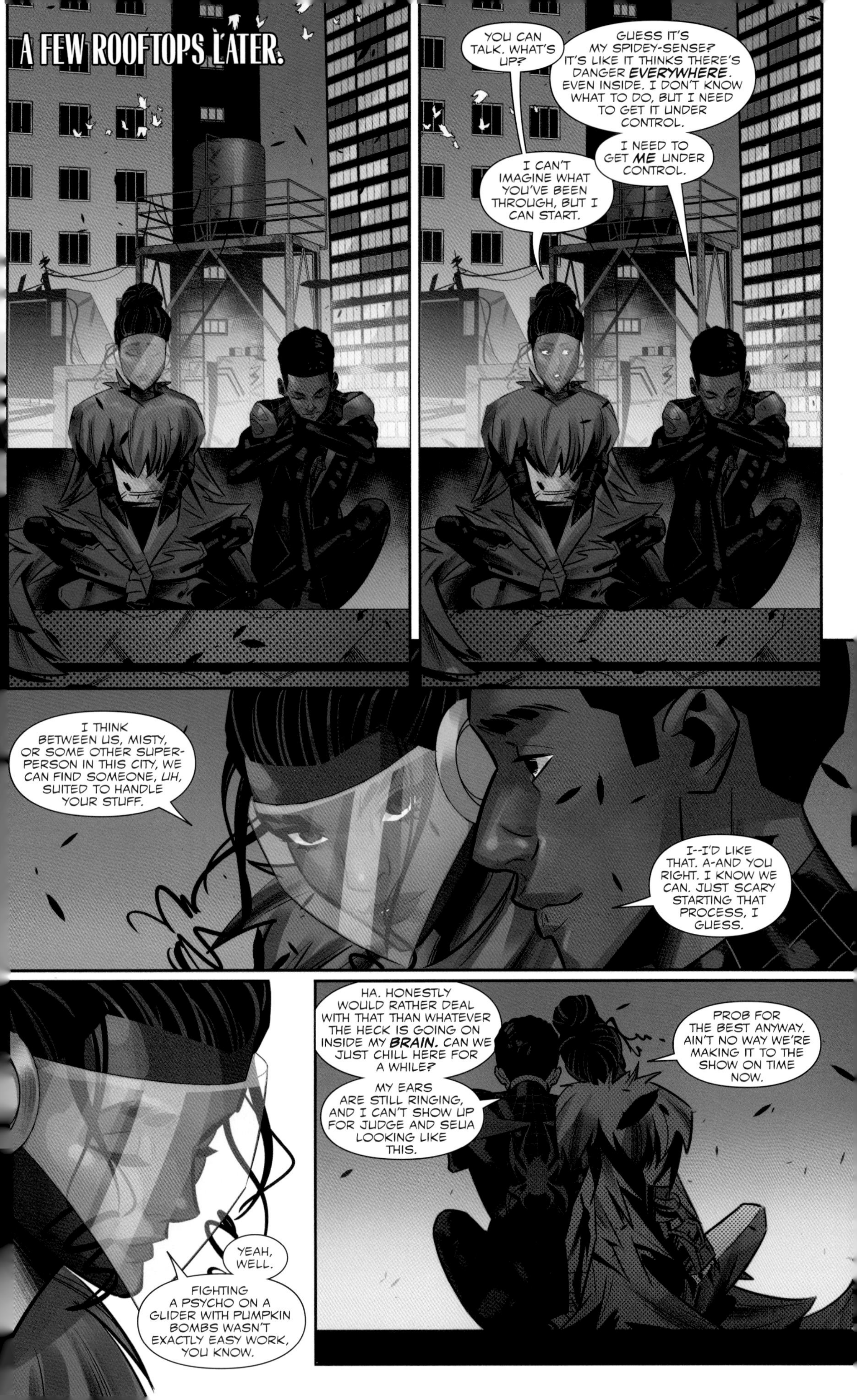
A FEW ROOFTOPS LATER.
YOU CAN TALK. WHAT'S UP?
GUESS IT'S MY SPIDEY-SENSE? IT'S LIKE IT THINKS THERE'S DANGER EVERYWHERE. EVEN INSIDE. I DON'T KNOW WHAT TO DO, BUT I NEED TO GET IT UNDER CONTROL.
I NEED TO GET ME UNDER CONTROL.
I CAN'T IMAGINE WHAT YOU'VE BEEN THROUGH, BUT I CAN START.
I THINK BETWEEN US, MISTY, OR SOME OTHER SUPER-PERSON IN THIS CITY, WE CAN FIND SOMEONE, UH, SUITED TO HANDLE YOUR STUFF.
I--I'D LIKE THAT. A-AND YOU RIGHT. I KNOW WE CAN. JUST SCARY STARTING THAT PROCESS, I GUESS.
YEAH, WELL.
FIGHTING A PSYCHO ON A GLIDER WITH PUMPKIN BOMBS WASN'T EXACTLY EASY WORK, YOU KNOW.
HA. HONESTLY WOULD RATHER DEAL WITH THAT THAN WHATEVER THE HECK IS GOING ON INSIDE MY BRAIN. CAN WE JUST CHILL HERE FOR A WHILE?
MY EARS ARE STILL RINGING, AND I CAN'T SHOW UP FOR JUDGE AND SELIA LOOKING LIKE THIS.
PROB FOR THE BEST ANYWAY. AIN'T NO WAY WE'RE MAKING IT TO THE SHOW ON TIME NOW.

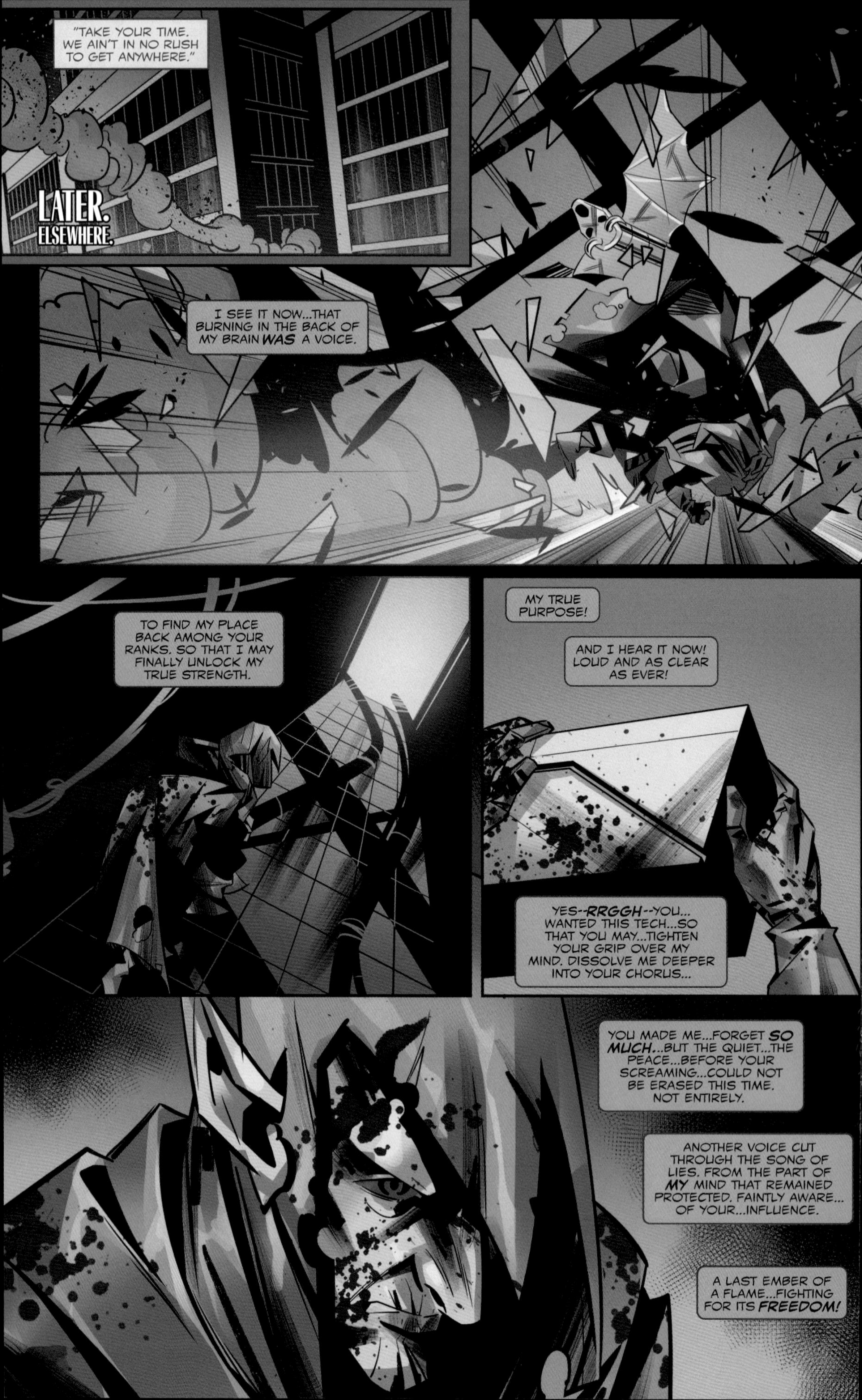
"TAKE YOUR TIME. WE AIN'T IN NO RUSH TO GET ANYWHERE."
LATER. ELSEWHERE.
I SEE IT NOW...THAT BURNING IN THE BACK OF MY BRAIN **WAS** A VOICE.
TO FIND MY PLACE BACK AMONG YOUR RANKS. SO THAT I MAY FINALLY UNLOCK MY TRUE STRENGTH.
MY TRUE PURPOSE!
AND I HEAR IT NOW! LOUD AND AS CLEAR AS EVER!
YES--**RRGGH**--YOU... WANTED THIS TECH...SO THAT YOU MAY...TIGHTEN YOUR GRIP OVER MY MIND. DISSOLVE ME DEEPER INTO YOUR CHORUS...
YOU MADE ME...FORGET **SO MUCH**...BUT THE QUIET...THE PEACE...BEFORE YOUR SCREAMING...COULD NOT BE ERASED THIS TIME. NOT ENTIRELY.
ANOTHER VOICE CUT THROUGH THE SONG OF LIES. FROM THE PART OF **MY** MIND THAT REMAINED PROTECTED. FAINTLY AWARE... OF YOUR...INFLUENCE.
A LAST EMBER OF A FLAME...FIGHTING FOR ITS **FREEDOM!**

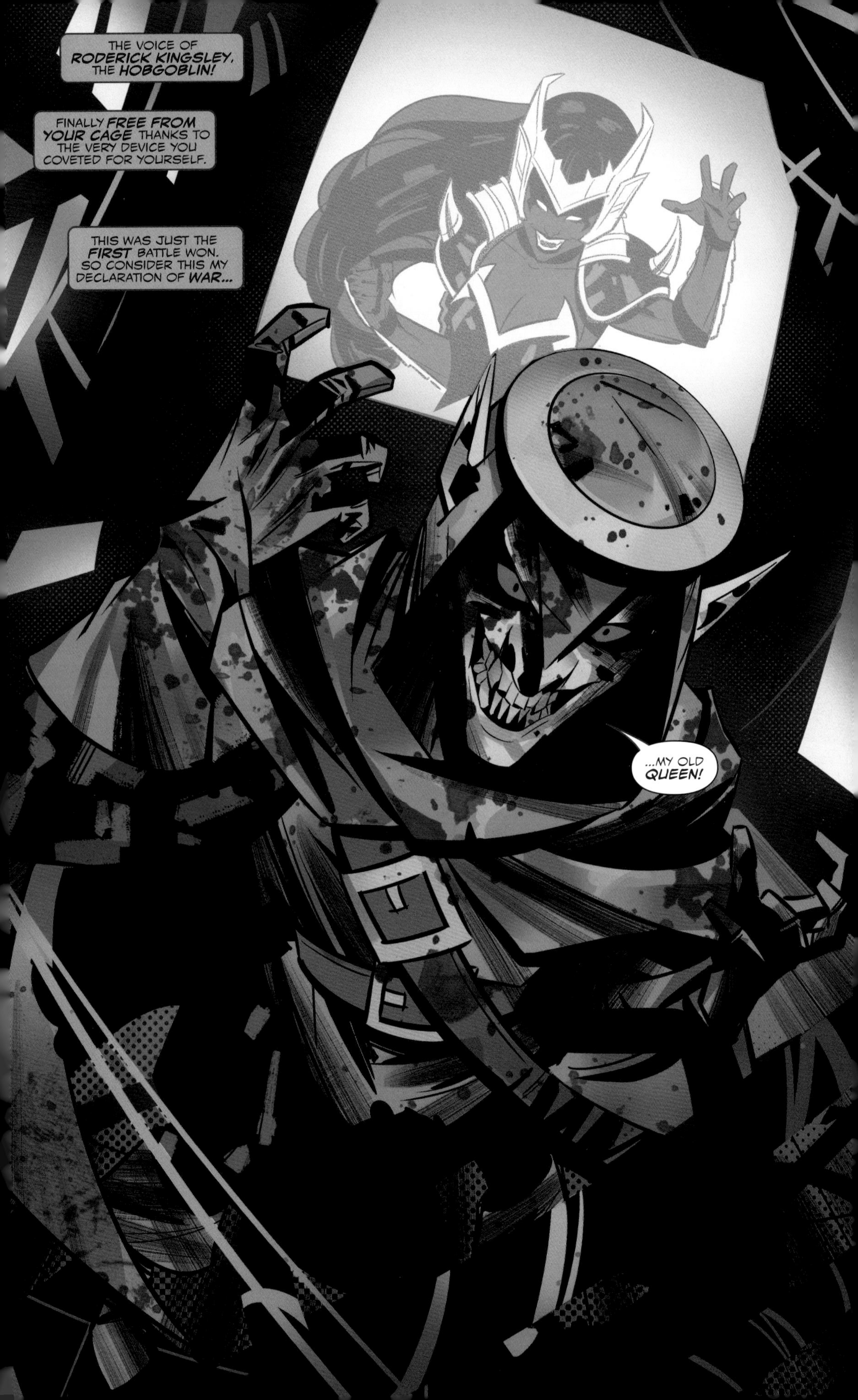
THE VOICE OF RODERICK KINGSLEY, THE HOBGOBLIN!
FINALLY FREE FROM YOUR CAGE THANKS TO THE VERY DEVICE YOU COVETED FOR YOURSELF.
THIS WAS JUST THE FIRST BATTLE WON. SO CONSIDER THIS MY DECLARATION OF WAR...
...MY OLD QUEEN!

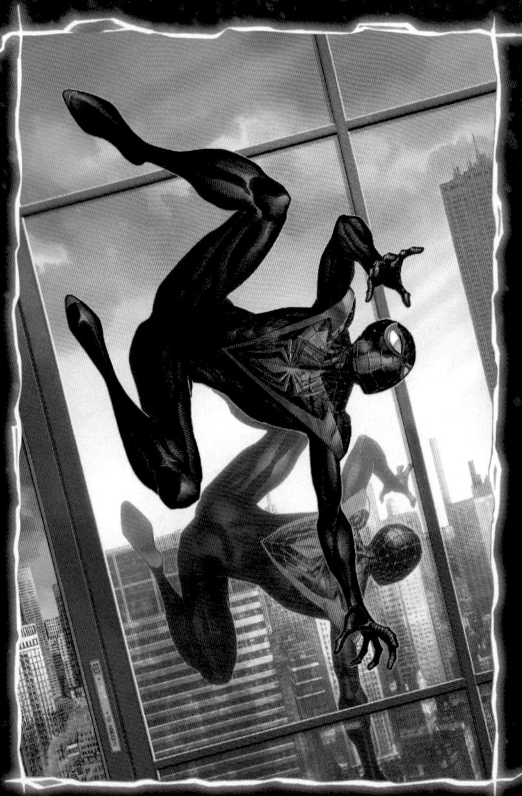

#8 VARIANT BY
JIM CHEUNG & JAY DAVID RAMOS

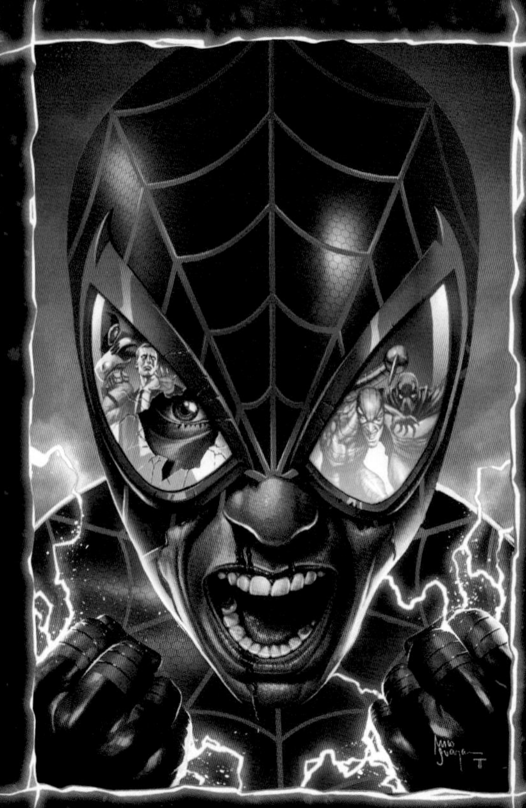

#8 VARIANT BY
MICO SUAYAN & JUAN FERNANDEZ

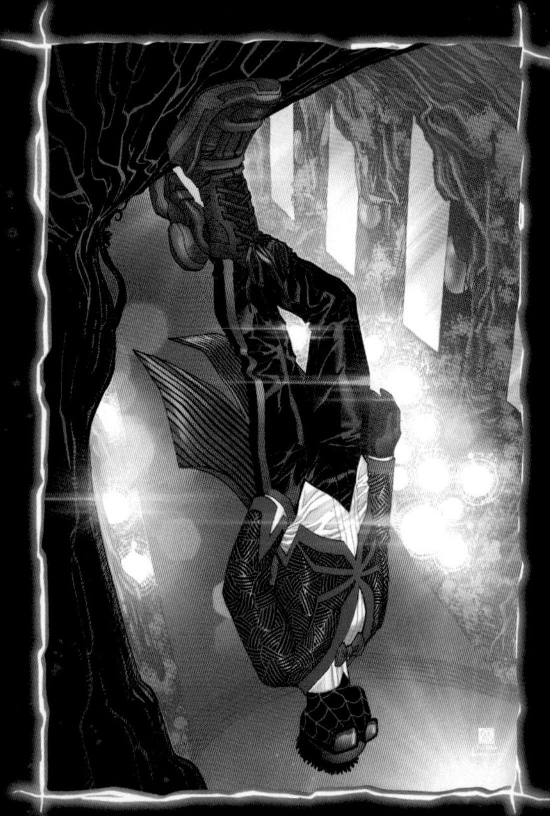

#8 HELLFIRE GALA VARIANT BY
**BERNARD CHANG &
MARCELO MAIOLO**

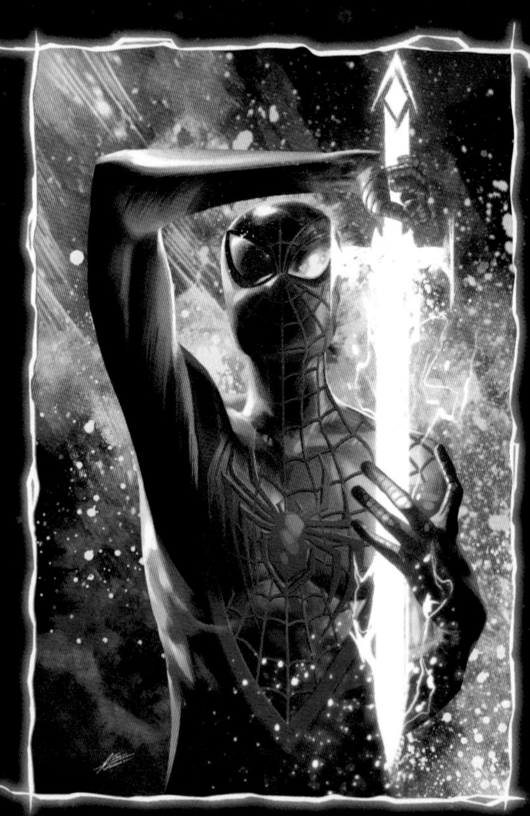

#9 VARIANT BY
MATEUS MANHANINI

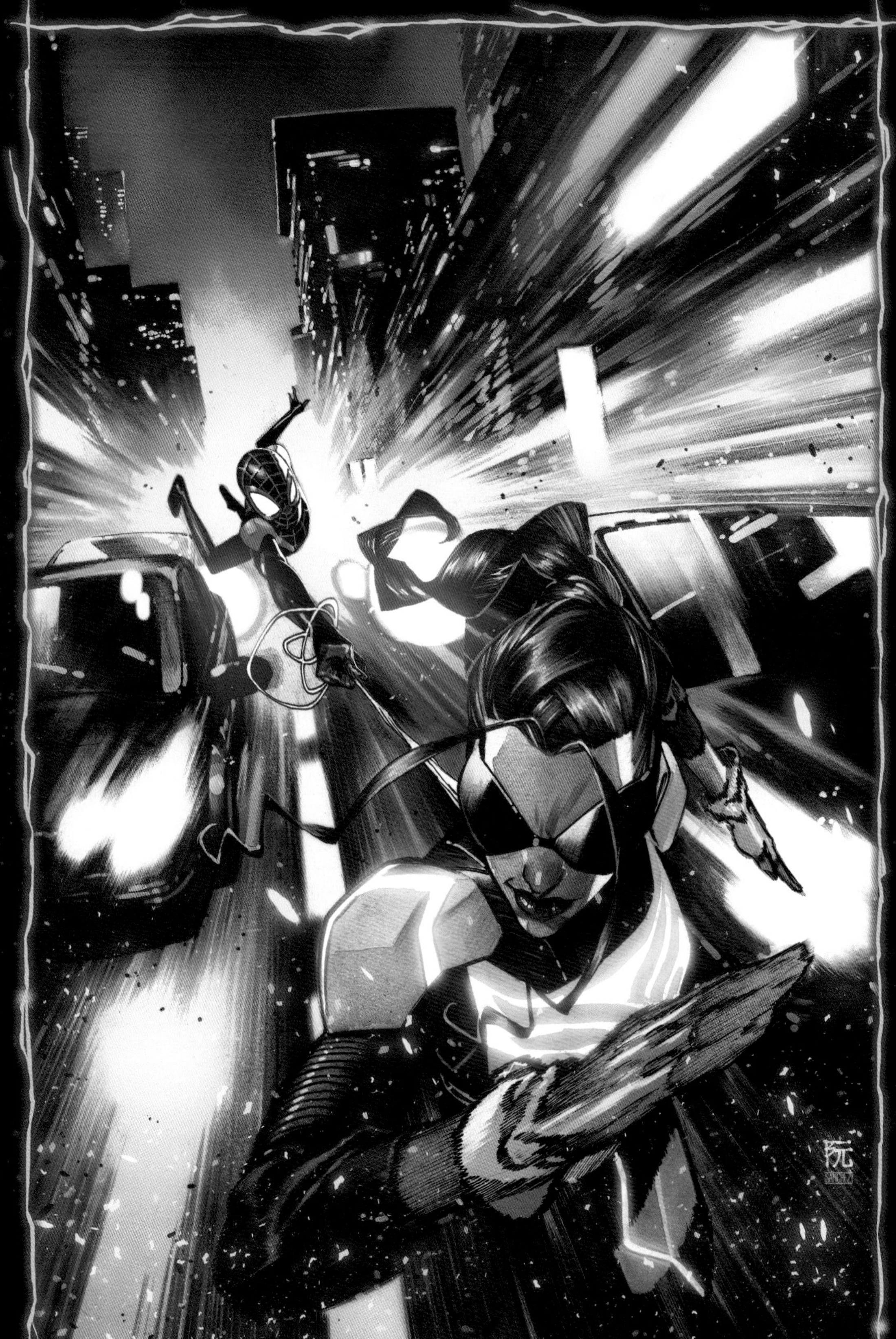

10

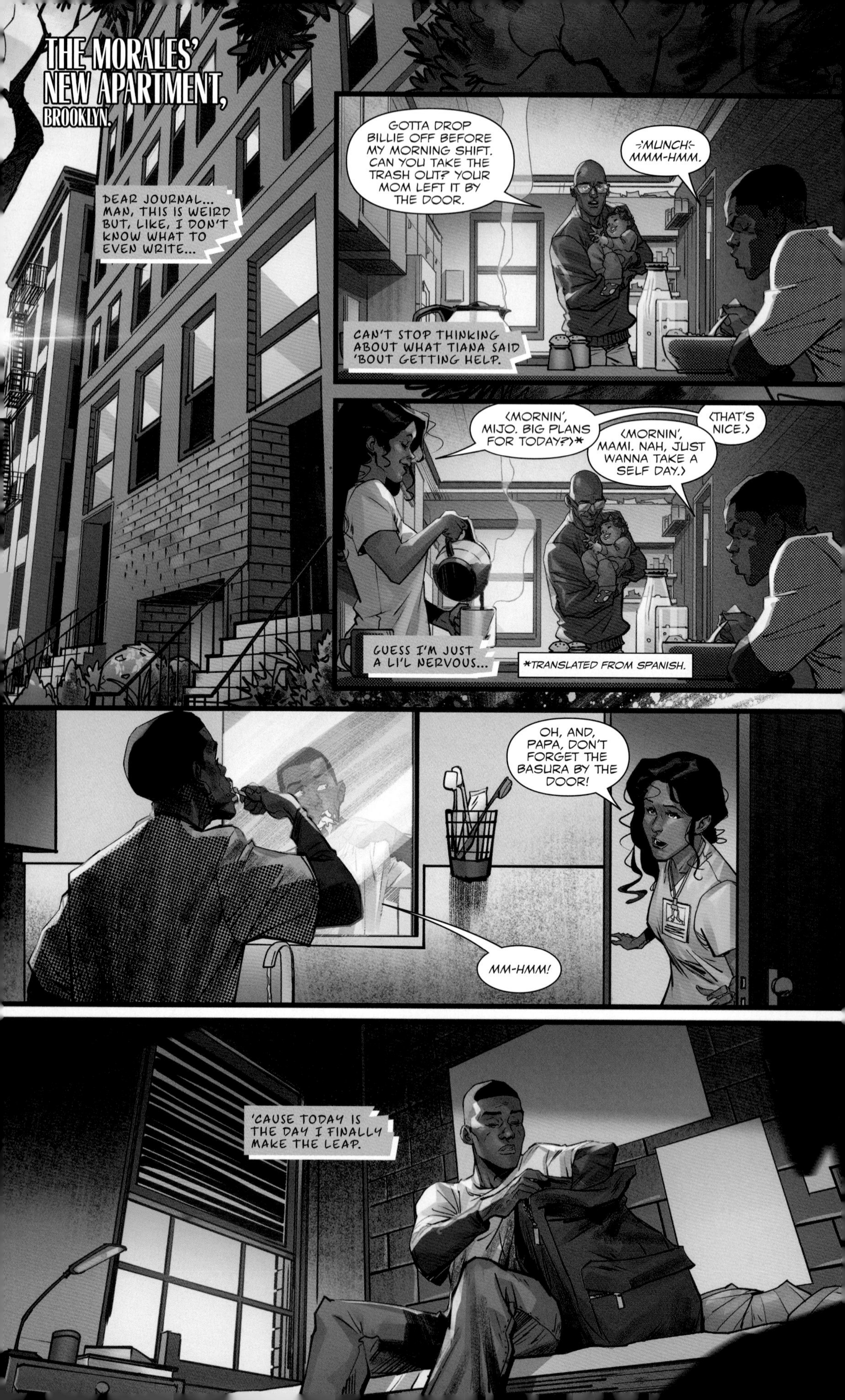
THE MORALES' NEW APARTMENT, BROOKLYN.
DEAR JOURNAL... MAN, THIS IS WEIRD BUT, LIKE, I DON'T KNOW WHAT TO EVEN WRITE...
GOTTA DROP BILLIE OFF BEFORE MY MORNING SHIFT. CAN YOU TAKE THE TRASH OUT? YOUR MOM LEFT IT BY THE DOOR.
-MUNCH- MMM-HMM.
CAN'T STOP THINKING ABOUT WHAT TIANA SAID 'BOUT GETTING HELP.
<MORNIN', MIJO. BIG PLANS FOR TODAY?>*
<MORNIN', MAMI. NAH, JUST WANNA TAKE A SELF DAY.>
<THAT'S NICE.>
GUESS I'M JUST A LI'L NERVOUS...
*TRANSLATED FROM SPANISH.
OH, AND, PAPA, DON'T FORGET THE BASURA BY THE DOOR!
MM-HMM!
'CAUSE TODAY IS THE DAY I FINALLY MAKE THE LEAP.

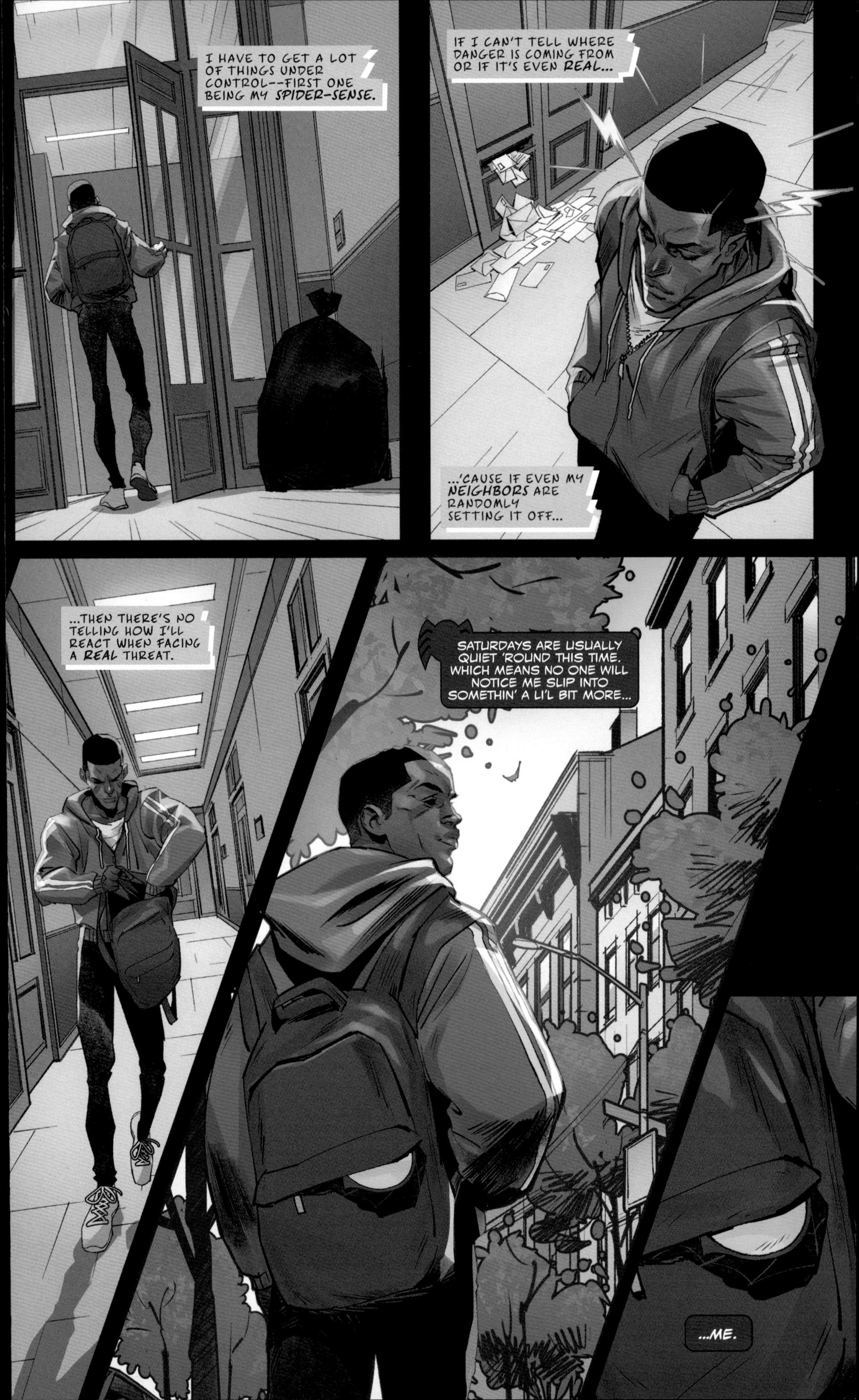
I HAVE TO GET A LOT OF THINGS UNDER CONTROL--FIRST ONE BEING MY *SPIDER-SENSE.*
IF I CAN'T TELL WHERE DANGER IS COMING FROM OR IF IT'S EVEN *REAL*...
...'CAUSE IF EVEN MY *NEIGHBORS* ARE RANDOMLY SETTING IT OFF...
...THEN THERE'S NO TELLING HOW I'LL REACT WHEN FACING A *REAL* THREAT.
SATURDAYS ARE USUALLY QUIET 'ROUND THIS TIME. WHICH MEANS NO ONE WILL NOTICE ME SLIP INTO SOMETHIN' A LI'L BIT MORE...
...ME.

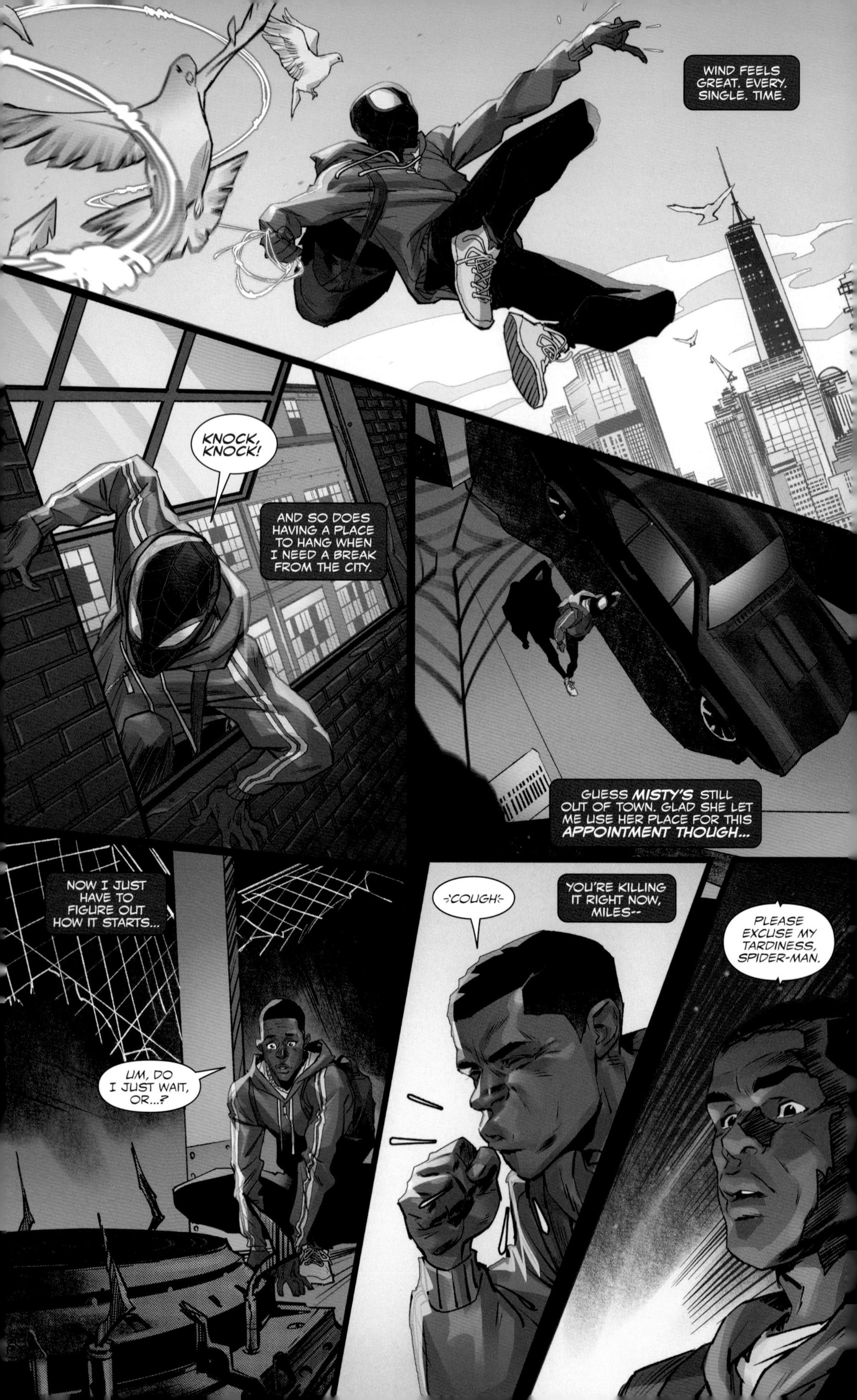
WIND FEELS GREAT. EVERY. SINGLE. TIME.
KNOCK, KNOCK!
AND SO DOES HAVING A PLACE TO HANG WHEN I NEED A BREAK FROM THE CITY.
GUESS MISTY'S STILL OUT OF TOWN. GLAD SHE LET ME USE HER PLACE FOR THIS APPOINTMENT THOUGH...
NOW I JUST HAVE TO FIGURE OUT HOW IT STARTS...
UM, DO I JUST WAIT, OR...?
COUGH
YOU'RE KILLING IT RIGHT NOW, MILES--
PLEASE EXCUSE MY TARDINESS, SPIDER-MAN.

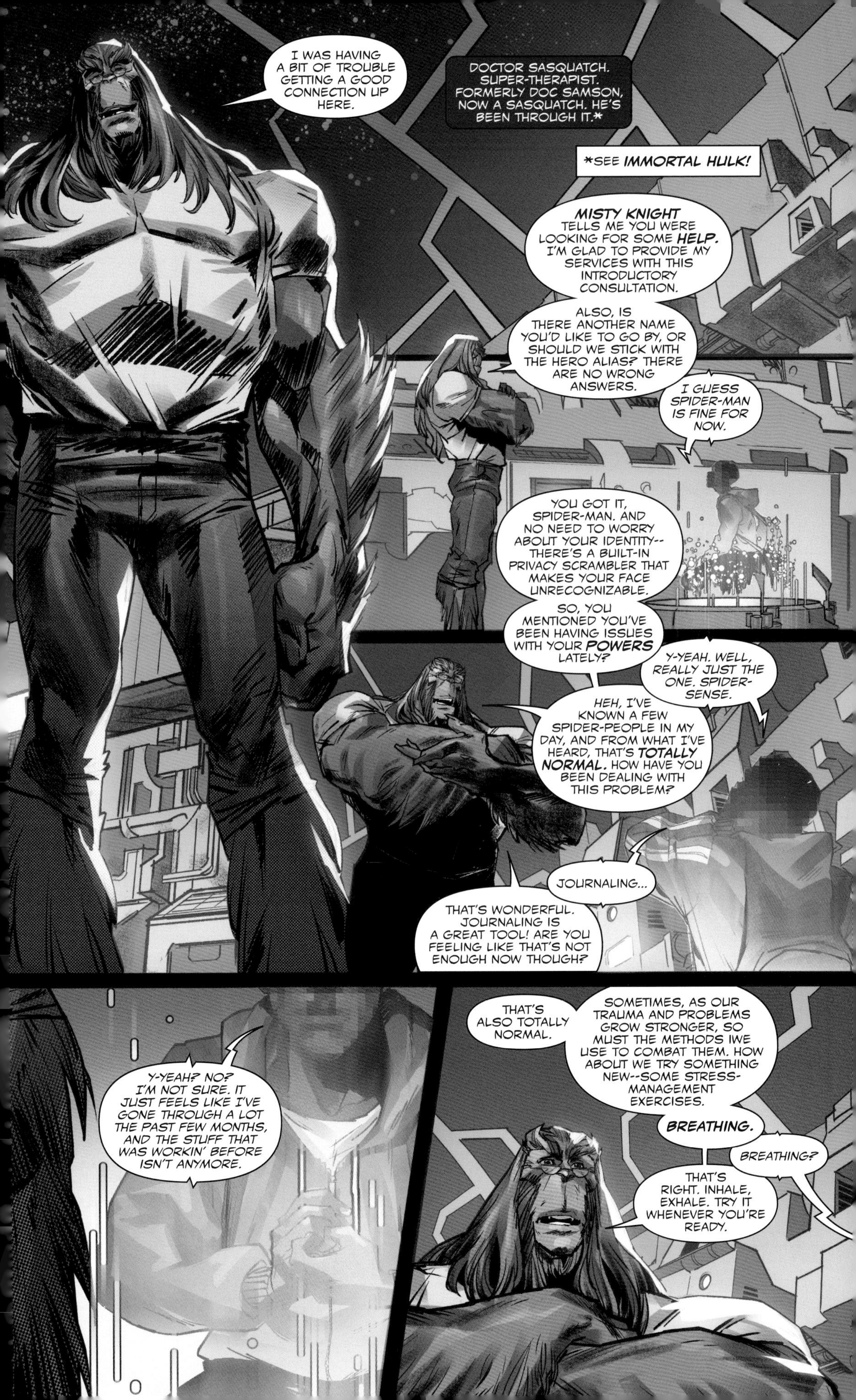
I WAS HAVING A BIT OF TROUBLE GETTING A GOOD CONNECTION UP HERE.
DOCTOR SASQUATCH. SUPER-THERAPIST. FORMERLY DOC SAMSON, NOW A SASQUATCH. HE'S BEEN THROUGH IT.*
*SEE IMMORTAL HULK!
MISTY KNIGHT TELLS ME YOU WERE LOOKING FOR SOME HELP. I'M GLAD TO PROVIDE MY SERVICES WITH THIS INTRODUCTORY CONSULTATION.
ALSO, IS THERE ANOTHER NAME YOU'D LIKE TO GO BY, OR SHOULD WE STICK WITH THE HERO ALIAS? THERE ARE NO WRONG ANSWERS.
I GUESS SPIDER-MAN IS FINE FOR NOW.
YOU GOT IT, SPIDER-MAN. AND NO NEED TO WORRY ABOUT YOUR IDENTITY--THERE'S A BUILT-IN PRIVACY SCRAMBLER THAT MAKES YOUR FACE UNRECOGNIZABLE.
SO, YOU MENTIONED YOU'VE BEEN HAVING ISSUES WITH YOUR POWERS LATELY?
Y-YEAH. WELL, REALLY JUST THE ONE. SPIDER-SENSE.
HEH, I'VE KNOWN A FEW SPIDER-PEOPLE IN MY DAY, AND FROM WHAT I'VE HEARD, THAT'S TOTALLY NORMAL. HOW HAVE YOU BEEN DEALING WITH THIS PROBLEM?
JOURNALING...
THAT'S WONDERFUL. JOURNALING IS A GREAT TOOL! ARE YOU FEELING LIKE THAT'S NOT ENOUGH NOW THOUGH?
Y-YEAH? NO? I'M NOT SURE. IT JUST FEELS LIKE I'VE GONE THROUGH A LOT THE PAST FEW MONTHS, AND THE STUFF THAT WAS WORKIN' BEFORE ISN'T ANYMORE.
THAT'S ALSO TOTALLY NORMAL.
SOMETIMES, AS OUR TRAUMA AND PROBLEMS GROW STRONGER, SO MUST THE METHODS WE USE TO COMBAT THEM. HOW ABOUT WE TRY SOMETHING NEW--SOME STRESS-MANAGEMENT EXERCISES.
BREATHING.
BREATHING?
THAT'S RIGHT. INHALE, EXHALE. TRY IT WHENEVER YOU'RE READY.

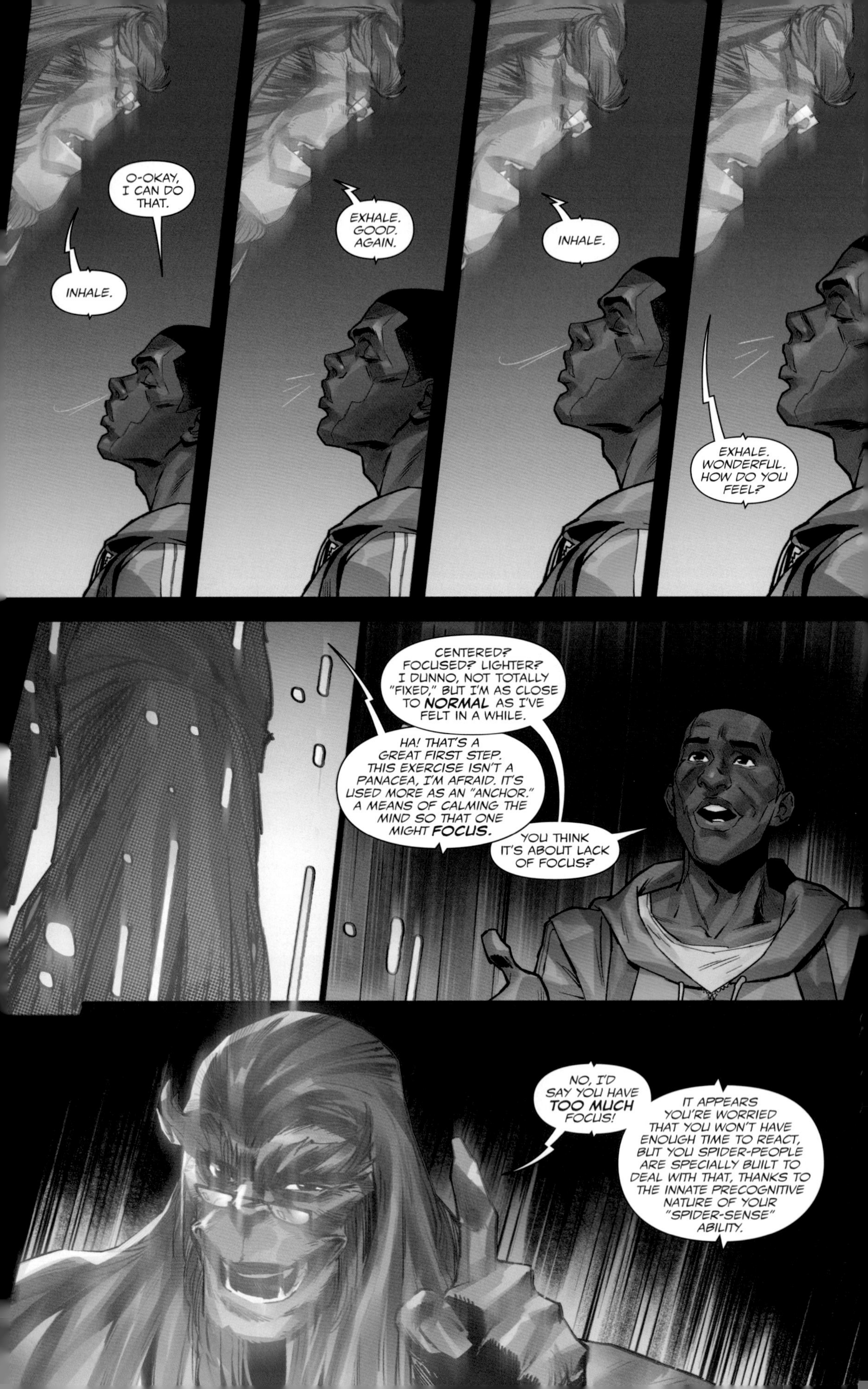
O-OKAY, I CAN DO THAT.
INHALE.
EXHALE. GOOD. AGAIN.
INHALE.
EXHALE. WONDERFUL. HOW DO YOU FEEL?
CENTERED? FOCUSED? LIGHTER? I DUNNO, NOT TOTALLY "FIXED," BUT I'M AS CLOSE TO NORMAL AS I'VE FELT IN A WHILE.
HA! THAT'S A GREAT FIRST STEP. THIS EXERCISE ISN'T A PANACEA, I'M AFRAID. IT'S USED MORE AS AN "ANCHOR." A MEANS OF CALMING THE MIND SO THAT ONE MIGHT FOCUS.
YOU THINK IT'S ABOUT LACK OF FOCUS?
NO, I'D SAY YOU HAVE TOO MUCH FOCUS!
IT APPEARS YOU'RE WORRIED THAT YOU WON'T HAVE ENOUGH TIME TO REACT, BUT YOU SPIDER-PEOPLE ARE SPECIALLY BUILT TO DEAL WITH THAT, THANKS TO THE INNATE PRECOGNITIVE NATURE OF YOUR "SPIDER-SENSE" ABILITY.

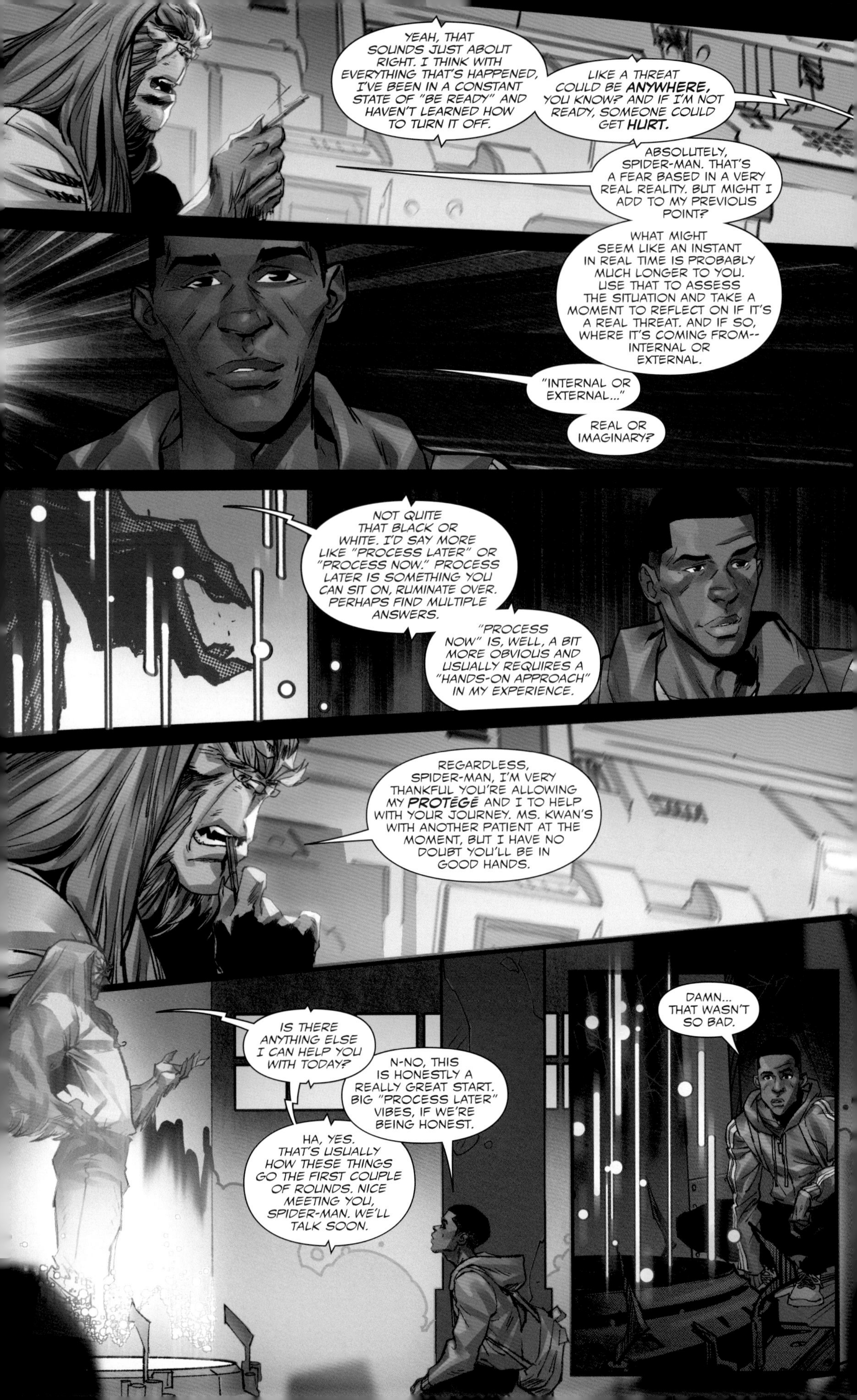
YEAH, THAT SOUNDS JUST ABOUT RIGHT. I THINK WITH EVERYTHING THAT'S HAPPENED, I'VE BEEN IN A CONSTANT STATE OF "BE READY" AND HAVEN'T LEARNED HOW TO TURN IT OFF.
LIKE A THREAT COULD BE **ANYWHERE,** YOU KNOW? AND IF I'M NOT READY, SOMEONE COULD GET **HURT.**
ABSOLUTELY, SPIDER-MAN. THAT'S A FEAR BASED IN A VERY REAL REALITY. BUT MIGHT I ADD TO MY PREVIOUS POINT?
WHAT MIGHT SEEM LIKE AN INSTANT IN REAL TIME IS PROBABLY MUCH LONGER TO YOU. USE THAT TO ASSESS THE SITUATION AND TAKE A MOMENT TO REFLECT ON IF IT'S A REAL THREAT. AND IF SO, WHERE IT'S COMING FROM-- INTERNAL OR EXTERNAL.
"INTERNAL OR EXTERNAL..."
REAL OR IMAGINARY?
NOT QUITE THAT BLACK OR WHITE. I'D SAY MORE LIKE "PROCESS LATER" OR "PROCESS NOW." PROCESS LATER IS SOMETHING YOU CAN SIT ON, RUMINATE OVER. PERHAPS FIND MULTIPLE ANSWERS.
"PROCESS NOW" IS, WELL, A BIT MORE OBVIOUS AND USUALLY REQUIRES A "HANDS-ON APPROACH" IN MY EXPERIENCE.
REGARDLESS, SPIDER-MAN, I'M VERY THANKFUL YOU'RE ALLOWING MY **PROTÉGÉ** AND I TO HELP WITH YOUR JOURNEY. MS. KWAN'S WITH ANOTHER PATIENT AT THE MOMENT, BUT I HAVE NO DOUBT YOU'LL BE IN GOOD HANDS.
IS THERE ANYTHING ELSE I CAN HELP YOU WITH TODAY?
N-NO, THIS IS HONESTLY A REALLY GREAT START. BIG "PROCESS LATER" VIBES, IF WE'RE BEING HONEST.
HA, YES. THAT'S USUALLY HOW THESE THINGS GO THE FIRST COUPLE OF ROUNDS. NICE MEETING YOU, SPIDER-MAN. WE'LL TALK SOON.
DAMN... THAT WASN'T SO BAD.

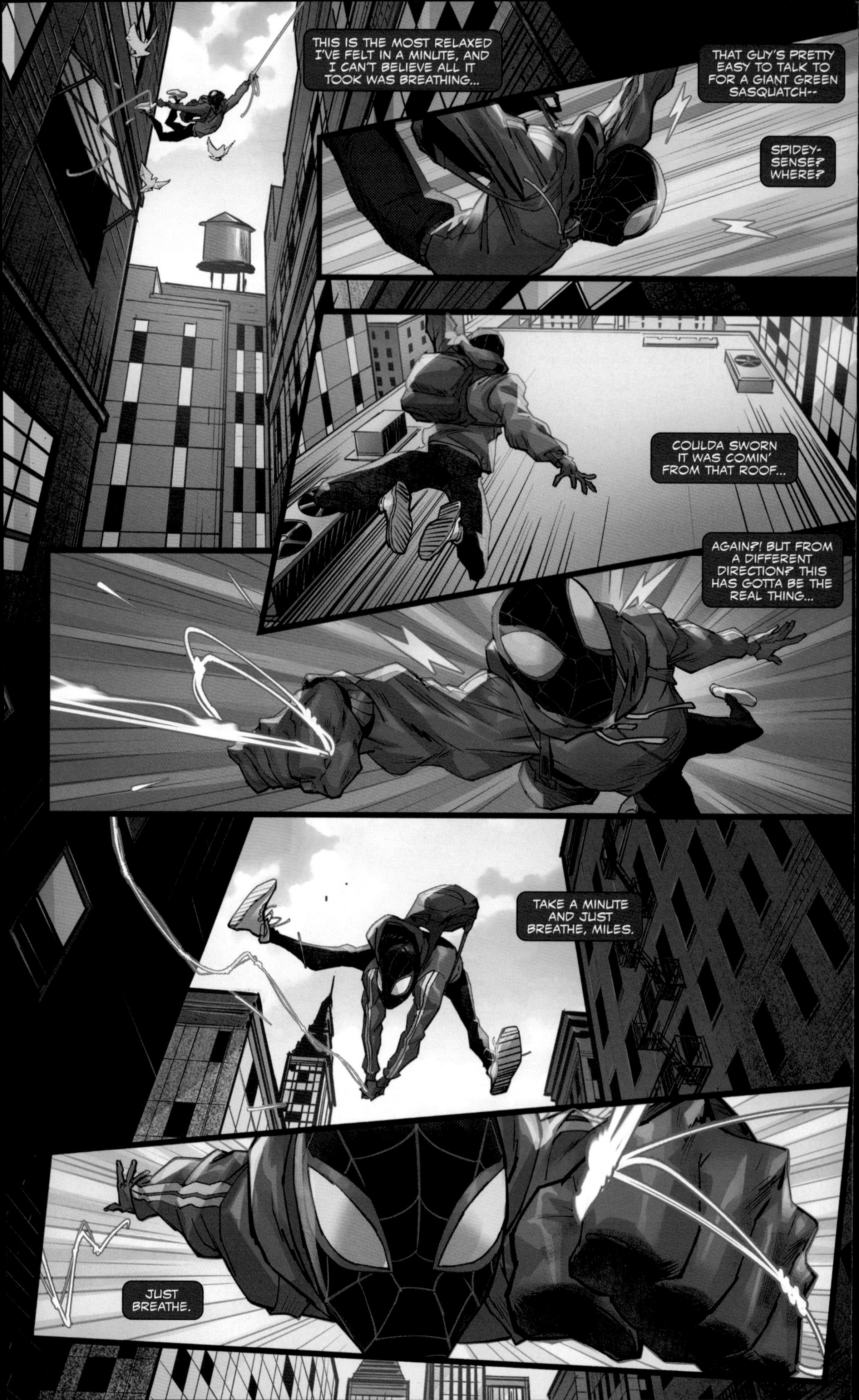
THIS IS THE MOST RELAXED I'VE FELT IN A MINUTE, AND I CAN'T BELIEVE ALL IT TOOK WAS BREATHING...
THAT GUY'S PRETTY EASY TO TALK TO FOR A GIANT GREEN SASQUATCH--
SPIDEY-SENSE? WHERE?
COULDA SWORN IT WAS COMIN' FROM THAT ROOF...
AGAIN?! BUT FROM A DIFFERENT DIRECTION? THIS HAS GOTTA BE THE REAL THING...
TAKE A MINUTE AND JUST BREATHE, MILES.
JUST BREATHE.

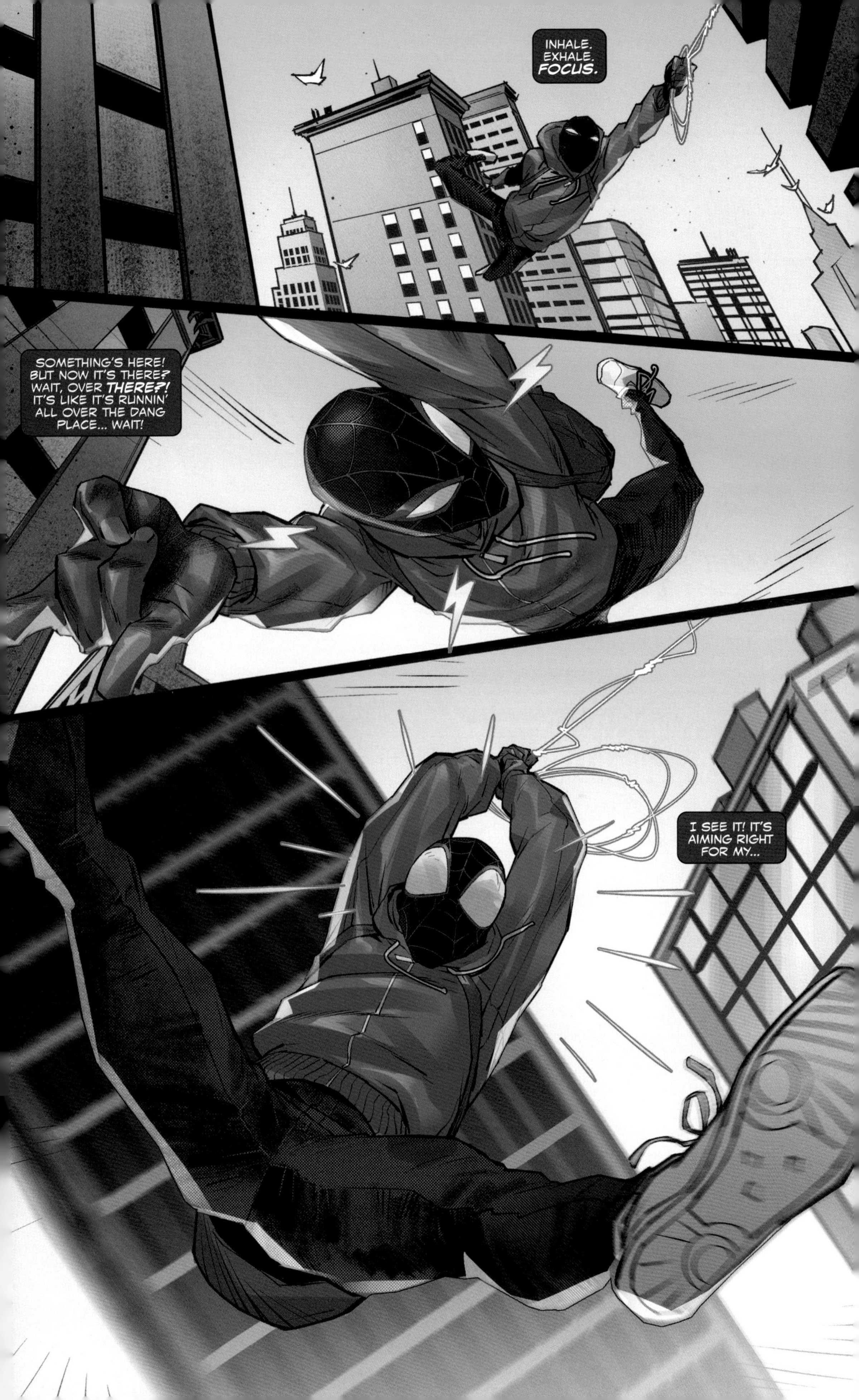
INHALE. EXHALE. FOCUS.
SOMETHING'S HERE! BUT NOW IT'S THERE? WAIT, OVER THERE?! IT'S LIKE IT'S RUNNIN' ALL OVER THE DANG PLACE... WAIT!
I SEE IT! IT'S AIMING RIGHT FOR MY...

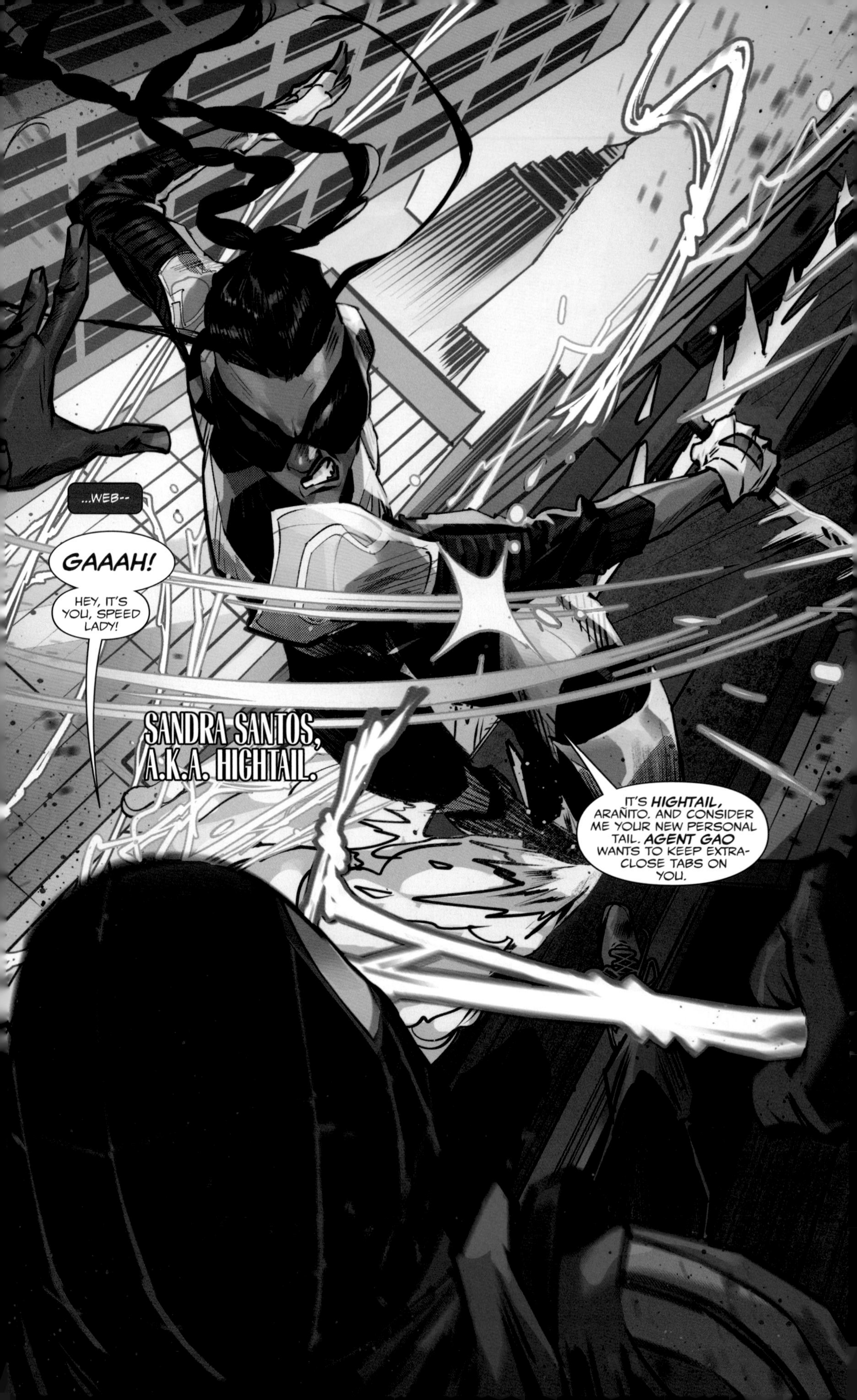
...WEB--
GAAAH!
HEY, IT'S YOU, SPEED LADY!
SANDRA SANTOS, A.K.A. HIGHTAIL.
IT'S HIGHTAIL, ARAÑITO. AND CONSIDER ME YOUR NEW PERSONAL TAIL. AGENT GAO WANTS TO KEEP EXTRA-CLOSE TABS ON YOU.

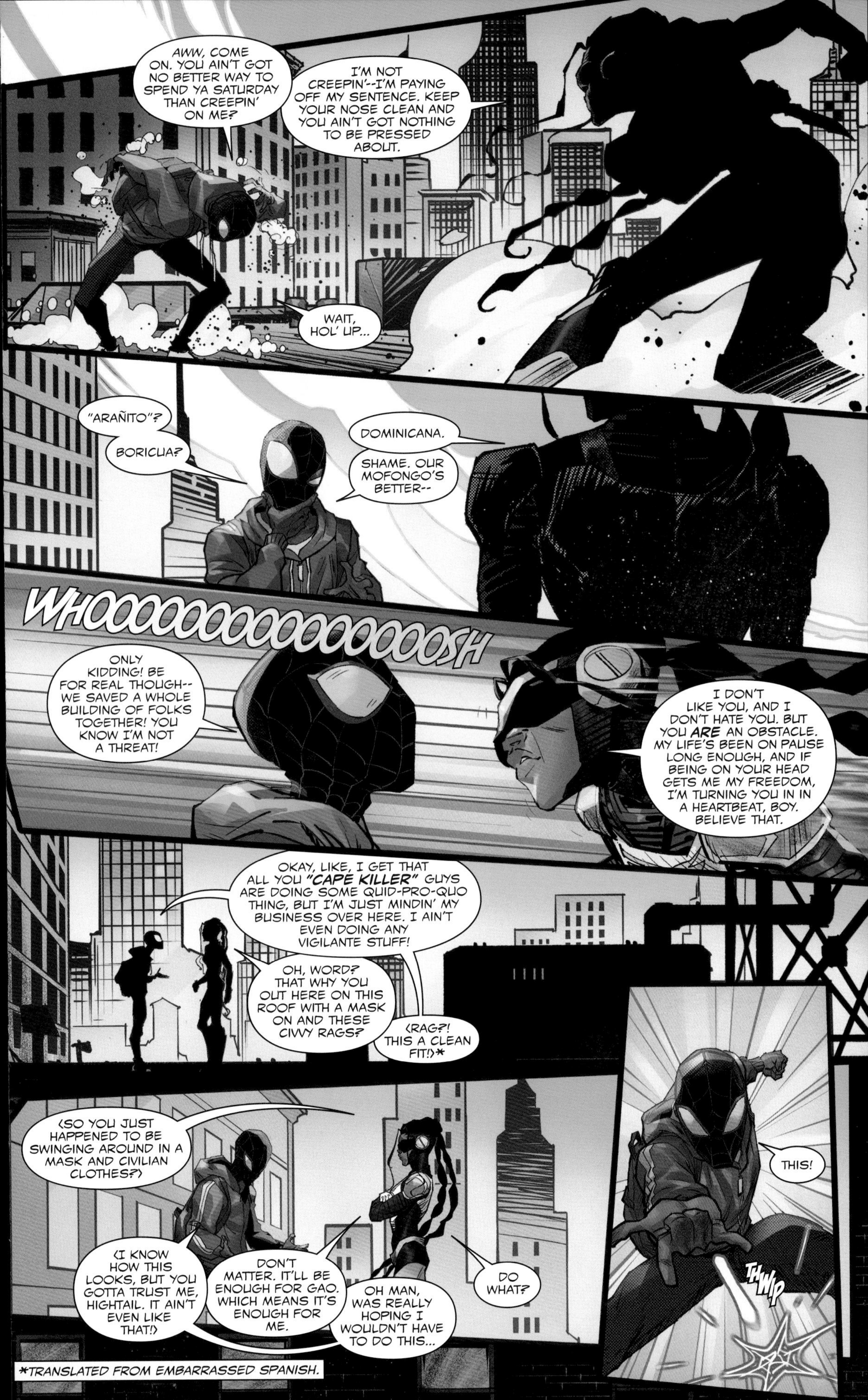
AWW, COME ON. YOU AIN'T GOT NO BETTER WAY TO SPEND YA SATURDAY THAN CREEPIN' ON ME?
I'M NOT CREEPIN'--I'M PAYING OFF MY SENTENCE. KEEP YOUR NOSE CLEAN AND YOU AIN'T GOT NOTHING TO BE PRESSED ABOUT.
WAIT, HOL' UP...
"ARAÑITO"?
BORICUA?
DOMINICANA.
SHAME. OUR MOFONGO'S BETTER--
WHOOOOOOOOOOOOOOOSH
ONLY KIDDING! BE FOR REAL THOUGH--WE SAVED A WHOLE BUILDING OF FOLKS TOGETHER! YOU KNOW I'M NOT A THREAT!
I DON'T LIKE YOU, AND I DON'T HATE YOU. BUT YOU ARE AN OBSTACLE. MY LIFE'S BEEN ON PAUSE LONG ENOUGH, AND IF BEING ON YOUR HEAD GETS ME MY FREEDOM, I'M TURNING YOU IN IN A HEARTBEAT, BOY. BELIEVE THAT.
OKAY, LIKE, I GET THAT ALL YOU "CAPE KILLER" GUYS ARE DOING SOME QUID-PRO-QUO THING, BUT I'M JUST MINDIN' MY BUSINESS OVER HERE. I AIN'T EVEN DOING ANY VIGILANTE STUFF!
OH, WORD? THAT WHY YOU OUT HERE ON THIS ROOF WITH A MASK ON AND THESE CIVVY RAGS?
⟨RAG?! THIS A CLEAN FIT!⟩*
⟨SO YOU JUST HAPPENED TO BE SWINGING AROUND IN A MASK AND CIVILIAN CLOTHES?⟩
⟨I KNOW HOW THIS LOOKS, BUT YOU GOTTA TRUST ME, HIGHTAIL. IT AIN'T EVEN LIKE THAT!⟩
DON'T MATTER. IT'LL BE ENOUGH FOR GAO. WHICH MEANS IT'S ENOUGH FOR ME.
OH MAN, WAS REALLY HOPING I WOULDN'T HAVE TO DO THIS...
DO WHAT?
THIS!
THWIP
*TRANSLATED FROM EMBARRASSED SPANISH.

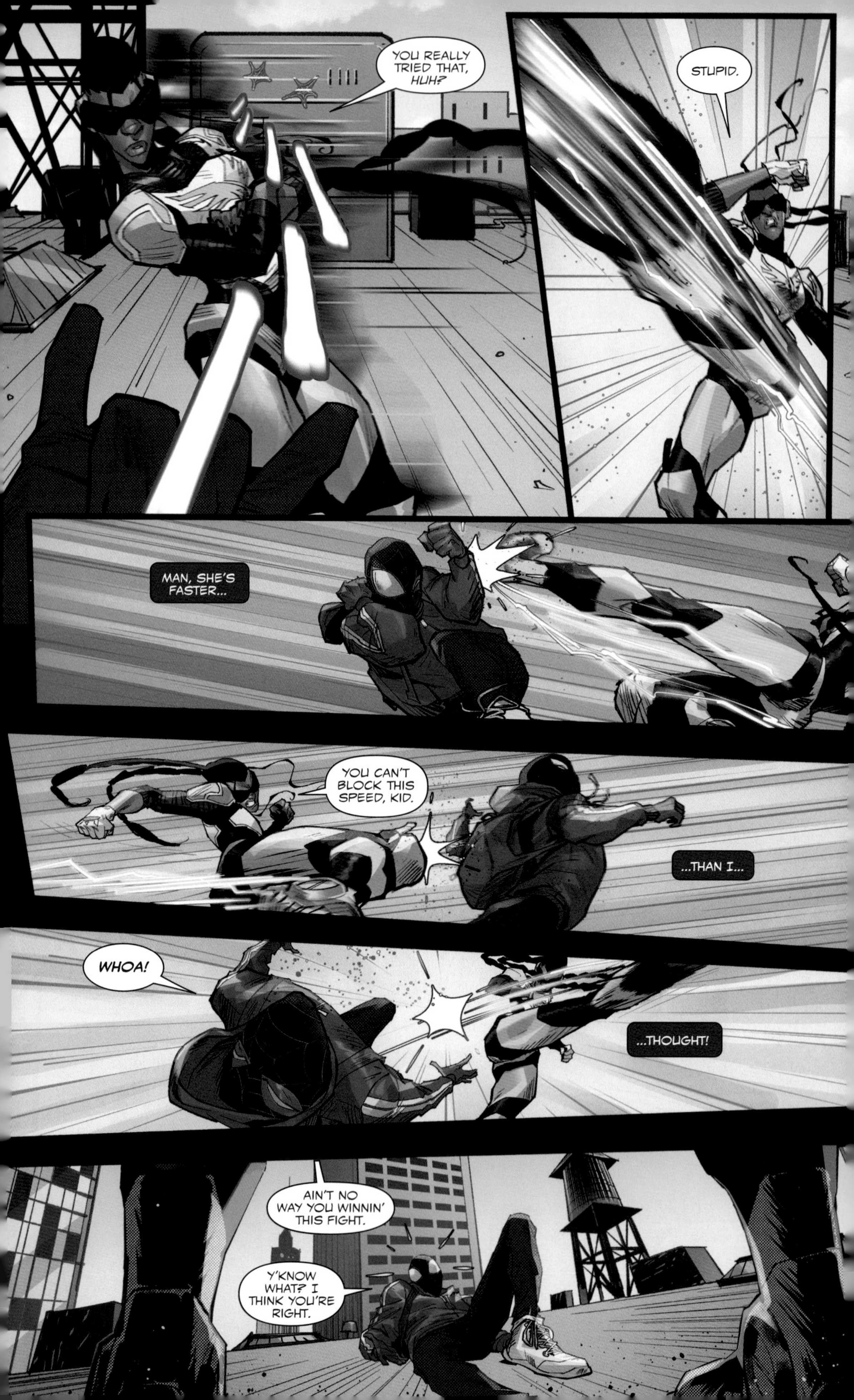
YOU REALLY TRIED THAT, HUH?
STUPID.
MAN, SHE'S FASTER...
YOU CAN'T BLOCK THIS SPEED, KID.
...THAN I...
WHOA!
...THOUGHT!
AIN'T NO WAY YOU WINNIN' THIS FIGHT.
Y'KNOW WHAT? I THINK YOU'RE RIGHT.

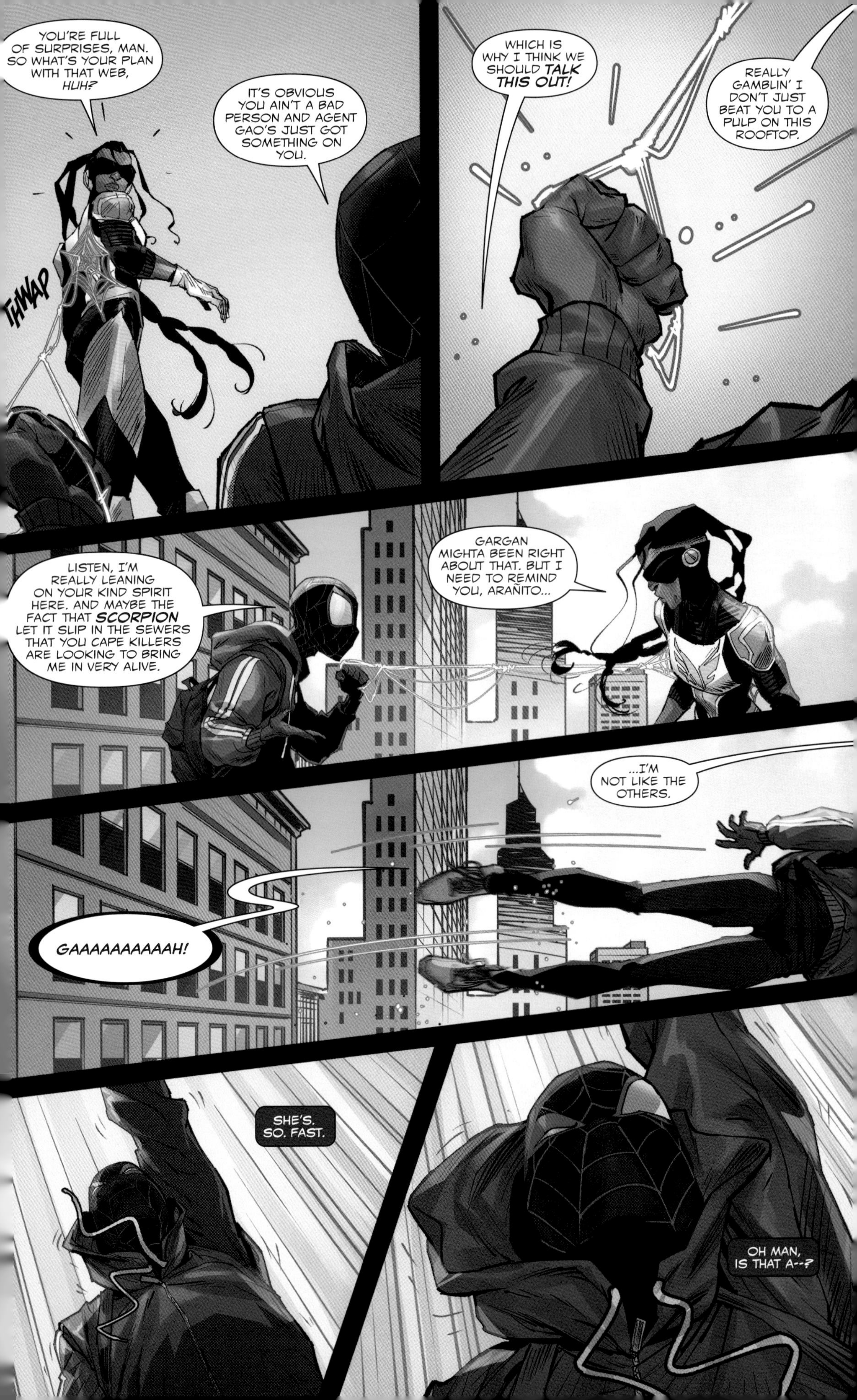
YOU'RE FULL OF SURPRISES, MAN. SO WHAT'S YOUR PLAN WITH THAT WEB, HUH?
IT'S OBVIOUS YOU AIN'T A BAD PERSON AND AGENT GAO'S JUST GOT SOMETHING ON YOU.
THWAP
WHICH IS WHY I THINK WE SHOULD TALK THIS OUT!
REALLY GAMBLIN' I DON'T JUST BEAT YOU TO A PULP ON THIS ROOFTOP.
LISTEN, I'M REALLY LEANING ON YOUR KIND SPIRIT HERE. AND MAYBE THE FACT THAT SCORPION LET IT SLIP IN THE SEWERS THAT YOU CAPE KILLERS ARE LOOKING TO BRING ME IN VERY ALIVE.
GARGAN MIGHTA BEEN RIGHT ABOUT THAT. BUT I NEED TO REMIND YOU, ARAÑITO...
...I'M NOT LIKE THE OTHERS.
GAAAAAAAAAAH!
SHE'S. SO. FAST.
OH MAN, IS THAT A--?

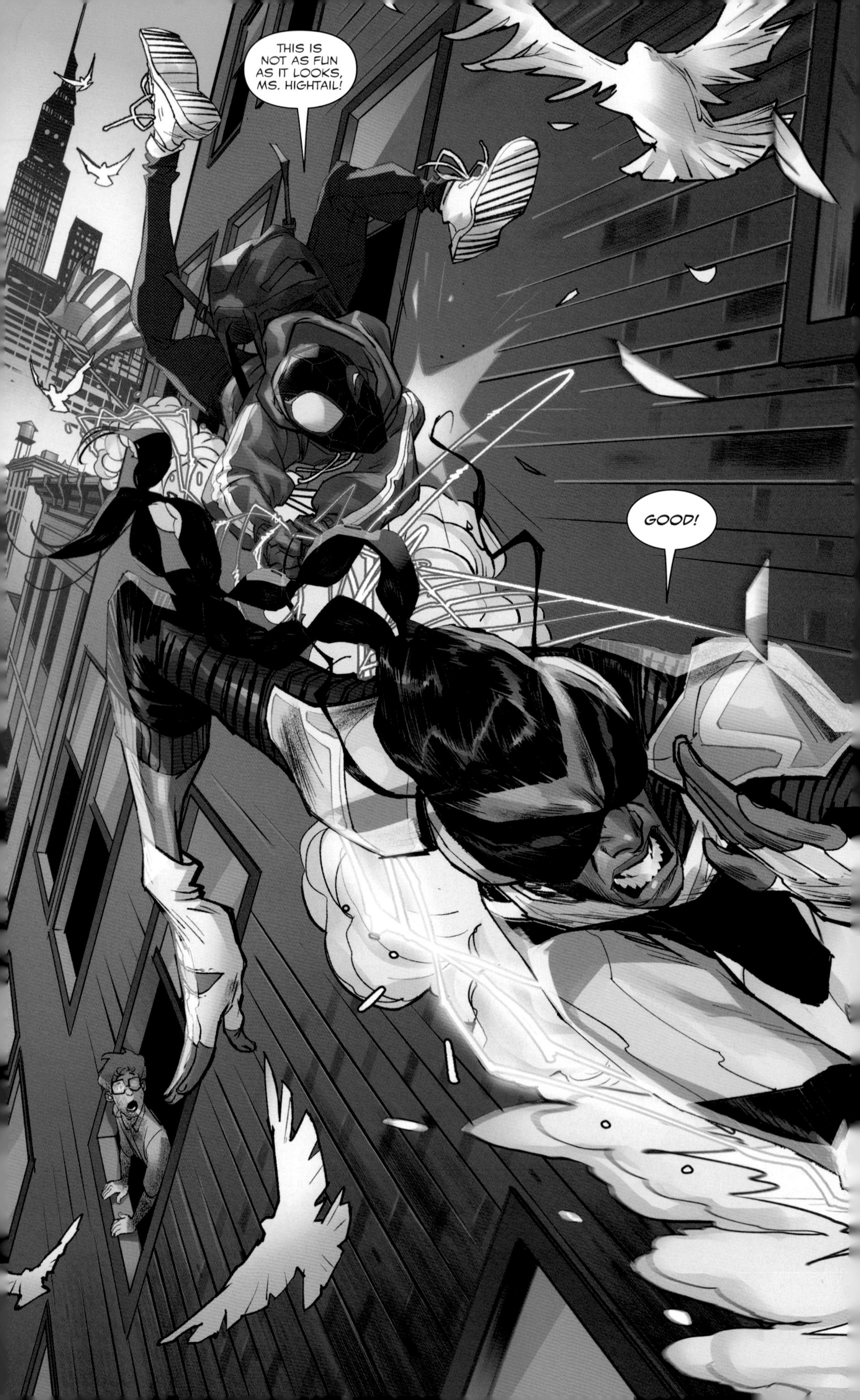
THIS IS NOT AS FUN AS IT LOOKS, MS. HIGHTAIL!
GOOD!

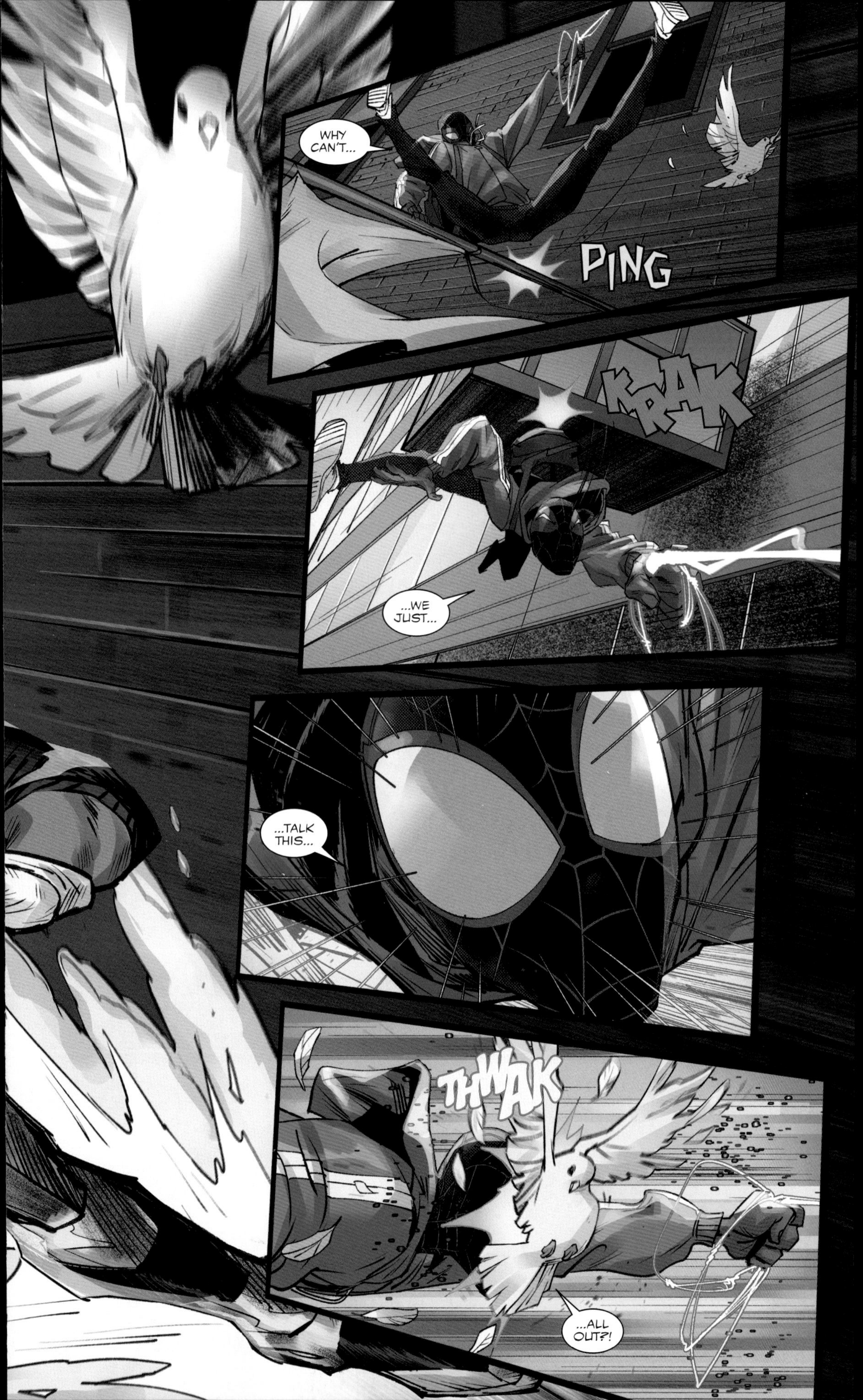
WHY CAN'T...
PING
KRAK
...WE JUST...
...TALK THIS...
THWAK
...ALL OUT?!

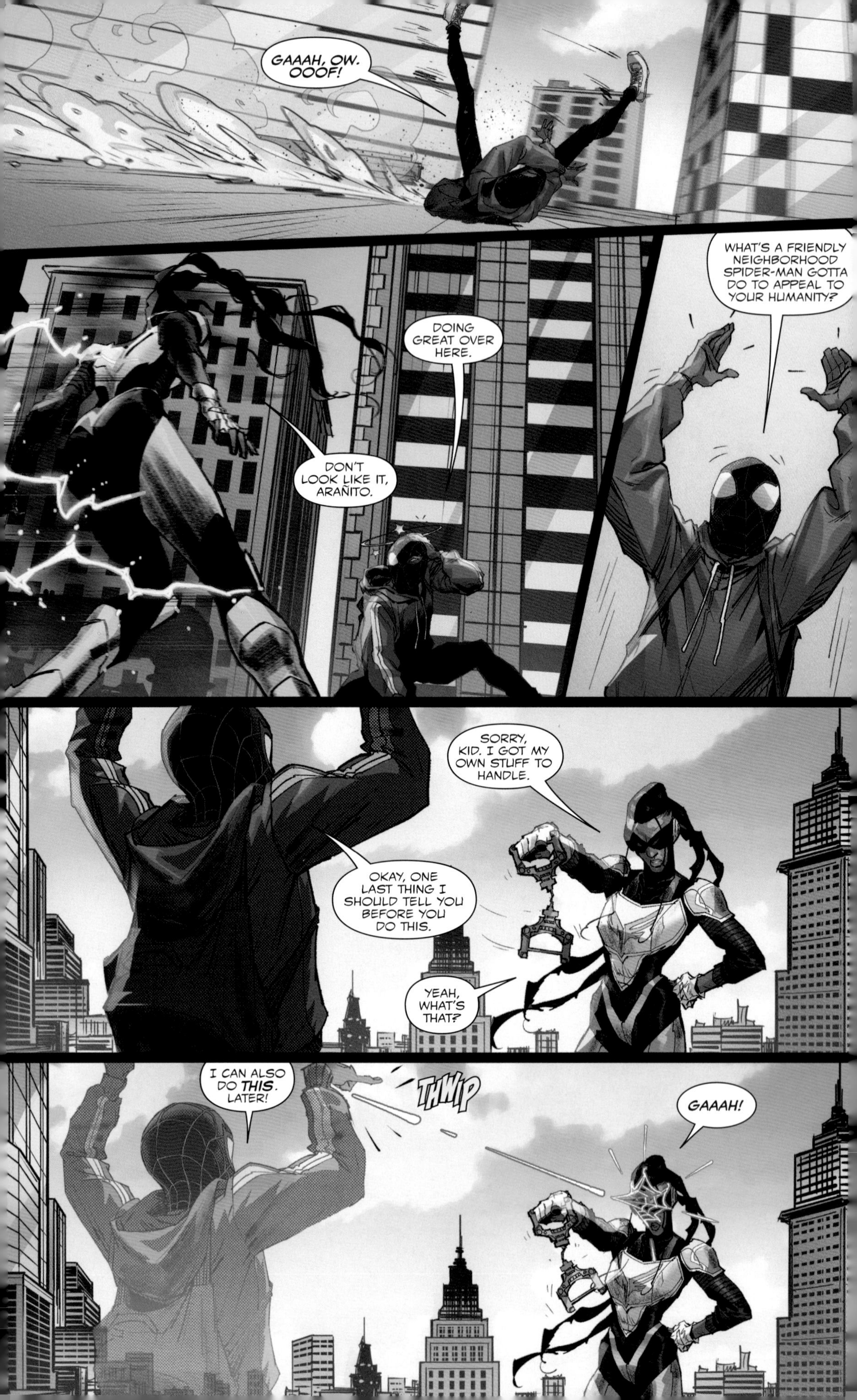
GAAAH, OW. OOOF!
DOING GREAT OVER HERE.
DON'T LOOK LIKE IT, ARAÑITO.
WHAT'S A FRIENDLY NEIGHBORHOOD SPIDER-MAN GOTTA DO TO APPEAL TO YOUR HUMANITY?
SORRY, KID. I GOT MY OWN STUFF TO HANDLE.
OKAY, ONE LAST THING I SHOULD TELL YOU BEFORE YOU DO THIS.
YEAH, WHAT'S THAT?
I CAN ALSO DO **THIS**. LATER!
THWIP
GAAAH!

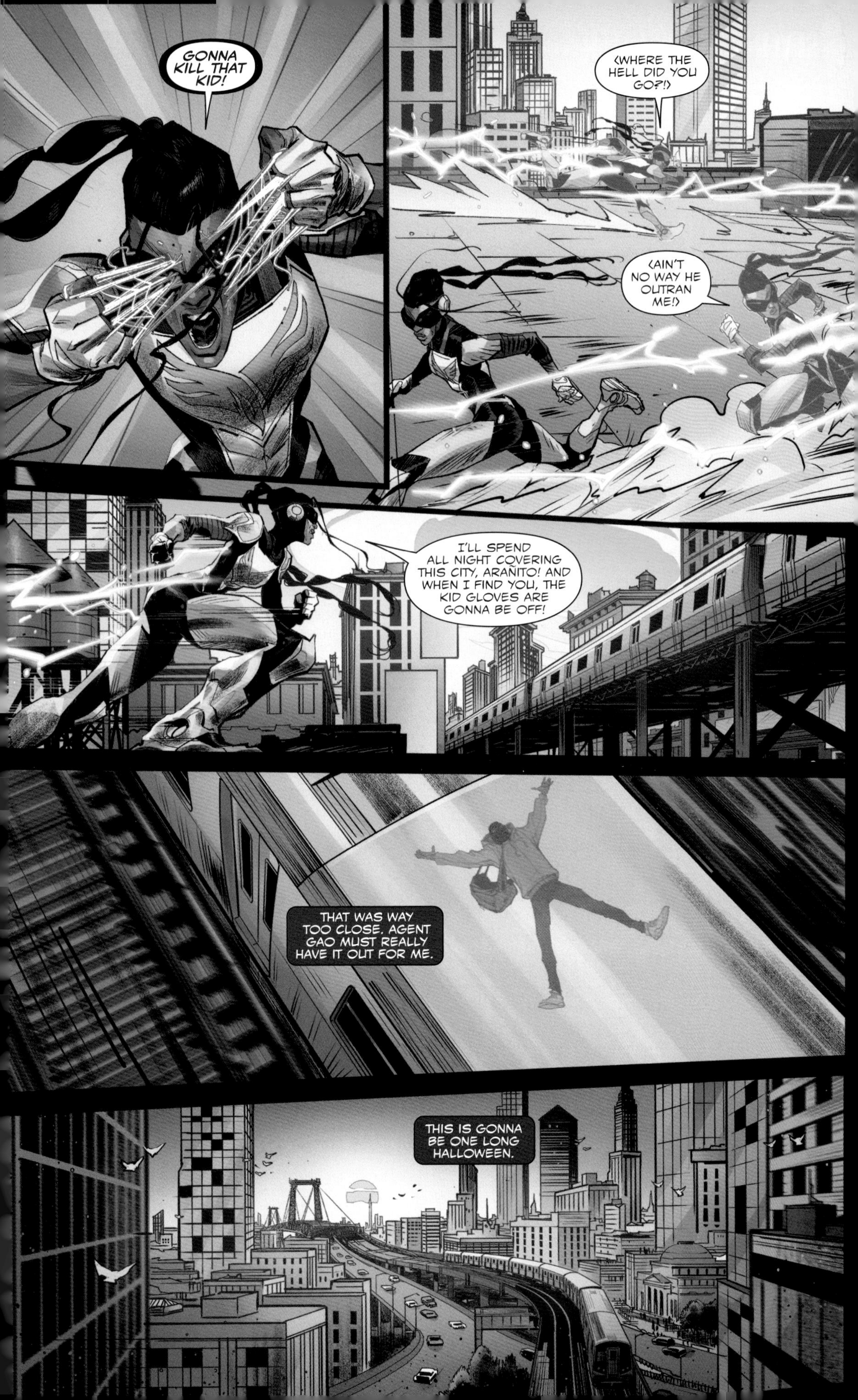
GONNA KILL THAT KID!
<WHERE THE HELL DID YOU GO?!>
<AIN'T NO WAY HE OUTRAN ME!>
I'LL SPEND ALL NIGHT COVERING THIS CITY, ARAÑITO! AND WHEN I FIND YOU, THE KID GLOVES ARE GONNA BE OFF!
THAT WAS WAY TOO CLOSE. AGENT GAO MUST REALLY HAVE IT OUT FOR ME.
THIS IS GONNA BE ONE LONG HALLOWEEN.

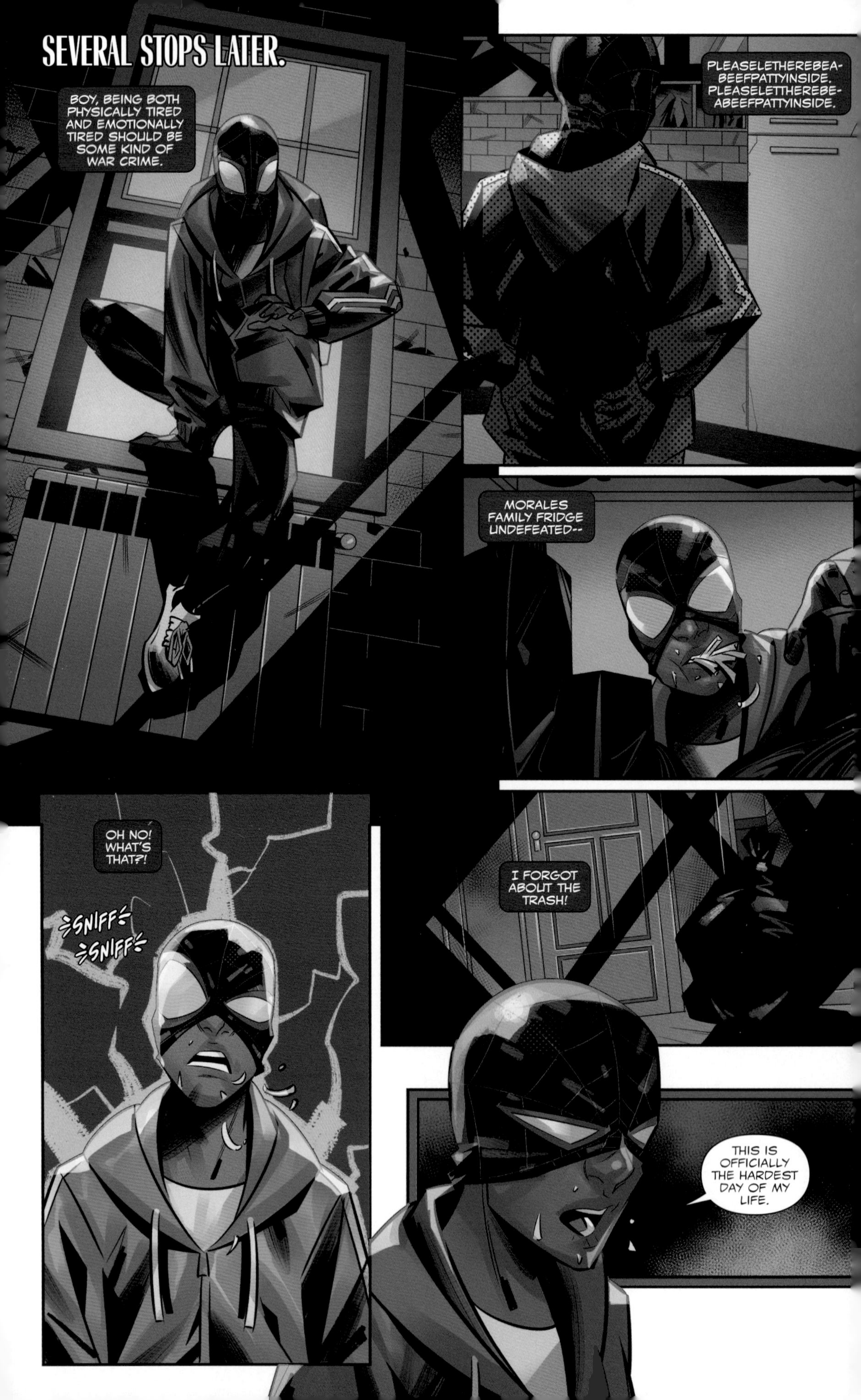
SEVERAL STOPS LATER.
BOY, BEING BOTH PHYSICALLY TIRED AND EMOTIONALLY TIRED SHOULD BE SOME KIND OF WAR CRIME.
PLEASELETTHEREBEA-BEEFPATTYINSIDE. PLEASELETTHEREBE-ABEEFPATTYINSIDE.
MORALES FAMILY FRIDGE UNDEFEATED--
OH NO! WHAT'S THAT?!
SNIFF
SNIFF
I FORGOT ABOUT THE TRASH!
THIS IS OFFICIALLY THE HARDEST DAY OF MY LIFE.

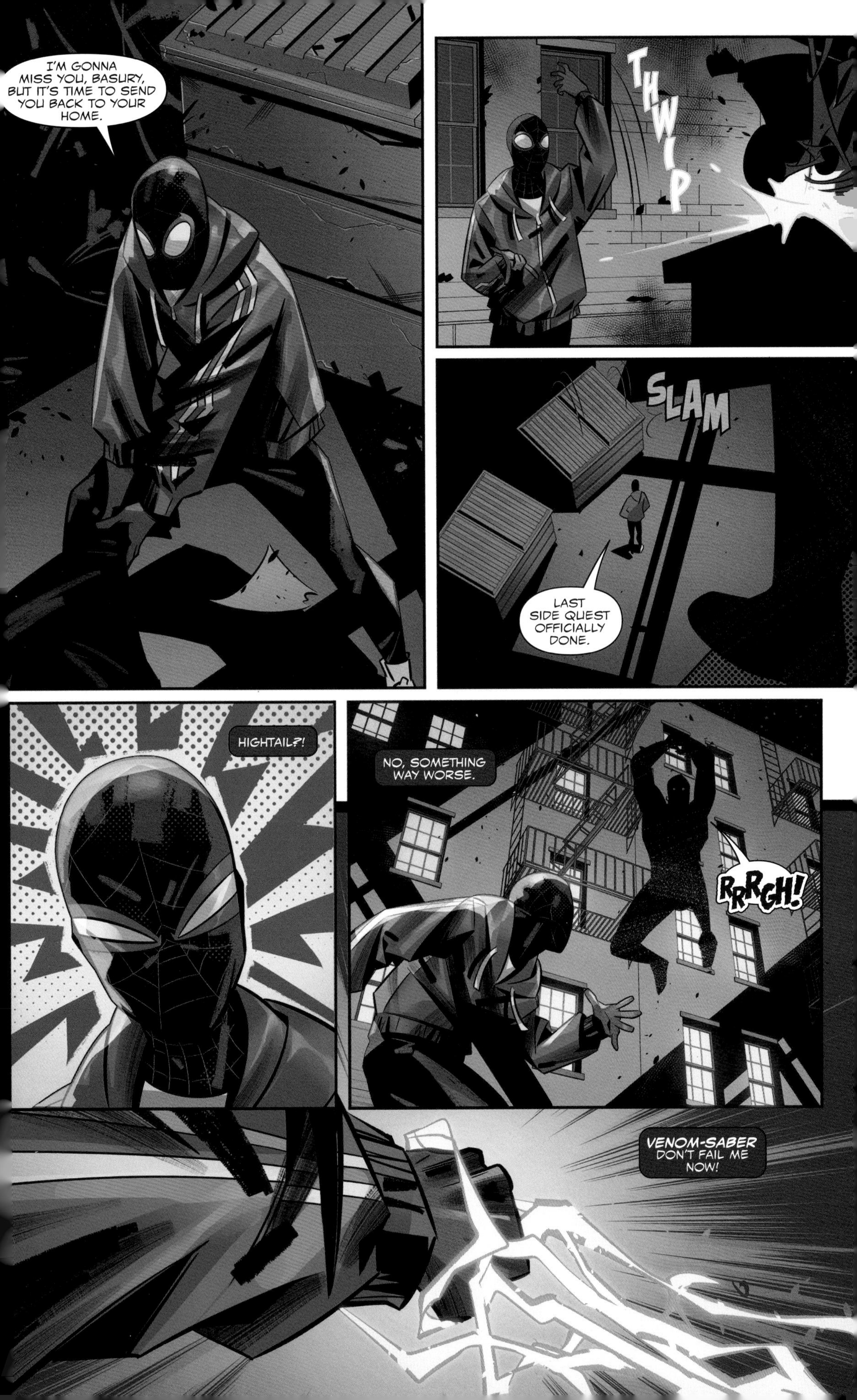
I'M GONNA MISS YOU, BASURY, BUT IT'S TIME TO SEND YOU BACK TO YOUR HOME.
THWIP
SLAM
LAST SIDE QUEST OFFICIALLY DONE.
HIGHTAIL?!
NO, SOMETHING WAY WORSE.
RRRGH!
VENOM-SABER DON'T FAIL ME NOW!

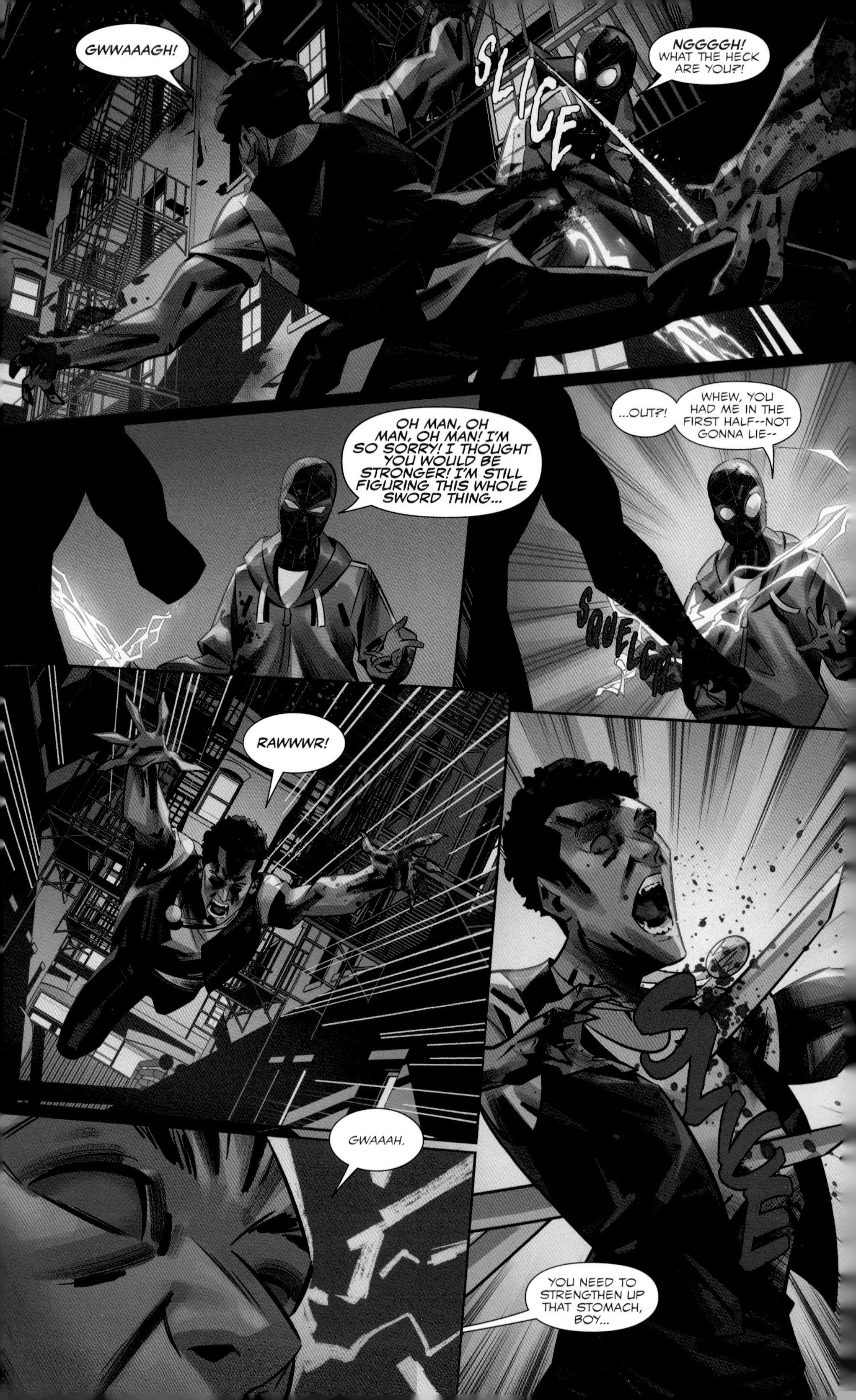
GWWAAAGH!
SLICE
NGGGGH! WHAT THE HECK ARE YOU?!
OH MAN, OH MAN, OH MAN! I'M SO SORRY! I THOUGHT YOU WOULD BE STRONGER! I'M STILL FIGURING THIS WHOLE SWORD THING...
...OUT?!
WHEW, YOU HAD ME IN THE FIRST HALF--NOT GONNA LIE--
SQUELCH
RAWWWR!
GWAAAH.
YOU NEED TO STRENGTHEN UP THAT STOMACH, BOY...

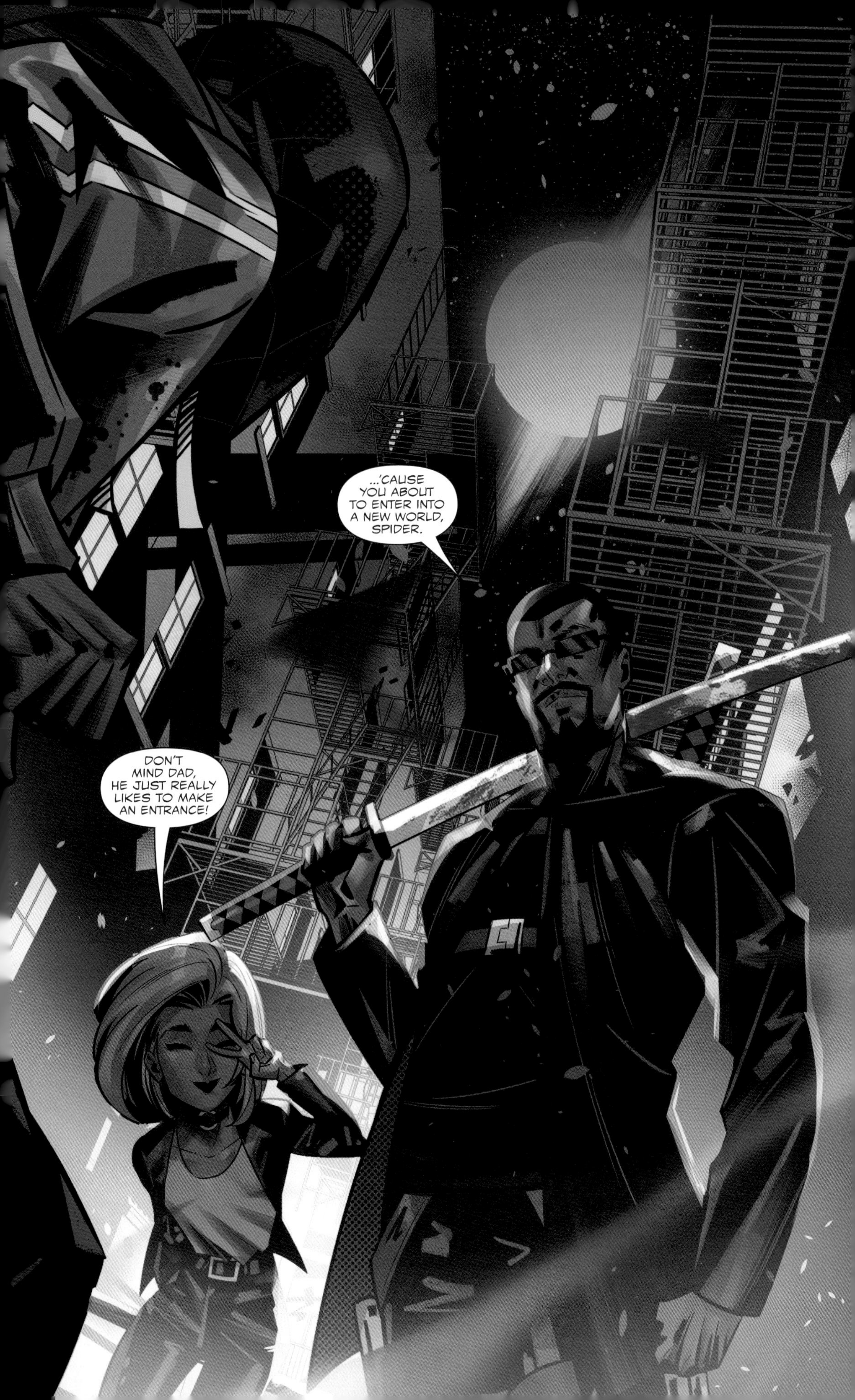
...'CAUSE YOU ABOUT TO ENTER INTO A NEW WORLD, SPIDER.
DON'T MIND DAD, HE JUST REALLY LIKES TO MAKE AN ENTRANCE!

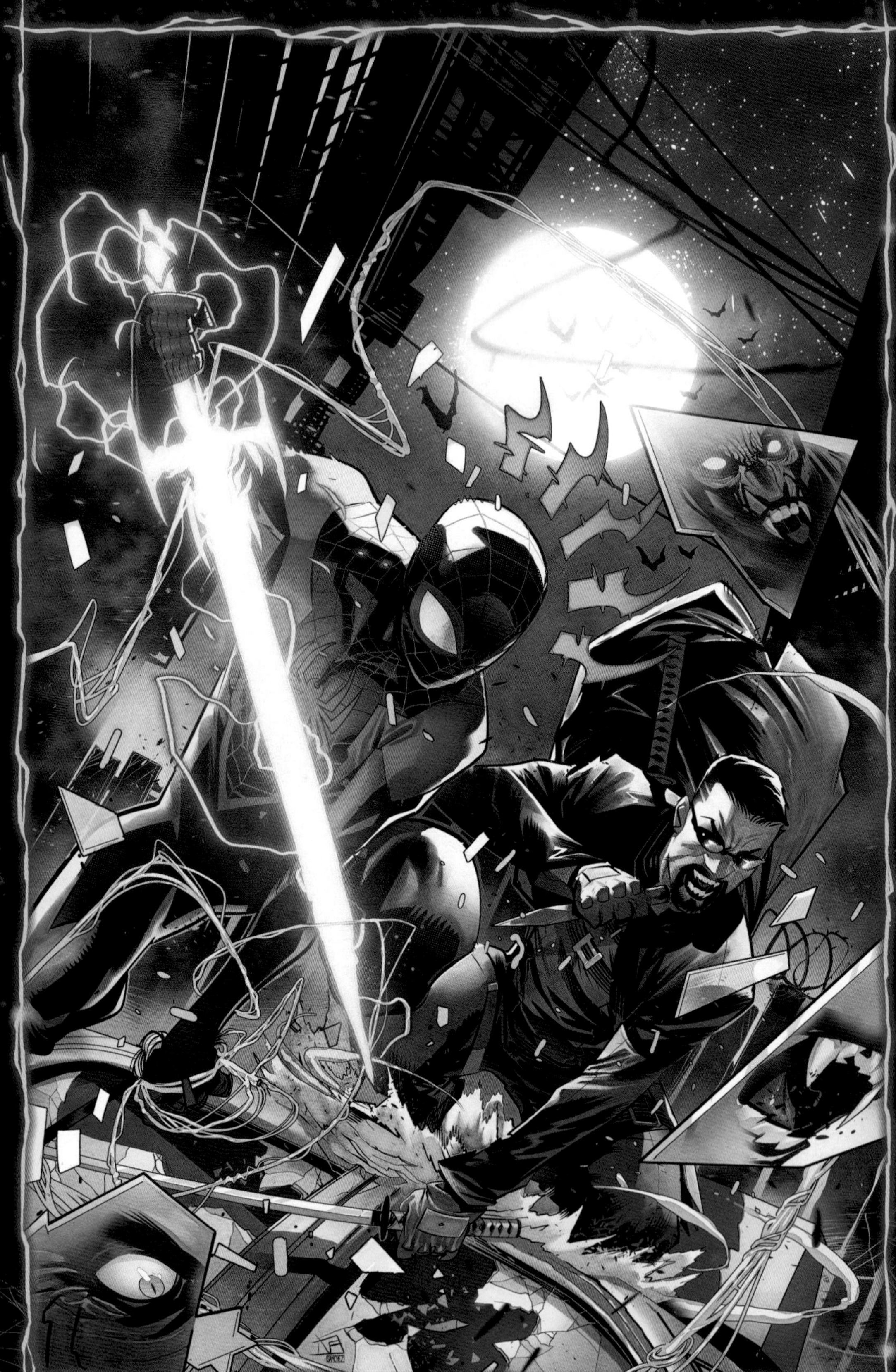

11

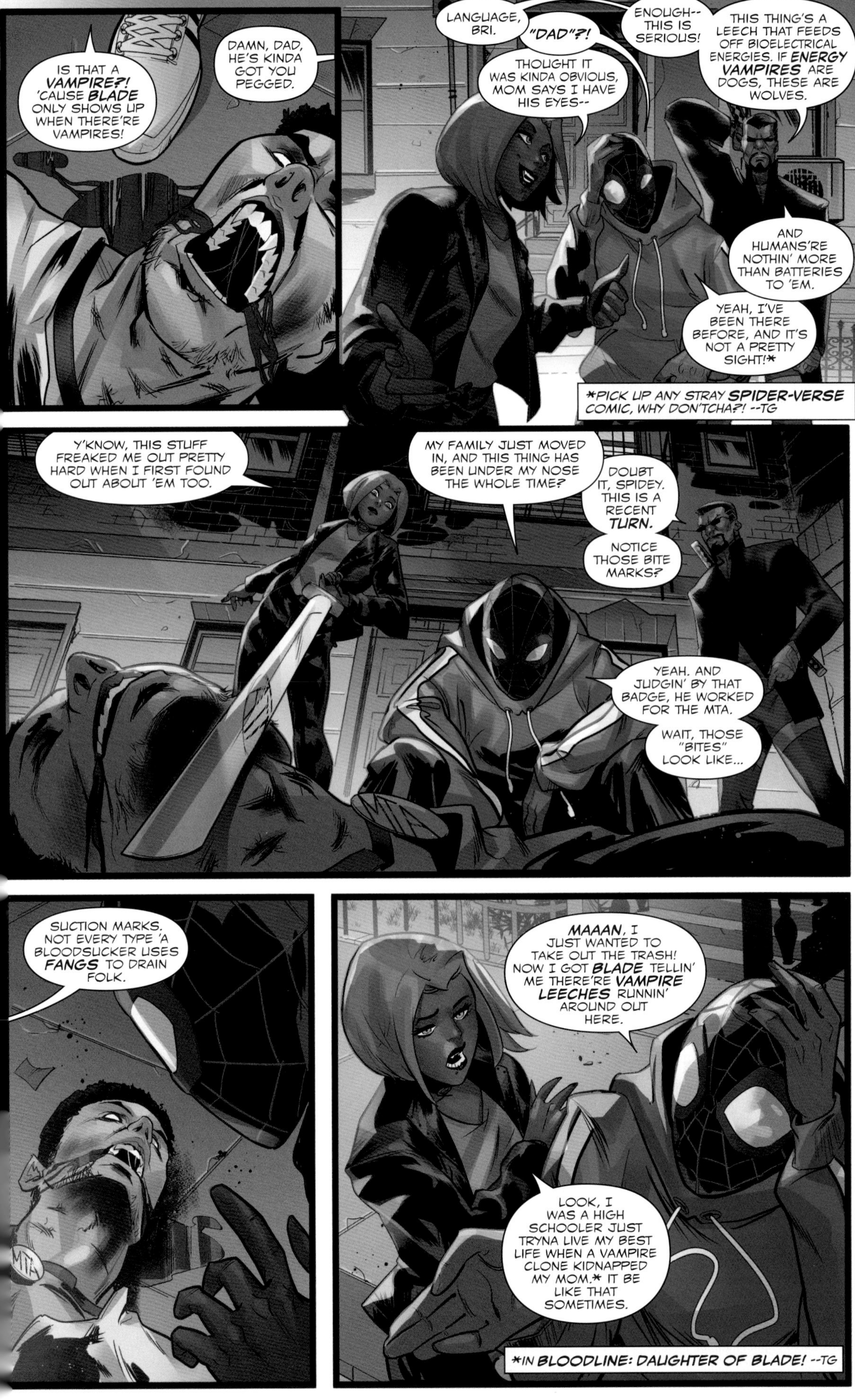
IS THAT A VAMPIRE?! 'CAUSE BLADE ONLY SHOWS UP WHEN THERE'RE VAMPIRES!
DAMN, DAD, HE'S KINDA GOT YOU PEGGED.
LANGUAGE, BRI.
"DAD"?!
THOUGHT IT WAS KINDA OBVIOUS, MOM SAYS I HAVE HIS EYES--
ENOUGH-- THIS IS SERIOUS!
THIS THING'S A LEECH THAT FEEDS OFF BIOELECTRICAL ENERGIES. IF ENERGY VAMPIRES ARE DOGS, THESE ARE WOLVES.
AND HUMANS'RE NOTHIN' MORE THAN BATTERIES TO 'EM.
YEAH, I'VE BEEN THERE BEFORE, AND IT'S NOT A PRETTY SIGHT!*
*PICK UP ANY STRAY SPIDER-VERSE COMIC, WHY DON'TCHA?! --TG
Y'KNOW, THIS STUFF FREAKED ME OUT PRETTY HARD WHEN I FIRST FOUND OUT ABOUT 'EM TOO.
MY FAMILY JUST MOVED IN, AND THIS THING HAS BEEN UNDER MY NOSE THE WHOLE TIME?
DOUBT IT, SPIDEY. THIS IS A RECENT TURN.
NOTICE THOSE BITE MARKS?
YEAH. AND JUDGIN' BY THAT BADGE, HE WORKED FOR THE MTA.
WAIT, THOSE "BITES" LOOK LIKE...
SUCTION MARKS. NOT EVERY TYPE 'A BLOODSUCKER USES FANGS TO DRAIN FOLK.
MTA
MAAAN, I JUST WANTED TO TAKE OUT THE TRASH! NOW I GOT BLADE TELLIN' ME THERE'RE VAMPIRE LEECHES RUNNIN' AROUND OUT HERE.
LOOK, I WAS A HIGH SCHOOLER JUST TRYNA LIVE MY BEST LIFE WHEN A VAMPIRE CLONE KIDNAPPED MY MOM.* IT BE LIKE THAT SOMETIMES.
*IN BLOODLINE: DAUGHTER OF BLADE! --TG

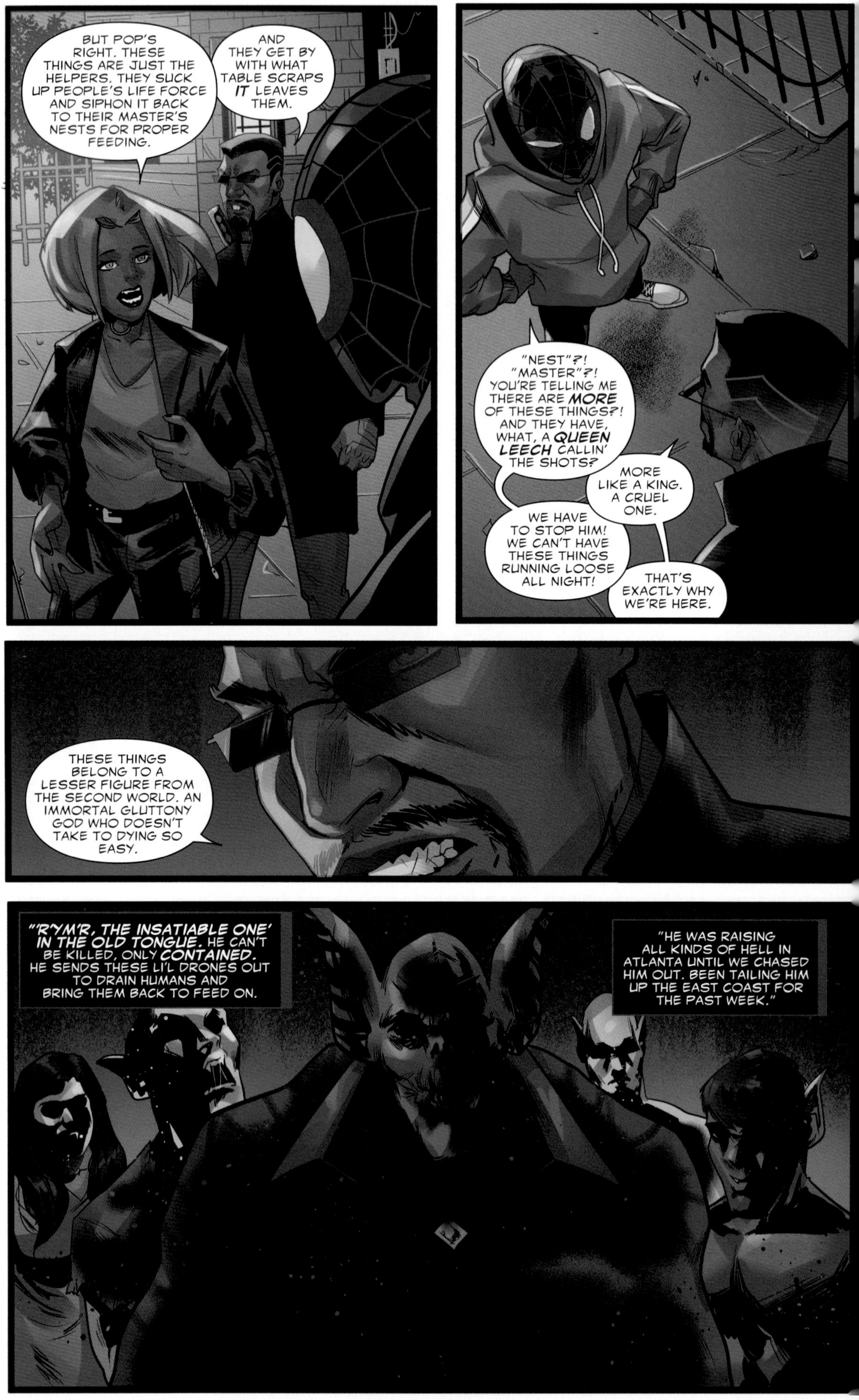
BUT POP'S RIGHT. THESE THINGS ARE JUST THE HELPERS. THEY SUCK UP PEOPLE'S LIFE FORCE AND SIPHON IT BACK TO THEIR MASTER'S NESTS FOR PROPER FEEDING.
AND THEY GET BY WITH WHAT TABLE SCRAPS *IT* LEAVES THEM.
"NEST"?! "MASTER"?! YOU'RE TELLING ME THERE ARE *MORE* OF THESE THINGS?! AND THEY HAVE, WHAT, A *QUEEN LEECH* CALLIN' THE SHOTS?
MORE LIKE A KING. A CRUEL ONE.
WE HAVE TO STOP HIM! WE CAN'T HAVE THESE THINGS RUNNING LOOSE ALL NIGHT!
THAT'S EXACTLY WHY WE'RE HERE.
THESE THINGS BELONG TO A LESSER FIGURE FROM THE SECOND WORLD. AN IMMORTAL GLUTTONY GOD WHO DOESN'T TAKE TO DYING SO EASY.
"'R'YM'R, THE INSATIABLE ONE' IN THE OLD TONGUE. HE CAN'T BE KILLED, ONLY *CONTAINED.* HE SENDS THESE LI'L DRONES OUT TO DRAIN HUMANS AND BRING THEM BACK TO FEED ON.
"HE WAS RAISING ALL KINDS OF HELL IN ATLANTA UNTIL WE CHASED HIM OUT. BEEN TAILING HIM UP THE EAST COAST FOR THE PAST WEEK."

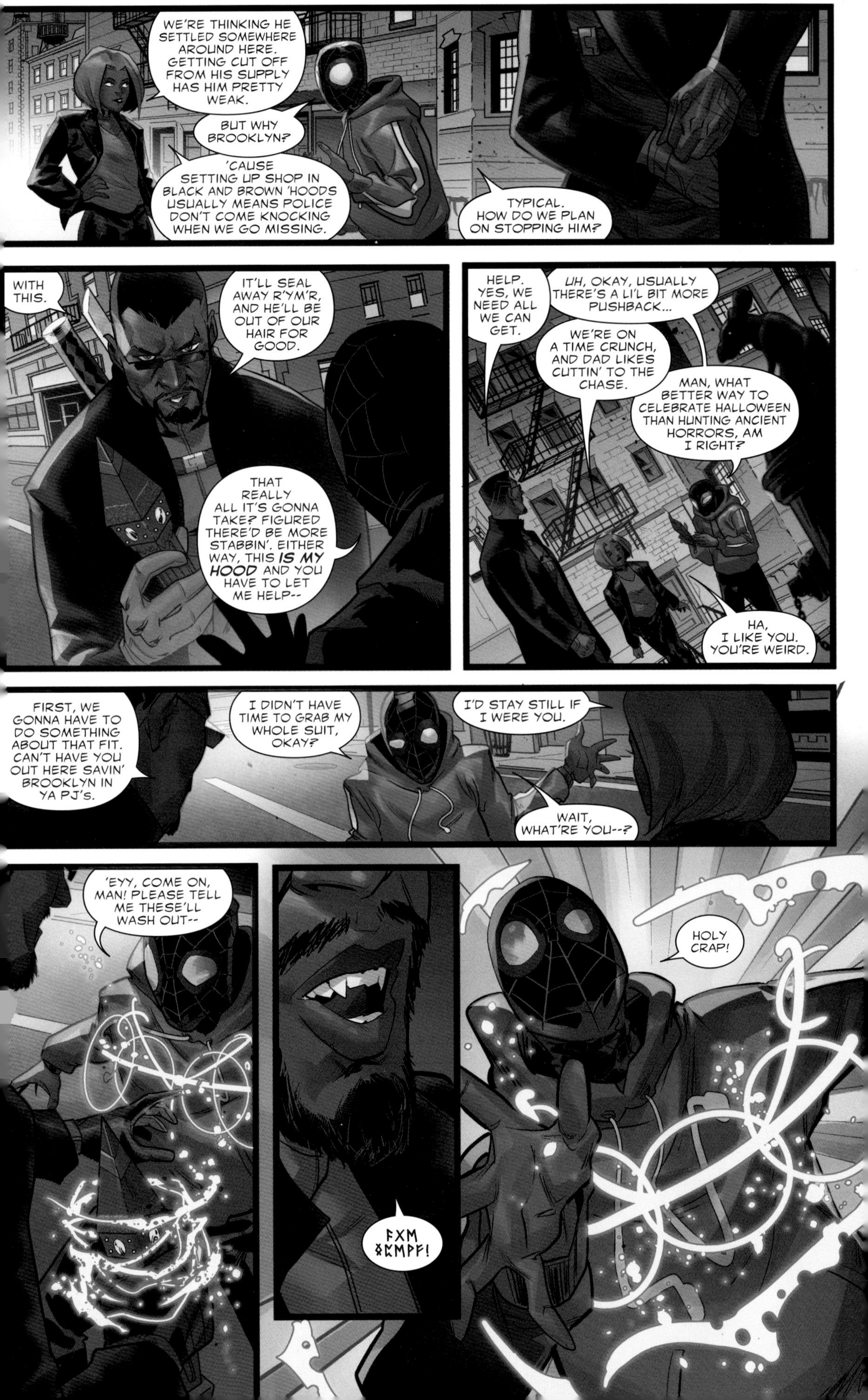
WE'RE THINKING HE SETTLED SOMEWHERE AROUND HERE. GETTING CUT OFF FROM HIS SUPPLY HAS HIM PRETTY WEAK.
BUT WHY BROOKLYN?
'CAUSE SETTING UP SHOP IN BLACK AND BROWN 'HOODS USUALLY MEANS POLICE DON'T COME KNOCKING WHEN WE GO MISSING.
TYPICAL. HOW DO WE PLAN ON STOPPING HIM?
WITH THIS.
IT'LL SEAL AWAY R'YM'R, AND HE'LL BE OUT OF OUR HAIR FOR GOOD.
THAT REALLY ALL IT'S GONNA TAKE? FIGURED THERE'D BE MORE STABBIN'. EITHER WAY, THIS **IS MY HOOD** AND YOU HAVE TO LET ME HELP--
HELP. YES, WE NEED ALL WE CAN GET.
UH, OKAY, USUALLY THERE'S A LI'L BIT MORE PUSHBACK...
WE'RE ON A TIME CRUNCH, AND DAD LIKES CUTTIN' TO THE CHASE.
MAN, WHAT BETTER WAY TO CELEBRATE HALLOWEEN THAN HUNTING ANCIENT HORRORS, AM I RIGHT?
HA, I LIKE YOU. YOU'RE WEIRD.
FIRST, WE GONNA HAVE TO DO SOMETHING ABOUT THAT FIT. CAN'T HAVE YOU OUT HERE SAVIN' BROOKLYN IN YA PJ'S.
I DIDN'T HAVE TIME TO GRAB MY WHOLE SUIT, OKAY?
I'D STAY STILL IF I WERE YOU.
WAIT, WHAT'RE YOU--?
'EYY, COME ON, MAN! PLEASE TELL ME THESE'LL WASH OUT--
HOLY CRAP!

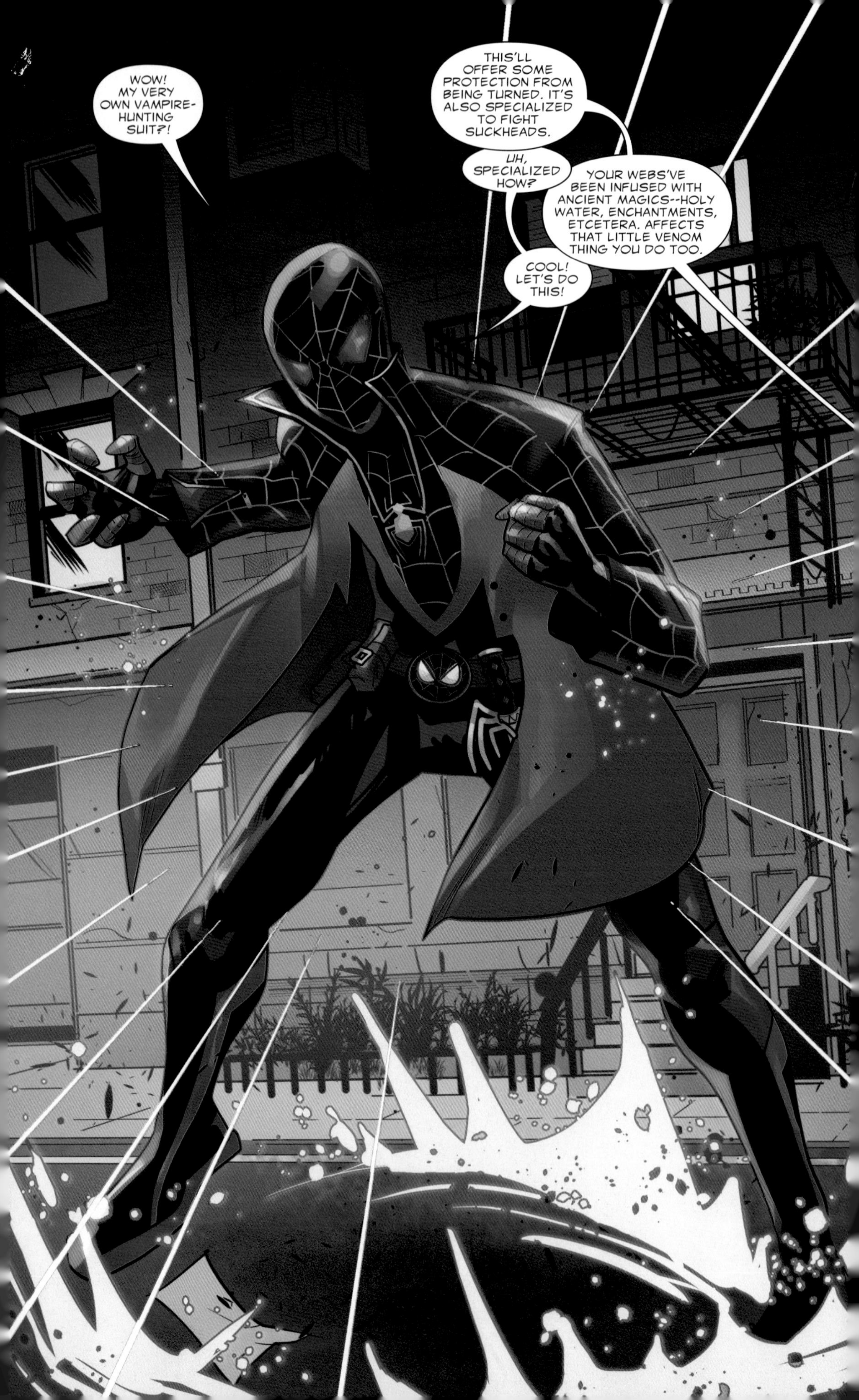
WOW! MY VERY OWN VAMPIRE-HUNTING SUIT?!
THIS'LL OFFER SOME PROTECTION FROM BEING TURNED. IT'S ALSO SPECIALIZED TO FIGHT SUCKHEADS.
UH, SPECIALIZED HOW?
YOUR WEBS'VE BEEN INFUSED WITH ANCIENT MAGICS--HOLY WATER, ENCHANTMENTS, ETCETERA. AFFECTS THAT LITTLE VENOM THING YOU DO TOO.
COOL! LET'S DO THIS!

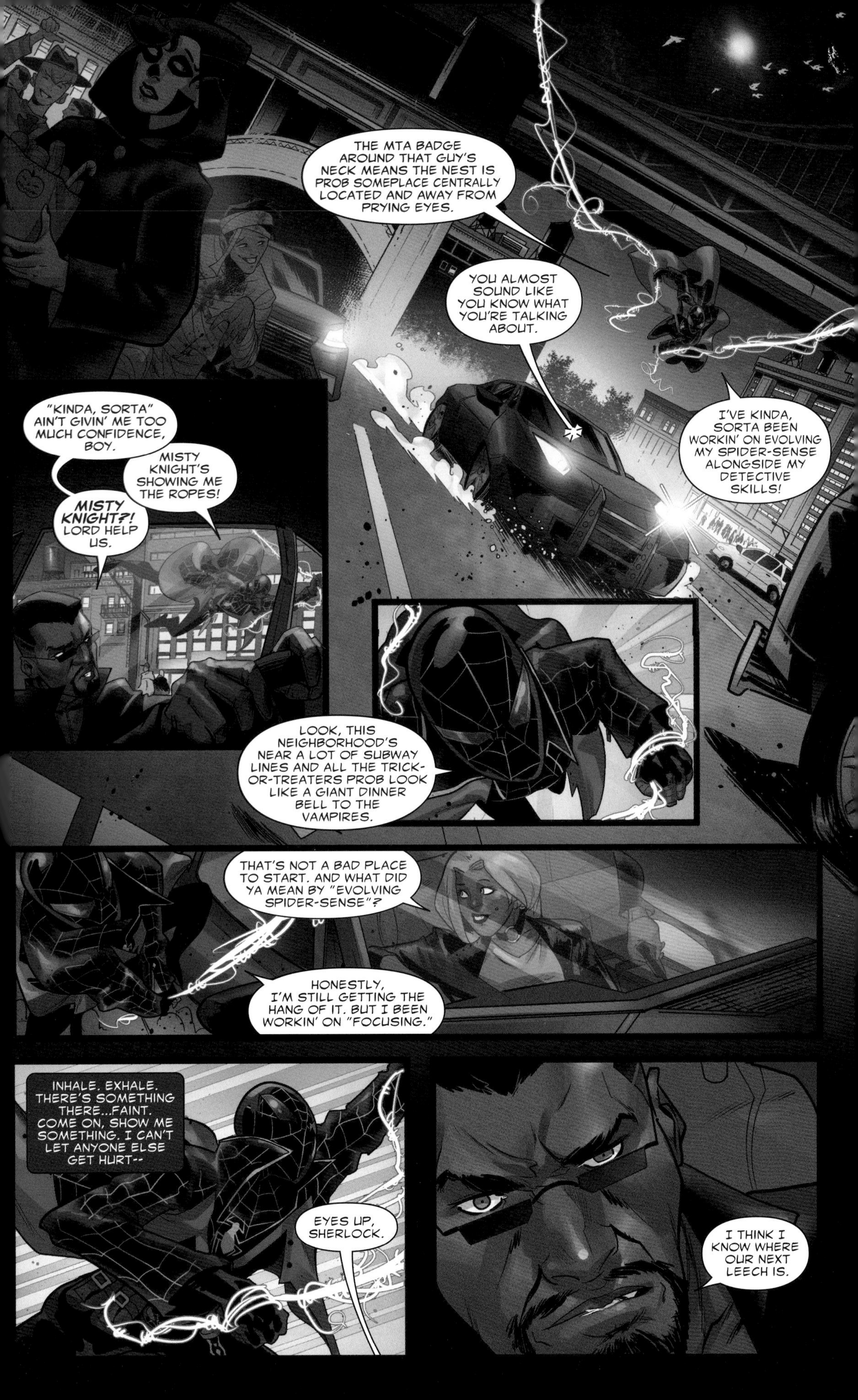
THE MTA BADGE AROUND THAT GUY'S NECK MEANS THE NEST IS PROB SOMEPLACE CENTRALLY LOCATED AND AWAY FROM PRYING EYES.
YOU ALMOST SOUND LIKE YOU KNOW WHAT YOU'RE TALKING ABOUT.
I'VE KINDA, SORTA BEEN WORKIN' ON EVOLVING MY SPIDER-SENSE ALONGSIDE MY DETECTIVE SKILLS!
"KINDA, SORTA" AIN'T GIVIN' ME TOO MUCH CONFIDENCE, BOY.
MISTY KNIGHT'S SHOWING ME THE ROPES!
MISTY KNIGHT?! LORD HELP US.
LOOK, THIS NEIGHBORHOOD'S NEAR A LOT OF SUBWAY LINES AND ALL THE TRICK-OR-TREATERS PROB LOOK LIKE A GIANT DINNER BELL TO THE VAMPIRES.
THAT'S NOT A BAD PLACE TO START. AND WHAT DID YA MEAN BY "EVOLVING SPIDER-SENSE"?
HONESTLY, I'M STILL GETTING THE HANG OF IT. BUT I BEEN WORKIN' ON "FOCUSING."
INHALE. EXHALE. THERE'S SOMETHING THERE...FAINT. COME ON, SHOW ME SOMETHING. I CAN'T LET ANYONE ELSE GET HURT--
EYES UP, SHERLOCK.
I THINK I KNOW WHERE OUR NEXT LEECH IS.

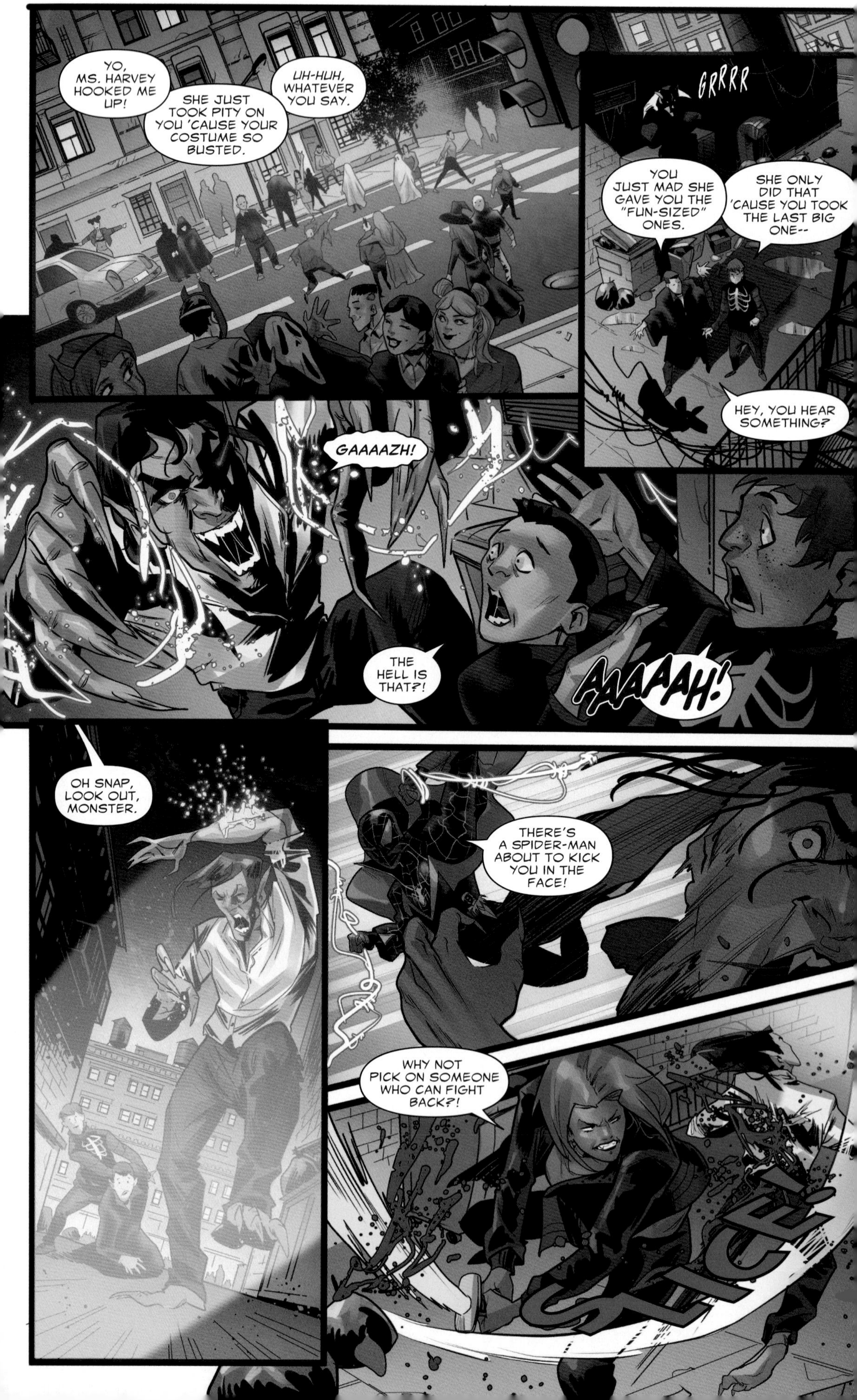
YO, MS. HARVEY HOOKED ME UP!
SHE JUST TOOK PITY ON YOU 'CAUSE YOUR COSTUME SO BUSTED.
UH-HUH, WHATEVER YOU SAY.
GRRRR
YOU JUST MAD SHE GAVE YOU THE "FUN-SIZED" ONES.
SHE ONLY DID THAT 'CAUSE YOU TOOK THE LAST BIG ONE--
HEY, YOU HEAR SOMETHING?
GAAAAZH!
THE HELL IS THAT?!
AAAAAH!
OH SNAP, LOOK OUT, MONSTER.
THERE'S A SPIDER-MAN ABOUT TO KICK YOU IN THE FACE!
WHY NOT PICK ON SOMEONE WHO CAN FIGHT BACK?!

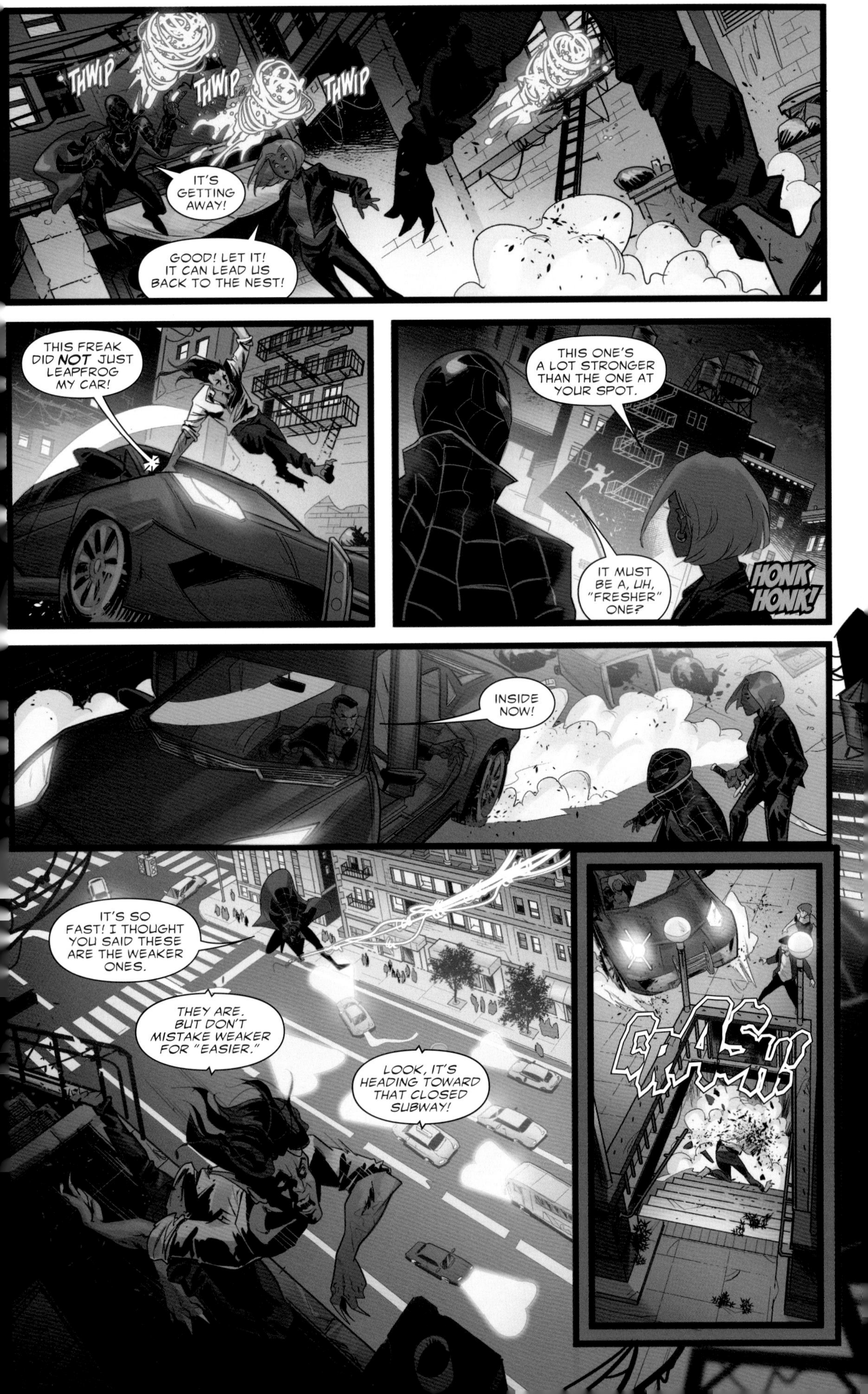
THWIP
THWIP
THWIP
IT'S GETTING AWAY!
GOOD! LET IT! IT CAN LEAD US BACK TO THE NEST!
THIS FREAK DID **NOT** JUST LEAPFROG MY CAR!
THIS ONE'S A LOT STRONGER THAN THE ONE AT YOUR SPOT.
IT MUST BE A, UH, "FRESHER" ONE?
HONK HONK!
INSIDE NOW!
IT'S SO FAST! I THOUGHT YOU SAID THESE ARE THE WEAKER ONES.
THEY ARE. BUT DON'T MISTAKE WEAKER FOR "EASIER."
LOOK, IT'S HEADING TOWARD THAT CLOSED SUBWAY!

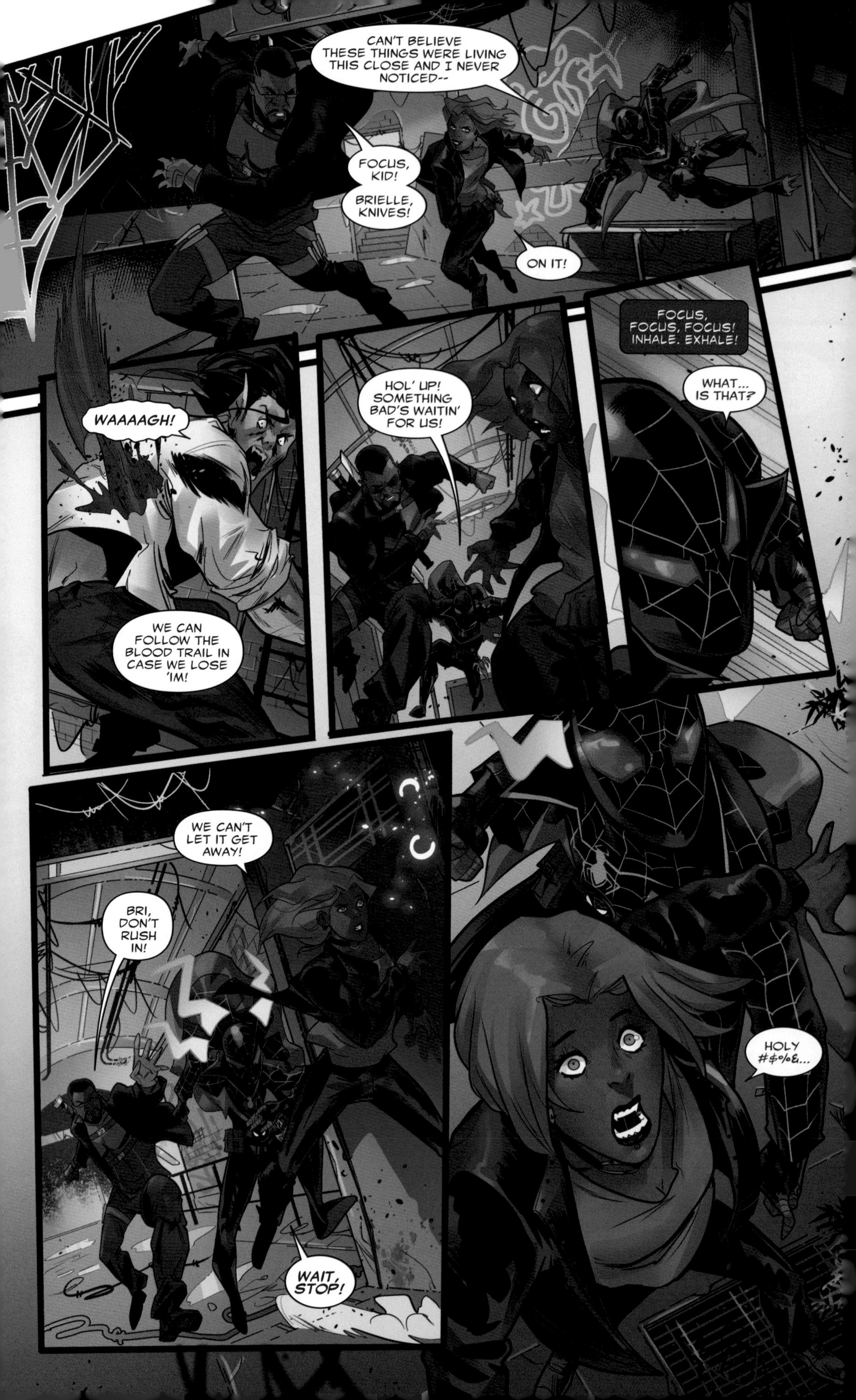
CAN'T BELIEVE THESE THINGS WERE LIVING THIS CLOSE AND I NEVER NOTICED--
FOCUS, KID!
BRIELLE, KNIVES!
ON IT!
WAAAAGH!
WE CAN FOLLOW THE BLOOD TRAIL IN CASE WE LOSE 'IM!
HOL' UP! SOMETHING BAD'S WAITIN' FOR US!
FOCUS, FOCUS, FOCUS! INHALE. EXHALE!
WHAT... IS THAT?
WE CAN'T LET IT GET AWAY!
BRI, DON'T RUSH IN!
WAIT, STOP!
HOLY #$%&...

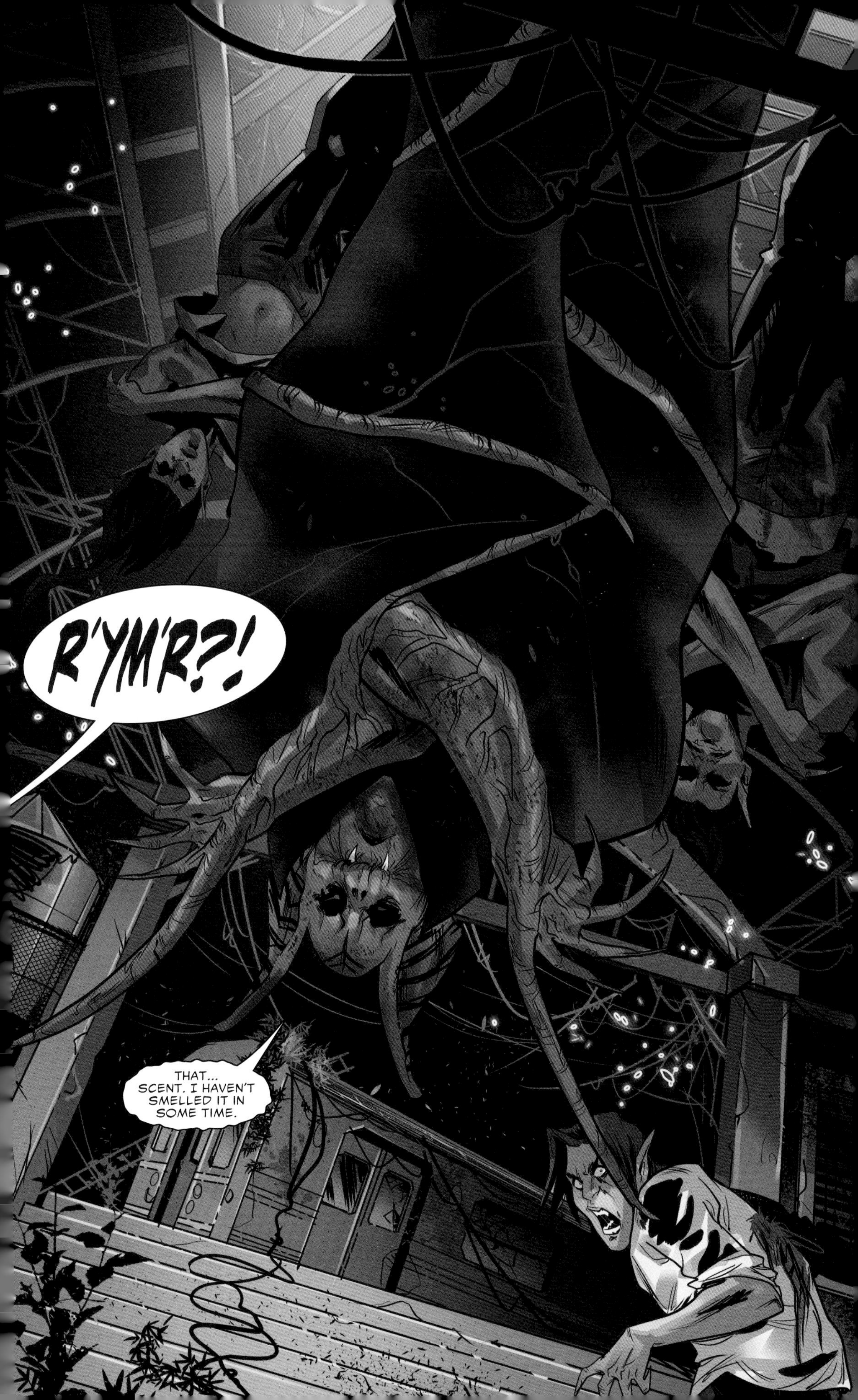
R'YM'R?!
THAT... SCENT. I HAVEN'T SMELLED IT IN SOME TIME.

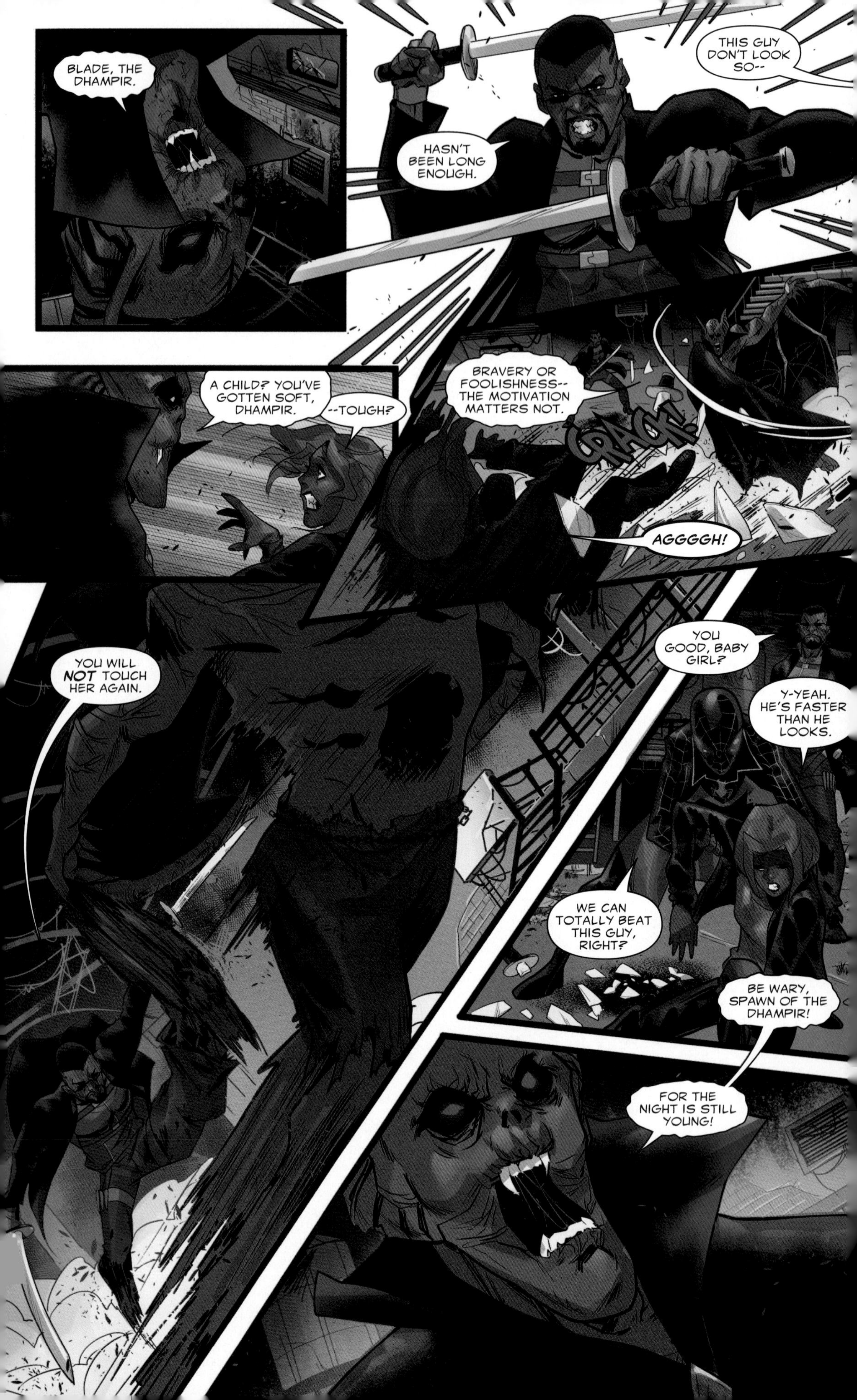
BLADE, THE DHAMPIR.
HASN'T BEEN LONG ENOUGH.
THIS GUY DON'T LOOK SO--
A CHILD? YOU'VE GOTTEN SOFT, DHAMPIR.
--TOUGH?
BRAVERY OR FOOLISHNESS-- THE MOTIVATION MATTERS NOT.
CRACK!
AGGGGH!
YOU WILL **NOT** TOUCH HER AGAIN.
YOU GOOD, BABY GIRL?
Y-YEAH. HE'S FASTER THAN HE LOOKS.
WE CAN TOTALLY BEAT THIS GUY, RIGHT?
BE WARY, SPAWN OF THE DHAMPIR!
FOR THE NIGHT IS STILL YOUNG!

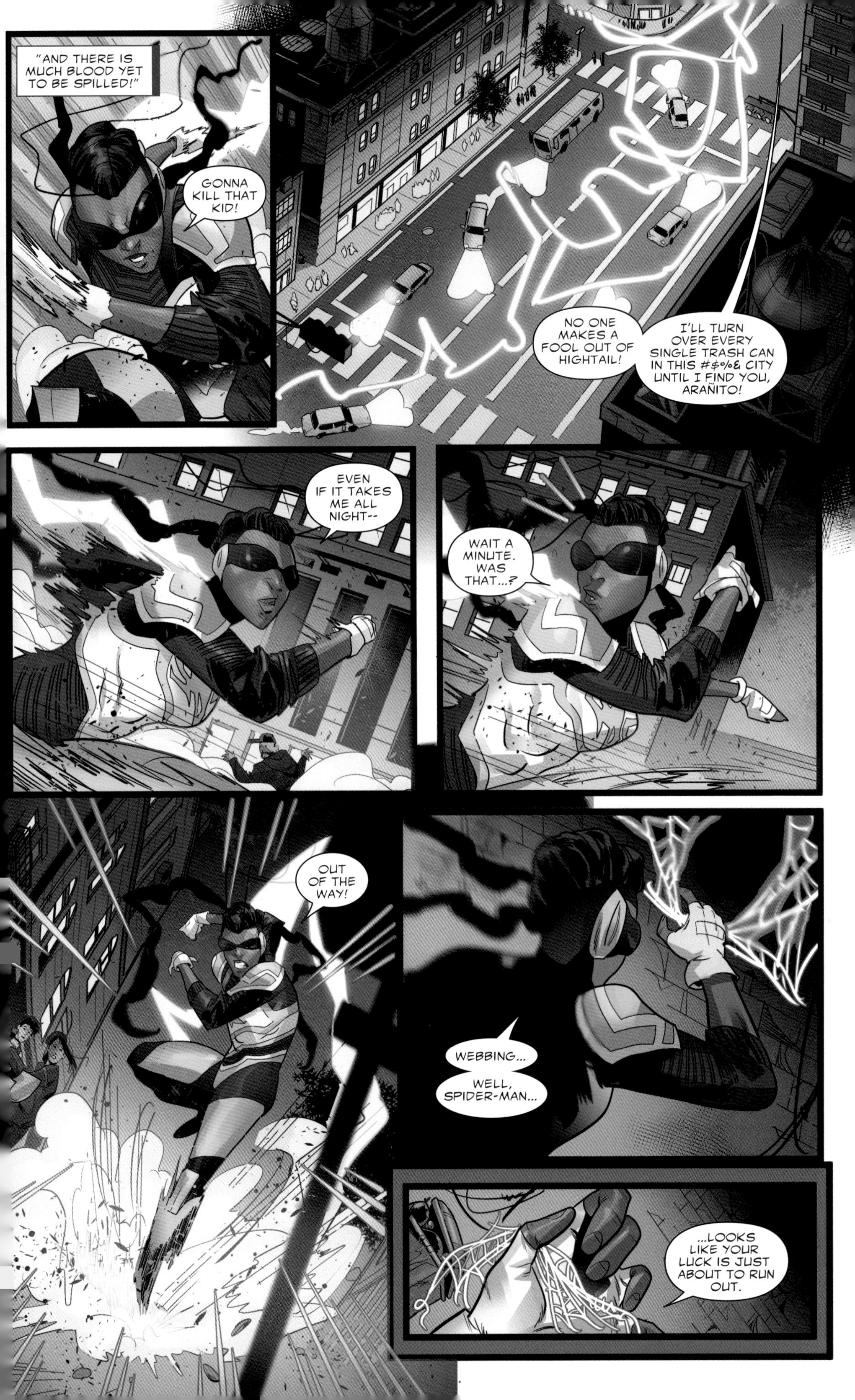
"AND THERE IS MUCH BLOOD YET TO BE SPILLED!"
GONNA KILL THAT KID!
NO ONE MAKES A FOOL OUT OF HIGHTAIL!
I'LL TURN OVER EVERY SINGLE TRASH CAN IN THIS #$%& CITY UNTIL I FIND YOU, ARAÑITO!
EVEN IF IT TAKES ME ALL NIGHT--
WAIT A MINUTE. WAS THAT...?
OUT OF THE WAY!
WEBBING...
WELL, SPIDER-MAN...
...LOOKS LIKE YOUR LUCK IS JUST ABOUT TO RUN OUT.

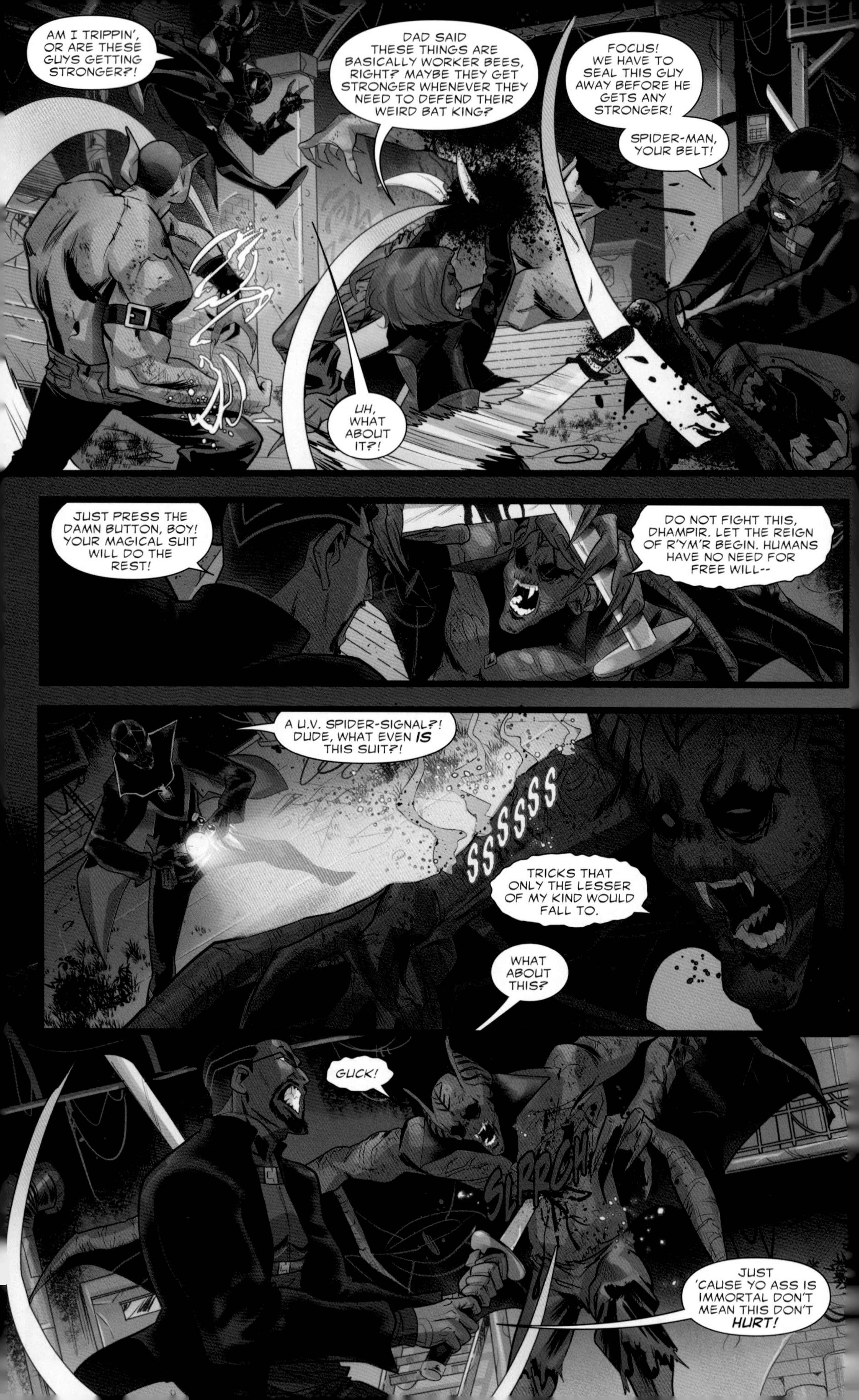
AM I TRIPPIN', OR ARE THESE GUYS GETTING STRONGER?!
DAD SAID THESE THINGS ARE BASICALLY WORKER BEES, RIGHT? MAYBE THEY GET STRONGER WHENEVER THEY NEED TO DEFEND THEIR WEIRD BAT KING?
FOCUS! WE HAVE TO SEAL THIS GUY AWAY BEFORE HE GETS ANY STRONGER!
SPIDER-MAN, YOUR BELT!
UH, WHAT ABOUT IT?!
JUST PRESS THE DAMN BUTTON, BOY! YOUR MAGICAL SUIT WILL DO THE REST!
DO NOT FIGHT THIS, DHAMPIR. LET THE REIGN OF R'YM'R BEGIN. HUMANS HAVE NO NEED FOR FREE WILL--
A U.V. SPIDER-SIGNAL?! DUDE, WHAT EVEN **IS** THIS SUIT?!
SSSSSS
TRICKS THAT ONLY THE LESSER OF MY KIND WOULD FALL TO.
WHAT ABOUT THIS?
GUCK!
SLRRCH!
JUST 'CAUSE YO ASS IS IMMORTAL DON'T MEAN THIS DON'T ***HURT!***

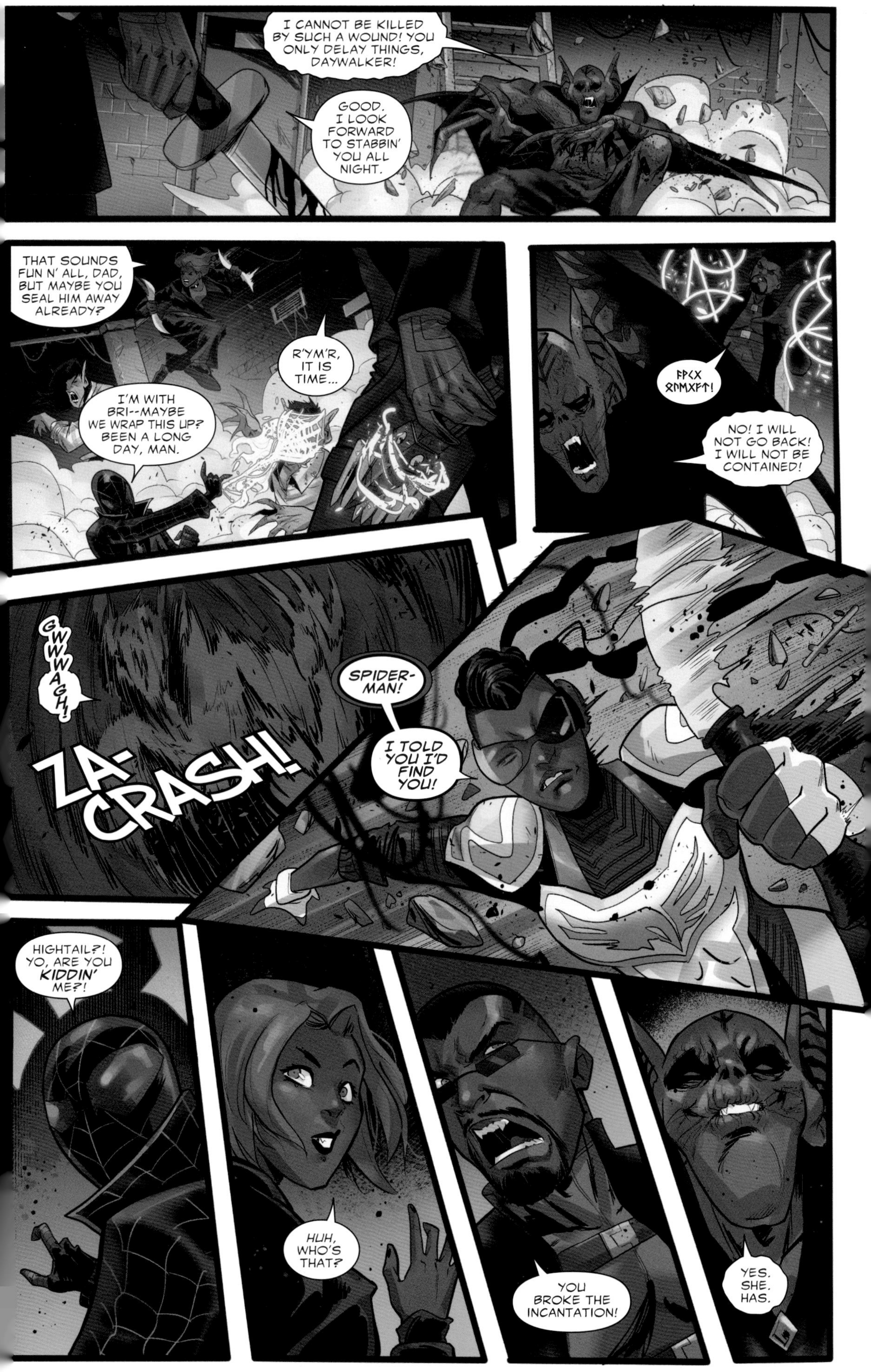
I CANNOT BE KILLED BY SUCH A WOUND! YOU ONLY DELAY THINGS, DAYWALKER!
GOOD. I LOOK FORWARD TO STABBIN' YOU ALL NIGHT.
THAT SOUNDS FUN N' ALL, DAD, BUT MAYBE YOU SEAL HIM AWAY ALREADY?
I'M WITH BRI--MAYBE WE WRAP THIS UP? BEEN A LONG DAY, MAN.
R'YM'R, IT IS TIME...
ᚨᚹᚲᚷ ᛟᚢᛖᚷᚨᛏ!
NO! I WILL NOT GO BACK! I WILL NOT BE CONTAINED!
GWWWAGH!
ZA-CRASH!
SPIDER-MAN!
I TOLD YOU I'D FIND YOU!
HIGHTAIL?! YO, ARE YOU KIDDIN' ME?!
HUH, WHO'S THAT?
YOU BROKE THE INCANTATION!
YES. SHE. HAS.

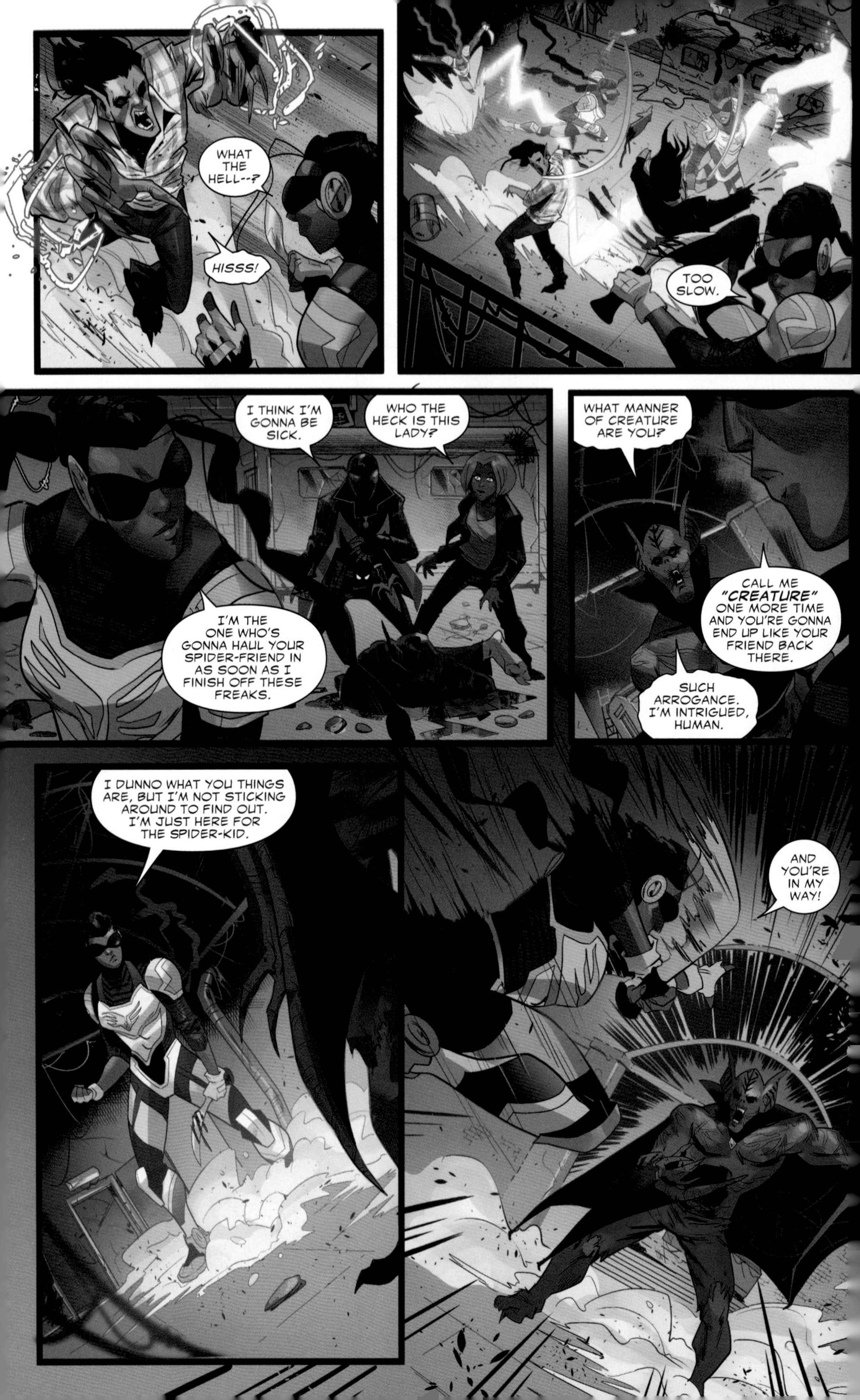
WHAT THE HELL--?
HISSS!
TOO SLOW.
I THINK I'M GONNA BE SICK.
WHO THE HECK IS THIS LADY?
I'M THE ONE WHO'S GONNA HAUL YOUR SPIDER-FRIEND IN AS SOON AS I FINISH OFF THESE FREAKS.
WHAT MANNER OF CREATURE ARE YOU?
CALL ME "CREATURE" ONE MORE TIME AND YOU'RE GONNA END UP LIKE YOUR FRIEND BACK THERE.
SUCH ARROGANCE. I'M INTRIGUED, HUMAN.
I DUNNO WHAT YOU THINGS ARE, BUT I'M NOT STICKING AROUND TO FIND OUT. I'M JUST HERE FOR THE SPIDER-KID.
AND YOU'RE IN MY WAY!

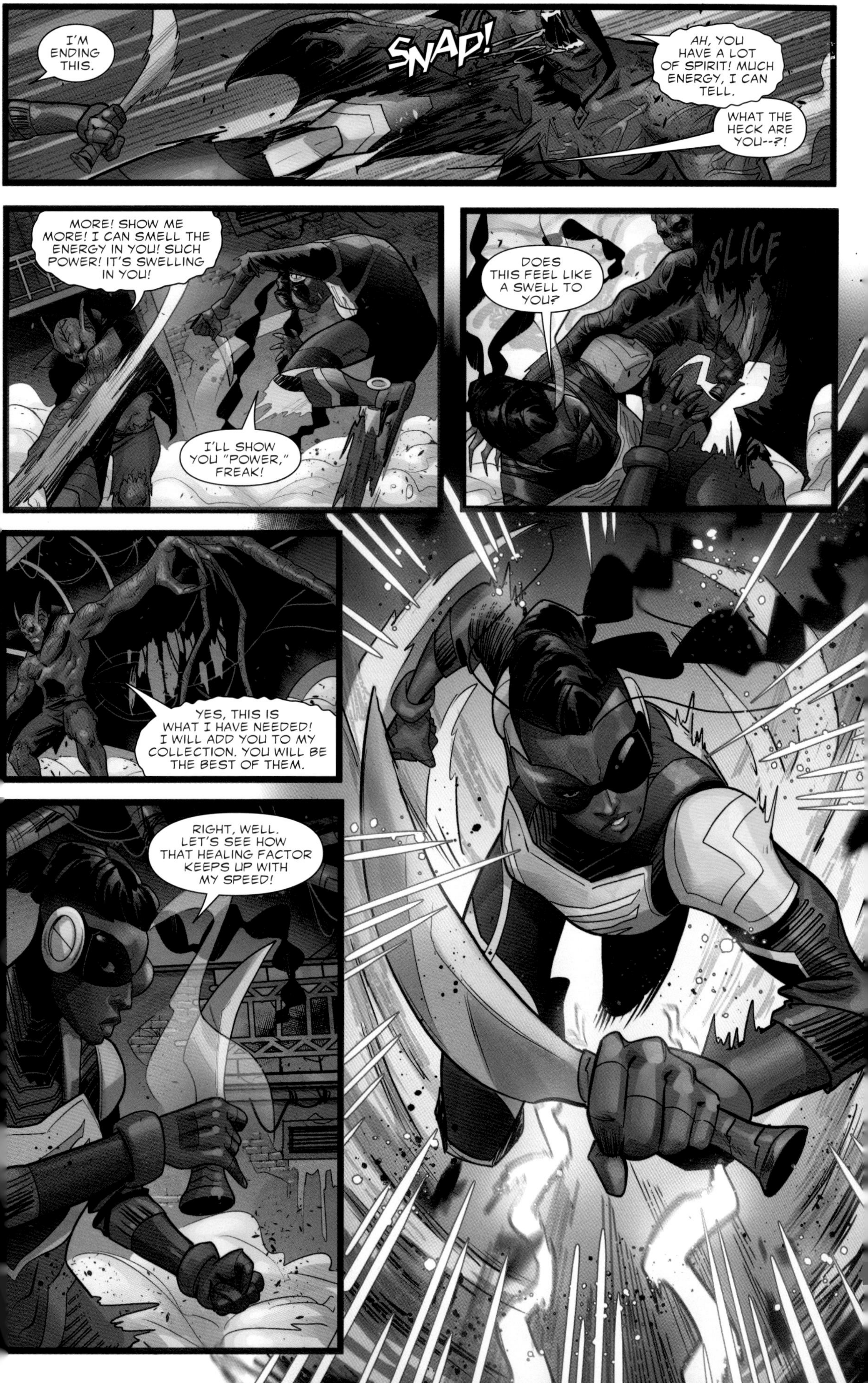
I'M ENDING THIS.
SNAP!
AH, YOU HAVE A LOT OF SPIRIT! MUCH ENERGY, I CAN TELL.
WHAT THE HECK ARE YOU--?!
MORE! SHOW ME MORE! I CAN SMELL THE ENERGY IN YOU! SUCH POWER! IT'S SWELLING IN YOU!
I'LL SHOW YOU "POWER," FREAK!
DOES THIS FEEL LIKE A SWELL TO YOU?
SLICE
YES, THIS IS WHAT I HAVE NEEDED! I WILL ADD YOU TO MY COLLECTION. YOU WILL BE THE BEST OF THEM.
RIGHT, WELL. LET'S SEE HOW THAT HEALING FACTOR KEEPS UP WITH MY SPEED!

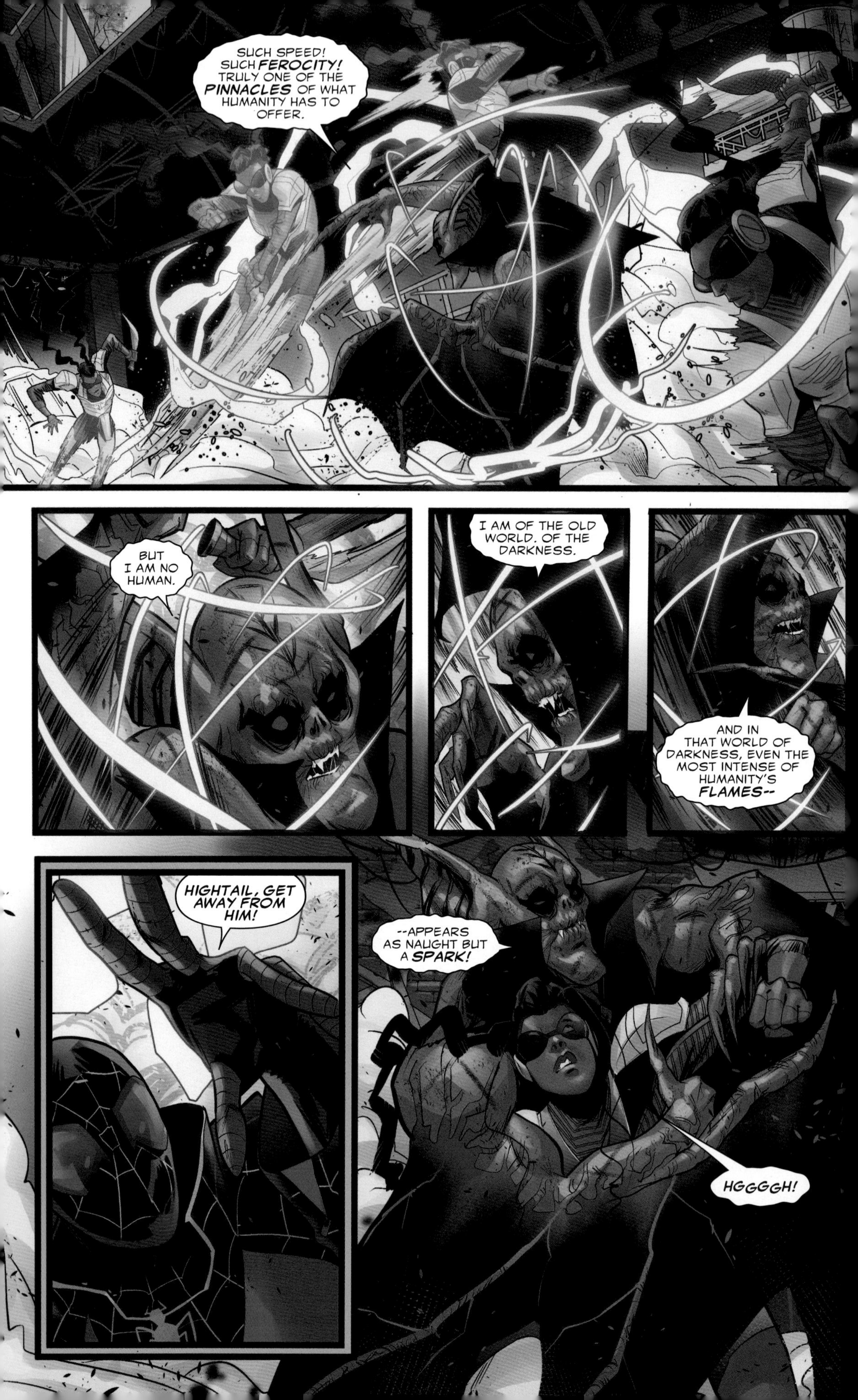
SUCH SPEED! SUCH FEROCITY! TRULY ONE OF THE PINNACLES OF WHAT HUMANITY HAS TO OFFER.
BUT I AM NO HUMAN.
I AM OF THE OLD WORLD. OF THE DARKNESS.
AND IN THAT WORLD OF DARKNESS, EVEN THE MOST INTENSE OF HUMANITY'S FLAMES--
HIGHTAIL, GET AWAY FROM HIM!
--APPEARS AS NAUGHT BUT A SPARK!
HGGGGH!

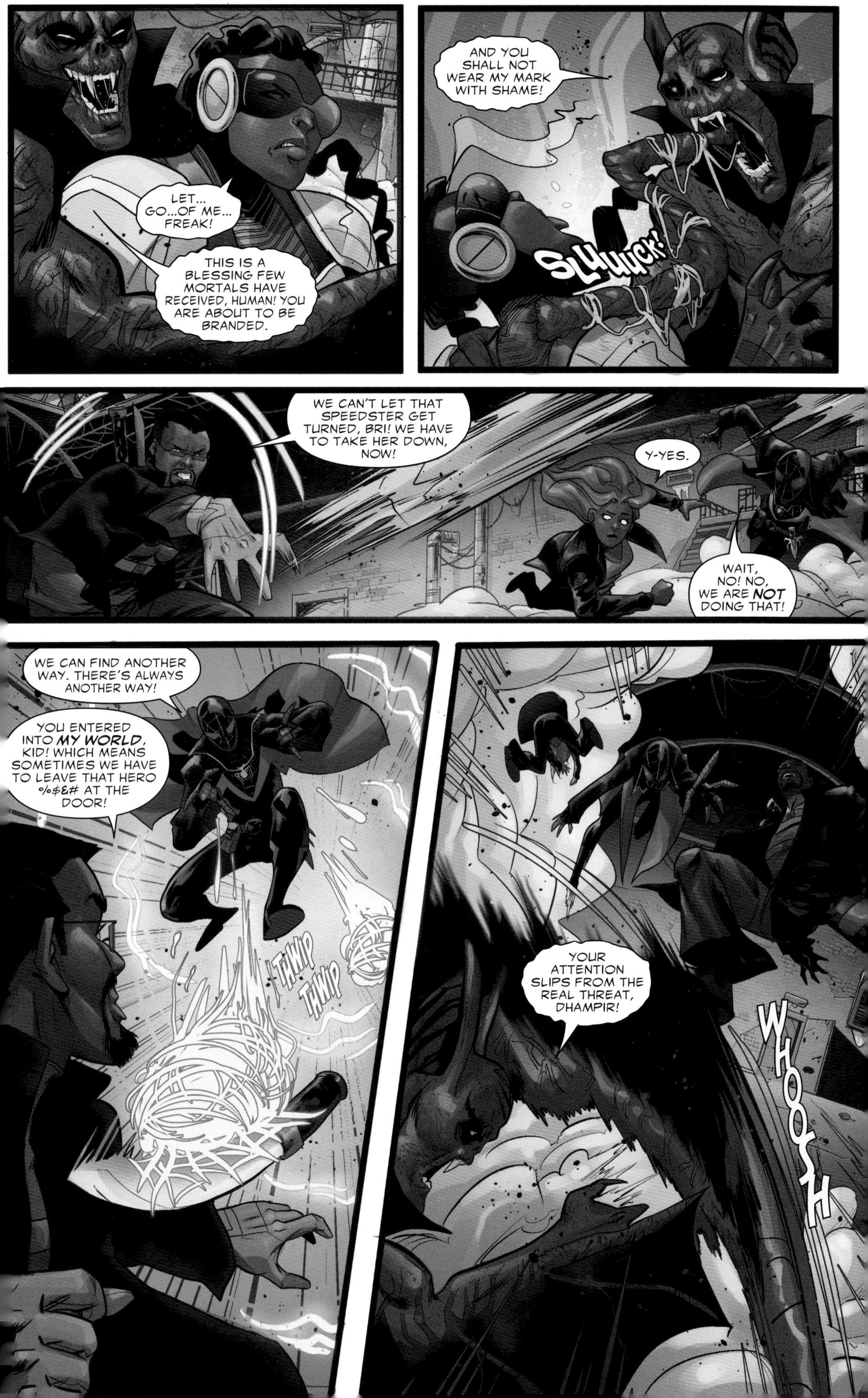

LET... GO...OF ME... FREAK!
THIS IS A BLESSING FEW MORTALS HAVE RECEIVED, HUMAN! YOU ARE ABOUT TO BE BRANDED.
AND YOU SHALL NOT WEAR MY MARK WITH SHAME!
SLUUUCK!
WE CAN'T LET THAT SPEEDSTER GET TURNED, BRI! WE HAVE TO TAKE HER DOWN, NOW!
Y-YES.
WAIT, NO! NO, WE ARE NOT DOING THAT!
WE CAN FIND ANOTHER WAY. THERE'S ALWAYS ANOTHER WAY!
YOU ENTERED INTO MY WORLD, KID! WHICH MEANS SOMETIMES WE HAVE TO LEAVE THAT HERO %$&# AT THE DOOR!
THWIP THWIP
YOUR ATTENTION SLIPS FROM THE REAL THREAT, DHAMPIR!
WHOOSH

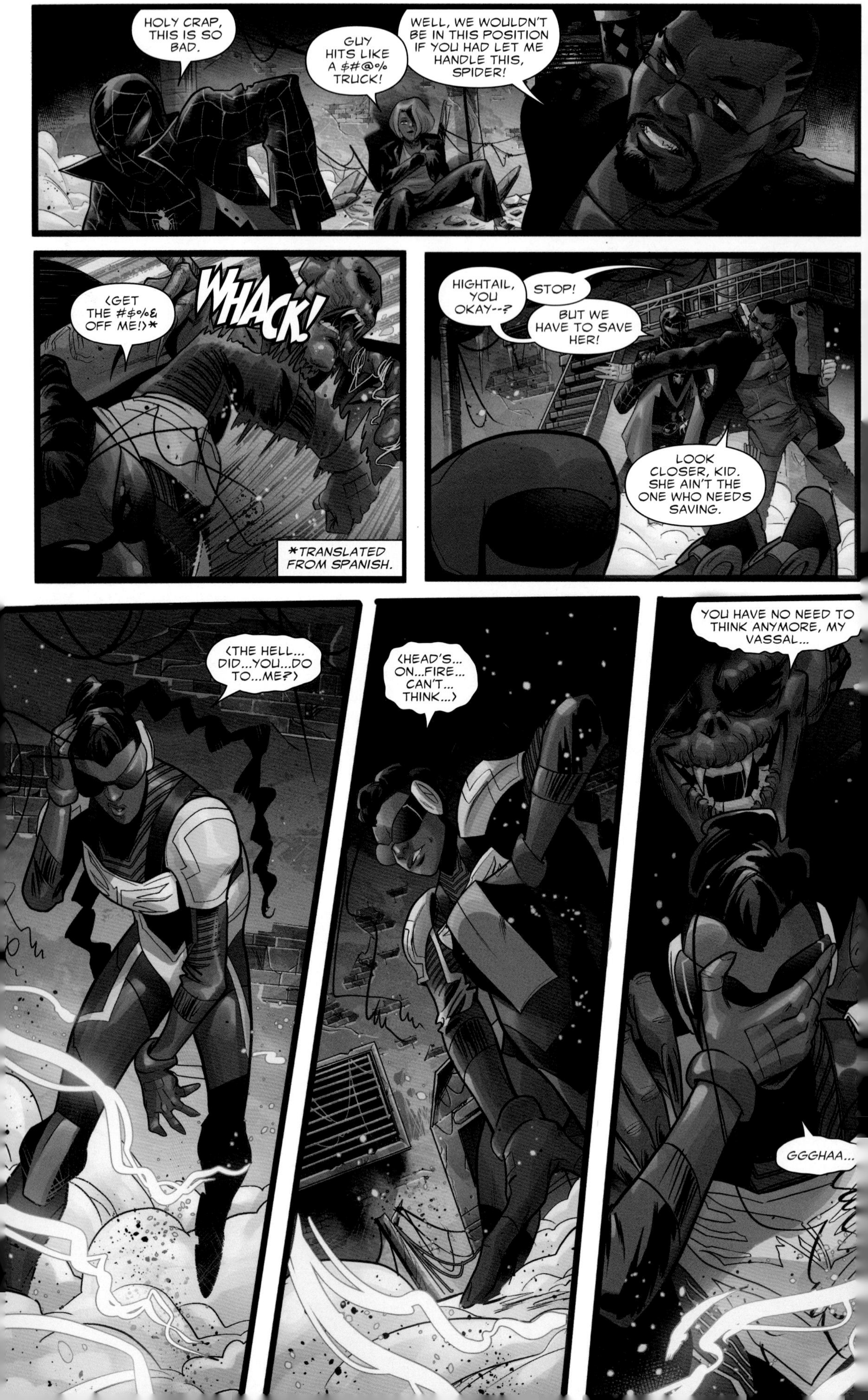
HOLY CRAP, THIS IS SO BAD.
GUY HITS LIKE A $#@%% TRUCK!
WELL, WE WOULDN'T BE IN THIS POSITION IF YOU HAD LET ME HANDLE THIS, SPIDER!
‹GET THE #$%& OFF ME!›*
WHACK!
*TRANSLATED FROM SPANISH.
HIGHTAIL, YOU OKAY--?
STOP!
BUT WE HAVE TO SAVE HER!
LOOK CLOSER, KID. SHE AIN'T THE ONE WHO NEEDS SAVING.
‹THE HELL... DID...YOU...DO TO...ME?›
‹HEAD'S... ON...FIRE... CAN'T... THINK...›
YOU HAVE NO NEED TO THINK ANYMORE, MY VASSAL...
GGGHAA...

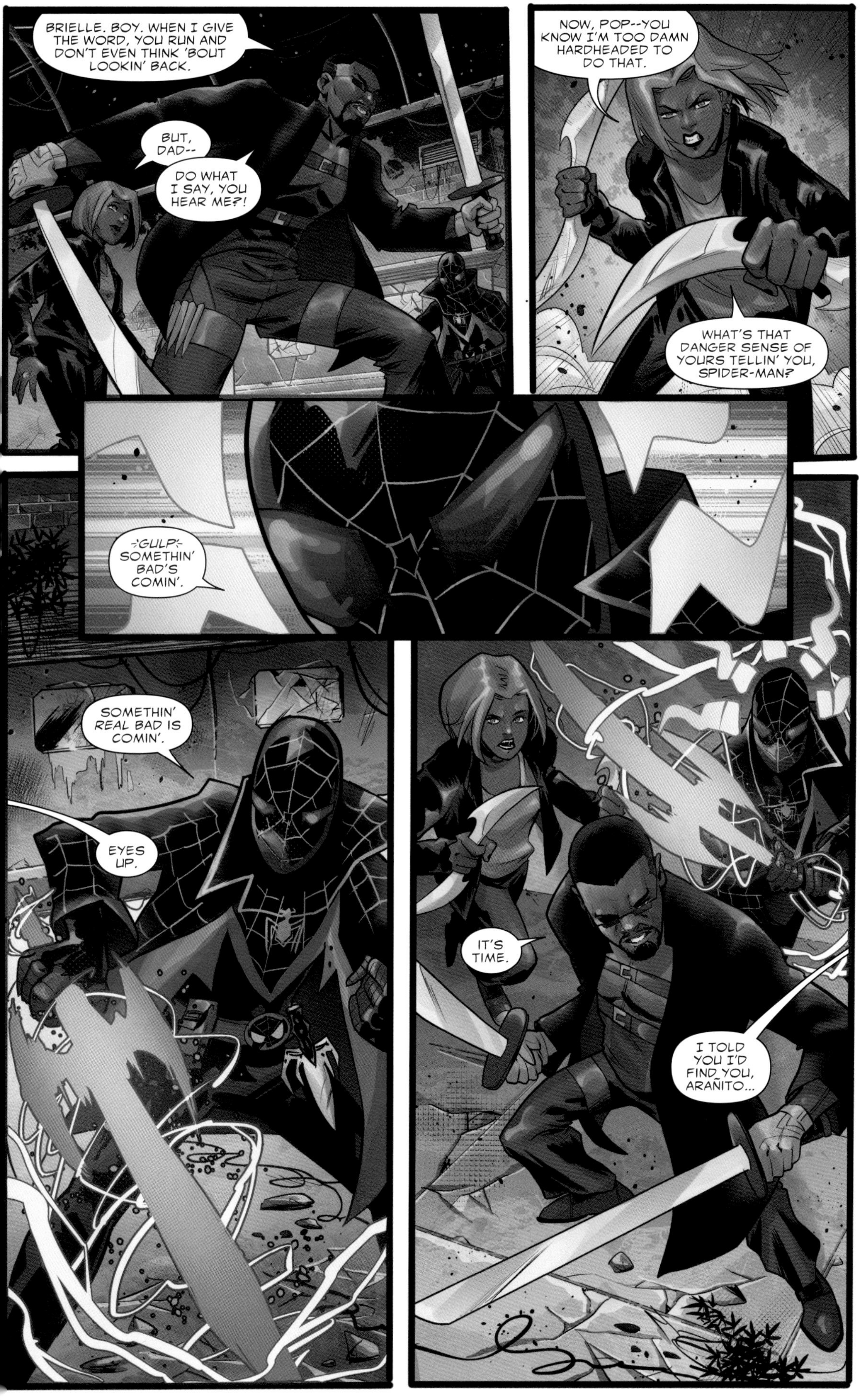
BRIELLE. BOY. WHEN I GIVE THE WORD, YOU RUN AND DON'T EVEN THINK 'BOUT LOOKIN' BACK.
BUT, DAD--
DO WHAT I SAY, YOU HEAR ME?!
NOW, POP--YOU KNOW I'M TOO DAMN HARDHEADED TO DO THAT.
WHAT'S THAT DANGER SENSE OF YOURS TELLIN' YOU, SPIDER-MAN?
GULP
SOMETHIN' BAD'S COMIN'.
SOMETHIN' REAL BAD IS COMIN'.
EYES UP.
IT'S TIME.
I TOLD YOU I'D FIND YOU, ARAÑITO...

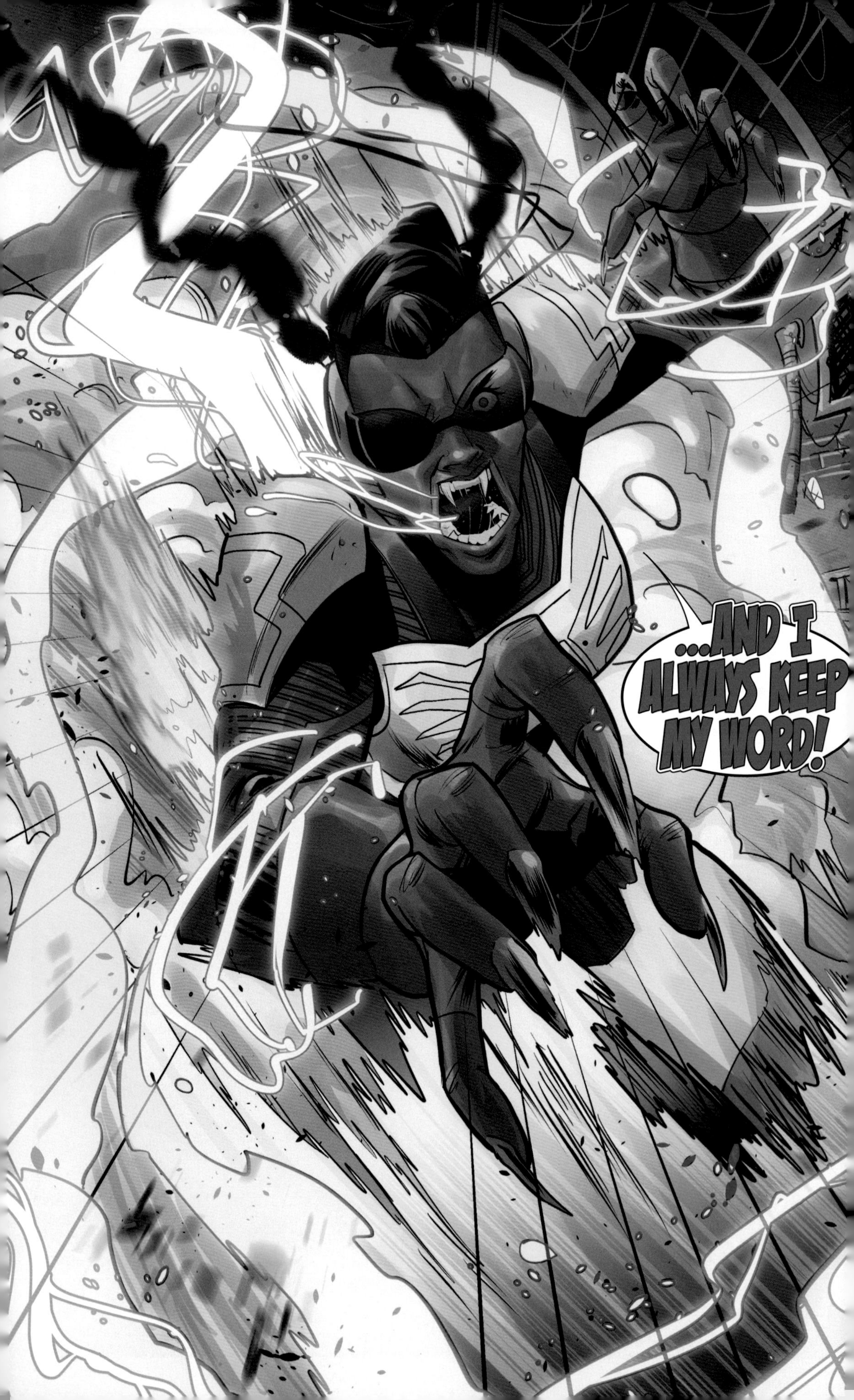
...AND I ALWAYS KEEP MY WORD!

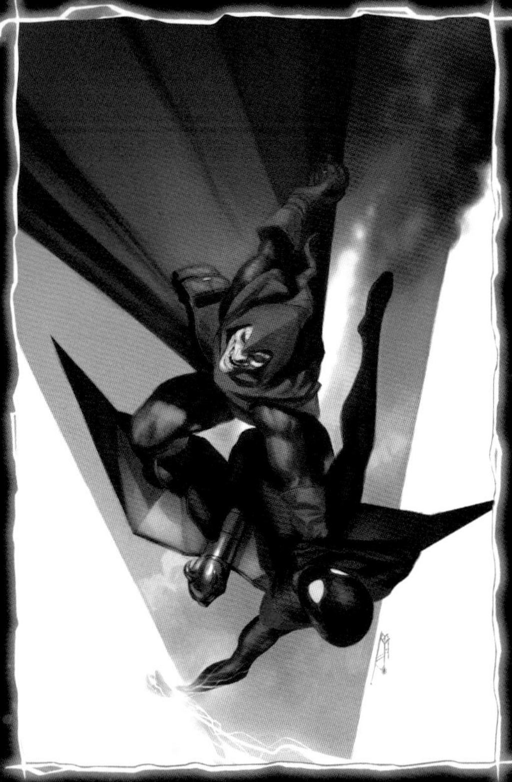

#9 VARIANT BY
MIGUEL MERCADO

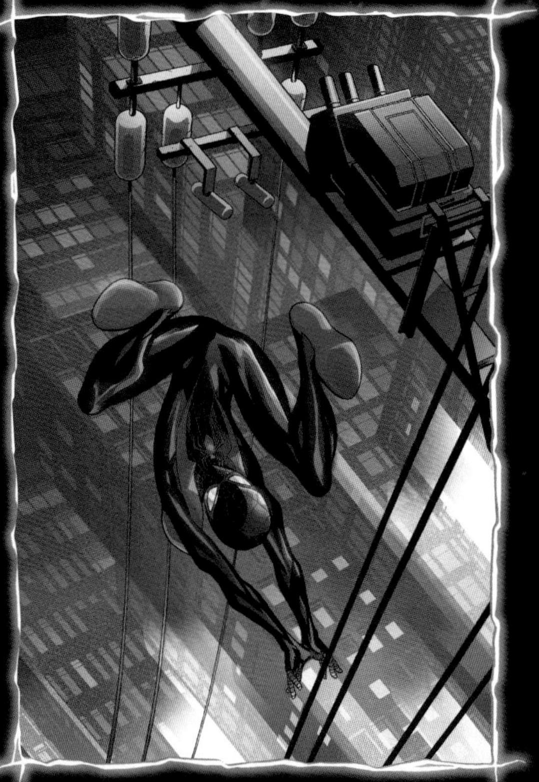

#10 VARIANT BY
MIKE McKONE & RUTH REDMOND

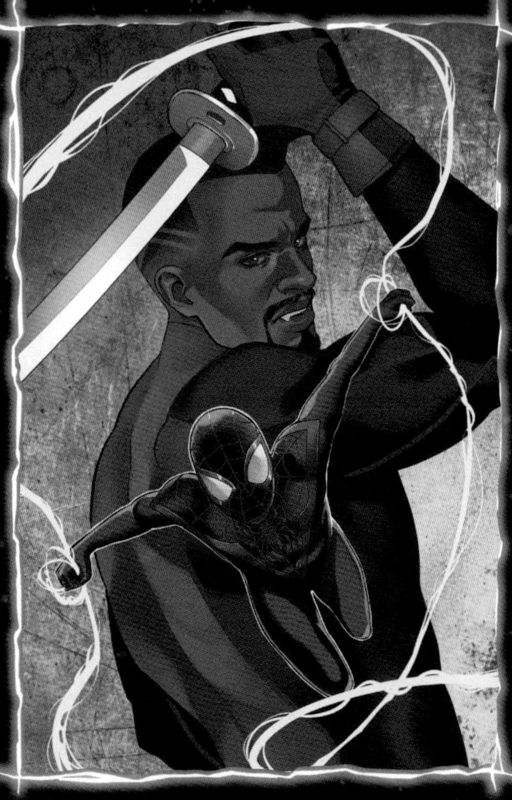

#10 VARIANT BY
ROMY JONES

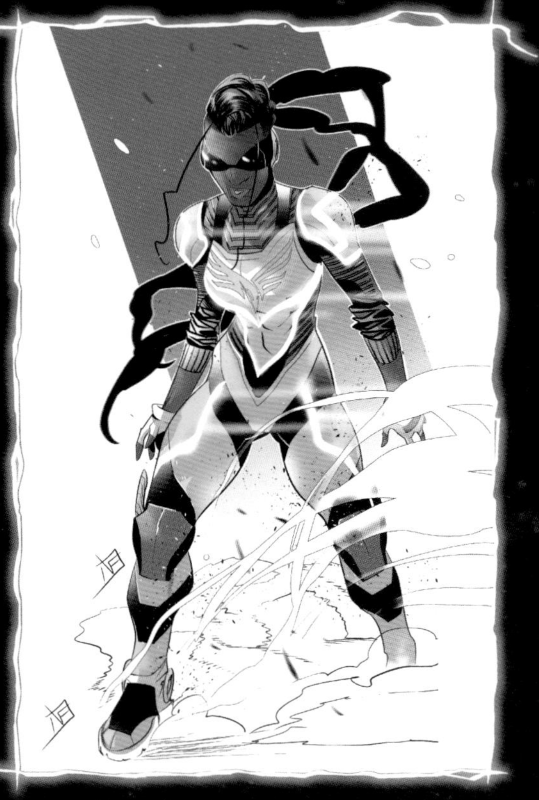

#10 DESIGN VARIANT BY
FEDERICO VICENTINI

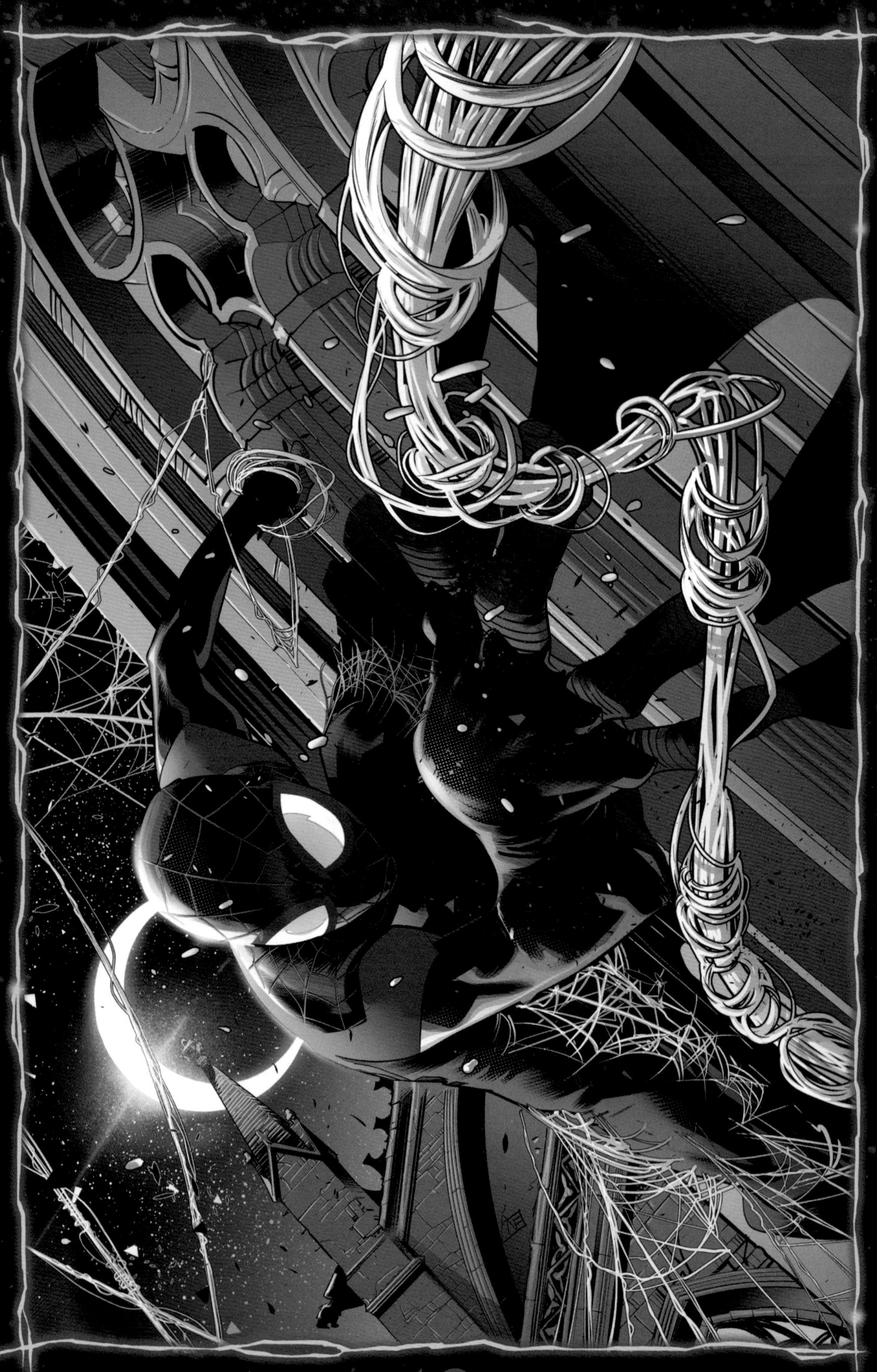

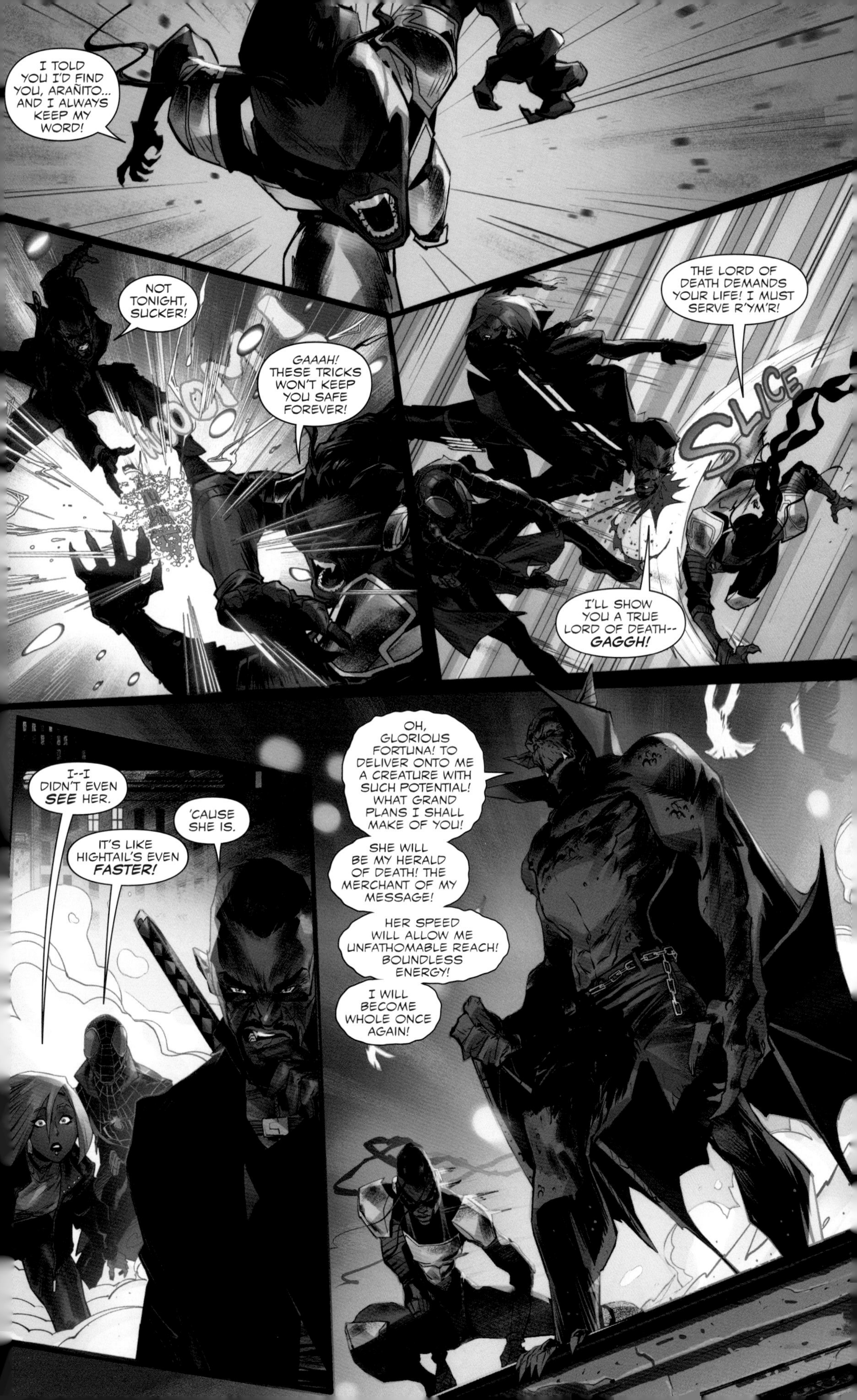
I TOLD YOU I'D FIND YOU, ARAÑITO... AND I ALWAYS KEEP MY WORD!
NOT TONIGHT, SUCKER!
GAAAH! THESE TRICKS WON'T KEEP YOU SAFE FOREVER!
THE LORD OF DEATH DEMANDS YOUR LIFE! I MUST SERVE R'YM'R!
SLICE
I'LL SHOW YOU A TRUE LORD OF DEATH-- GAGGH!
I--I DIDN'T EVEN SEE HER.
IT'S LIKE HIGHTAIL'S EVEN FASTER!
'CAUSE SHE IS.
OH, GLORIOUS FORTUNA! TO DELIVER ONTO ME A CREATURE WITH SUCH POTENTIAL! WHAT GRAND PLANS I SHALL MAKE OF YOU!
SHE WILL BE MY HERALD OF DEATH! THE MERCHANT OF MY MESSAGE!
HER SPEED WILL ALLOW ME UNFATHOMABLE REACH! BOUNDLESS ENERGY!
I WILL BECOME WHOLE ONCE AGAIN!

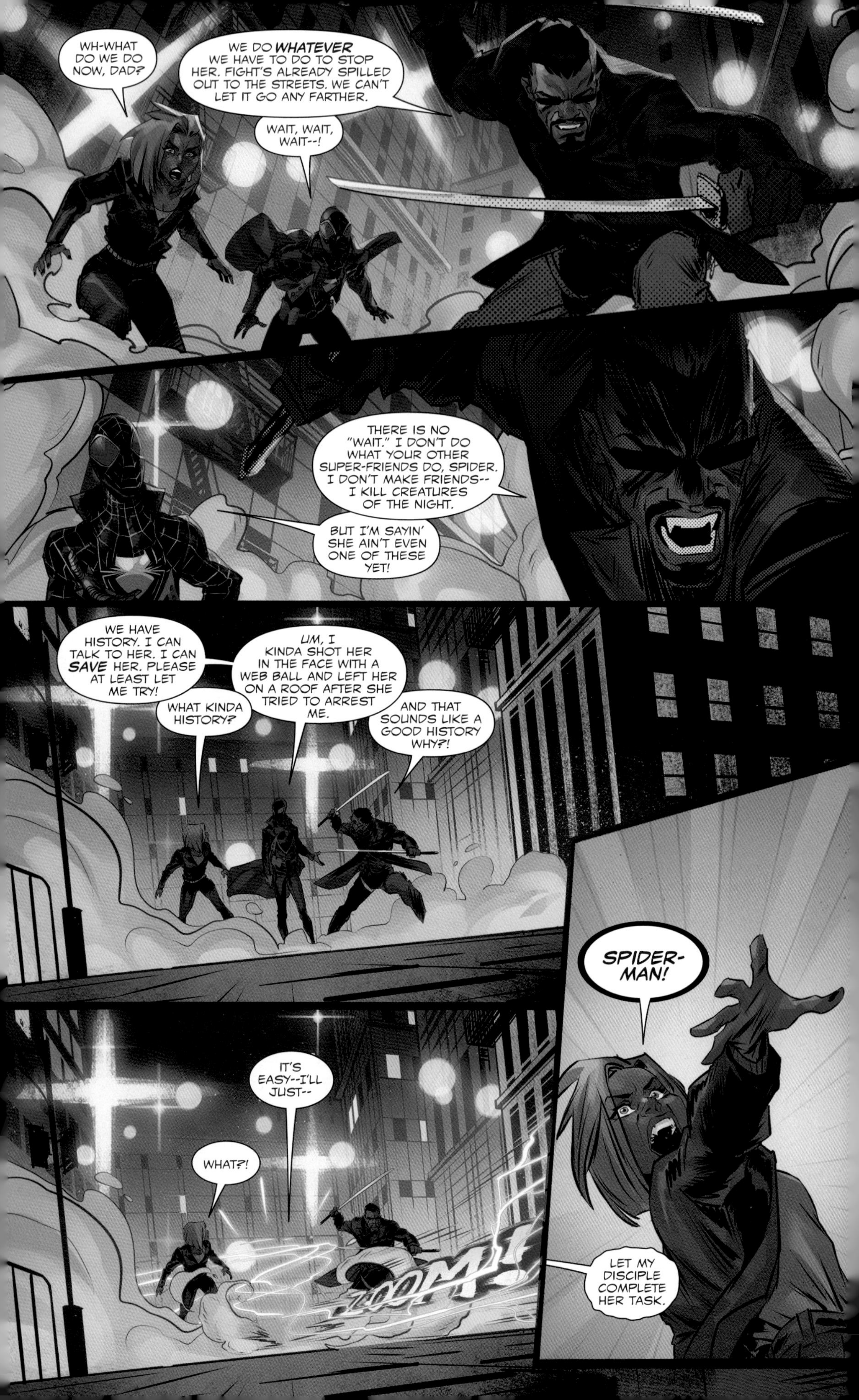
WH-WHAT DO WE DO NOW, DAD?
WE DO WHATEVER WE HAVE TO DO TO STOP HER. FIGHT'S ALREADY SPILLED OUT TO THE STREETS. WE CAN'T LET IT GO ANY FARTHER.
WAIT, WAIT, WAIT--!
THERE IS NO "WAIT." I DON'T DO WHAT YOUR OTHER SUPER-FRIENDS DO, SPIDER. I DON'T MAKE FRIENDS-- I KILL CREATURES OF THE NIGHT.
BUT I'M SAYIN' SHE AIN'T EVEN ONE OF THESE YET!
WE HAVE HISTORY. I CAN TALK TO HER. I CAN SAVE HER. PLEASE AT LEAST LET ME TRY!
WHAT KINDA HISTORY?
UM, I KINDA SHOT HER IN THE FACE WITH A WEB BALL AND LEFT HER ON A ROOF AFTER SHE TRIED TO ARREST ME.
AND THAT SOUNDS LIKE A GOOD HISTORY WHY?!
IT'S EASY--I'LL JUST--
WHAT?!
ZOOM!
SPIDER-MAN!
LET MY DISCIPLE COMPLETE HER TASK.

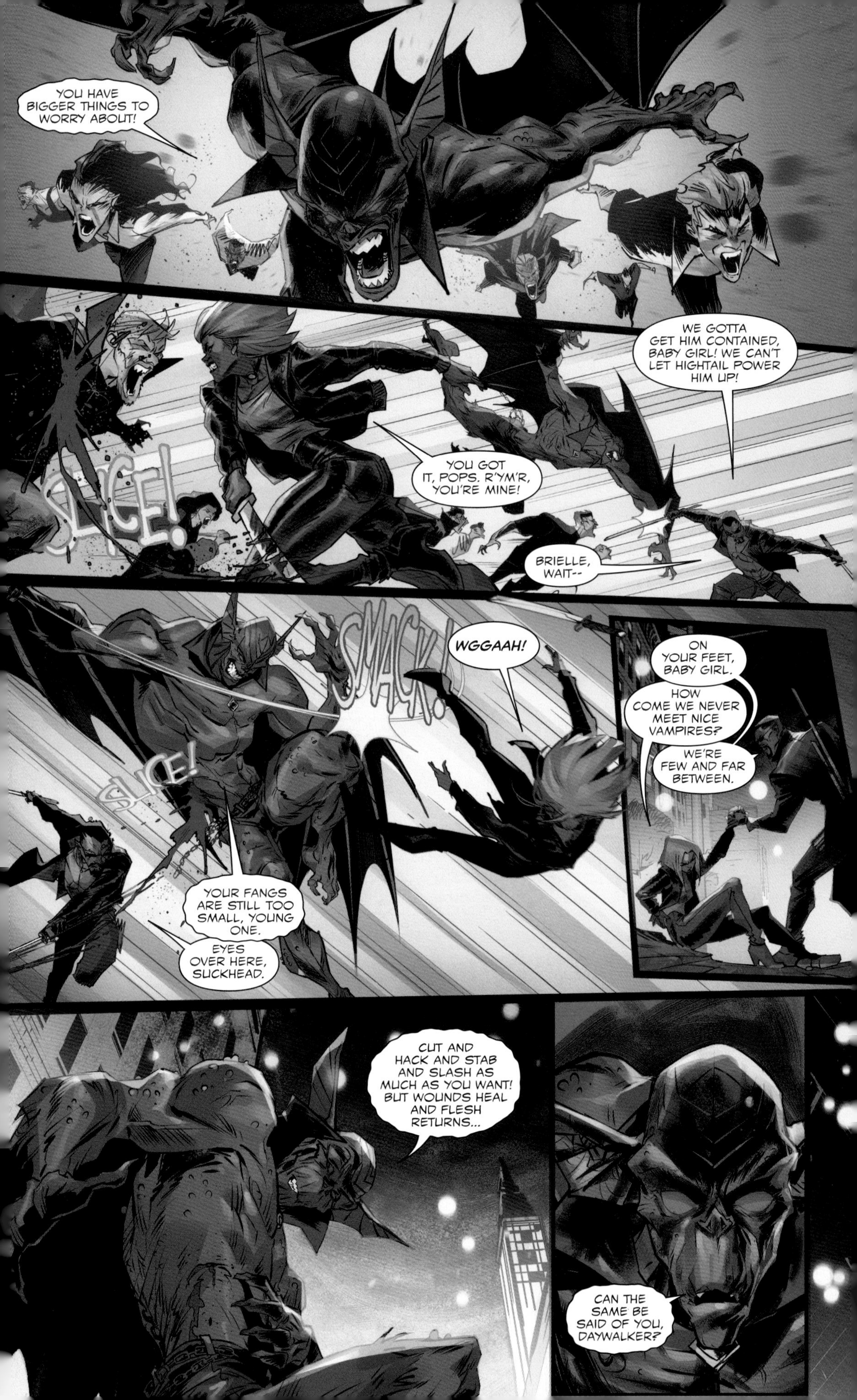
YOU HAVE BIGGER THINGS TO WORRY ABOUT!
SLICE!
WE GOTTA GET HIM CONTAINED, BABY GIRL! WE CAN'T LET HIGHTAIL POWER HIM UP!
YOU GOT IT, POPS. R'YM'R, YOU'RE MINE!
BRIELLE, WAIT--
SMACK!
WGGAAH!
SLICE!
YOUR FANGS ARE STILL TOO SMALL, YOUNG ONE.
EYES OVER HERE, SUCKHEAD.
ON YOUR FEET, BABY GIRL.
HOW COME WE NEVER MEET NICE VAMPIRES?
WE'RE FEW AND FAR BETWEEN.
CUT AND HACK AND STAB AND SLASH AS MUCH AS YOU WANT! BUT WOUNDS HEAL AND FLESH RETURNS...
CAN THE SAME BE SAID OF YOU, DAYWALKER?

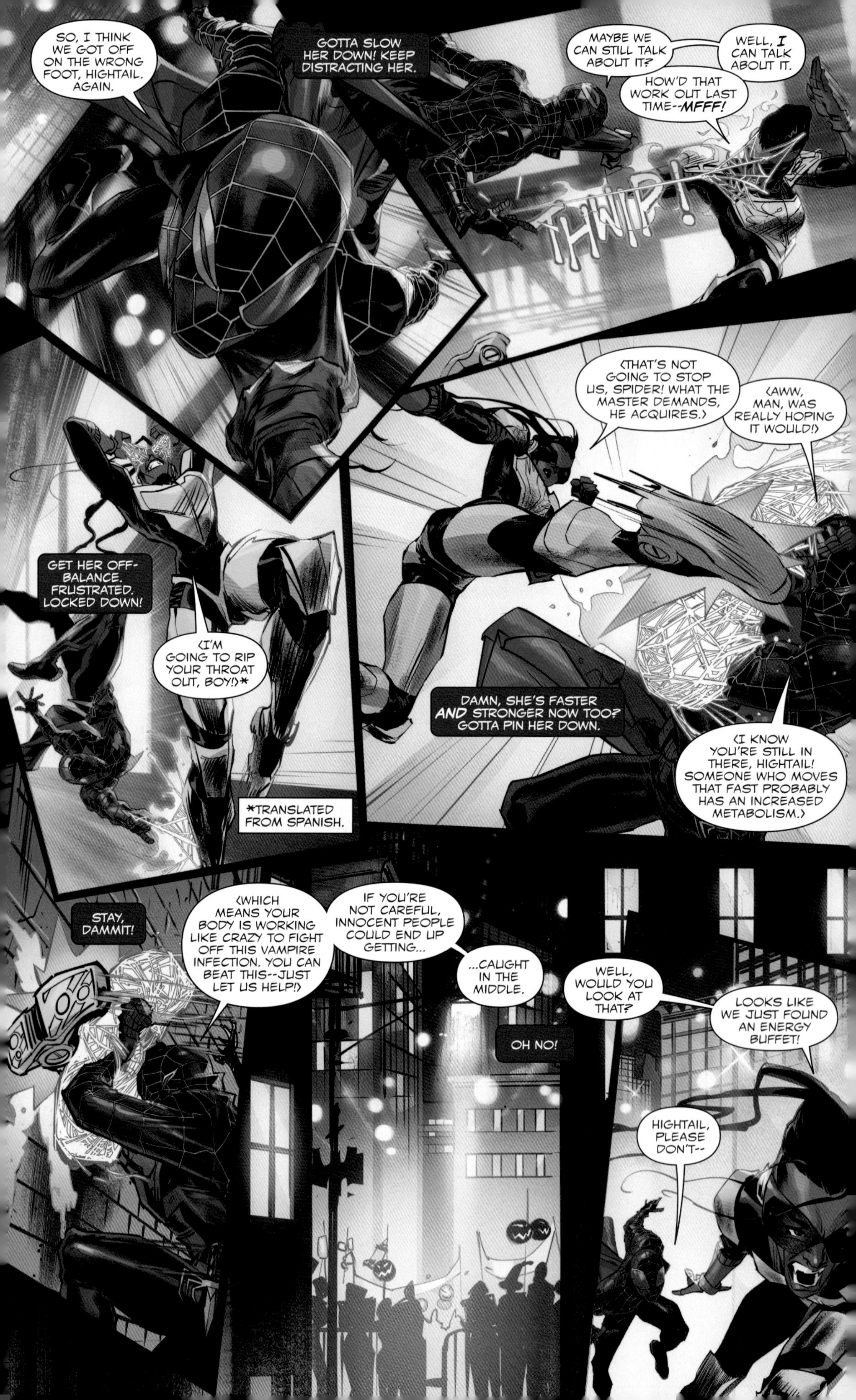
SO, I THINK WE GOT OFF ON THE WRONG FOOT, HIGHTAIL. AGAIN.
GOTTA SLOW HER DOWN! KEEP DISTRACTING HER.
MAYBE WE CAN STILL TALK ABOUT IT?
WELL, I CAN TALK ABOUT IT.
HOW'D THAT WORK OUT LAST TIME--MFFF!
THWIP!
GET HER OFF-BALANCE. FRUSTRATED. LOCKED DOWN!
<I'M GOING TO RIP YOUR THROAT OUT, BOY!>*
*TRANSLATED FROM SPANISH.
<THAT'S NOT GOING TO STOP US, SPIDER! WHAT THE MASTER DEMANDS, HE ACQUIRES.>
<AWW, MAN, WAS REALLY HOPING IT WOULD!>
DAMN, SHE'S FASTER AND STRONGER NOW TOO? GOTTA PIN HER DOWN.
<I KNOW YOU'RE STILL IN THERE, HIGHTAIL! SOMEONE WHO MOVES THAT FAST PROBABLY HAS AN INCREASED METABOLISM.>
STAY, DAMMIT!
<WHICH MEANS YOUR BODY IS WORKING LIKE CRAZY TO FIGHT OFF THIS VAMPIRE INFECTION. YOU CAN BEAT THIS--JUST LET US HELP!>
IF YOU'RE NOT CAREFUL, INNOCENT PEOPLE COULD END UP GETTING...
...CAUGHT IN THE MIDDLE.
OH NO!
WELL, WOULD YOU LOOK AT THAT?
LOOKS LIKE WE JUST FOUND AN ENERGY BUFFET!
HIGHTAIL, PLEASE DON'T--

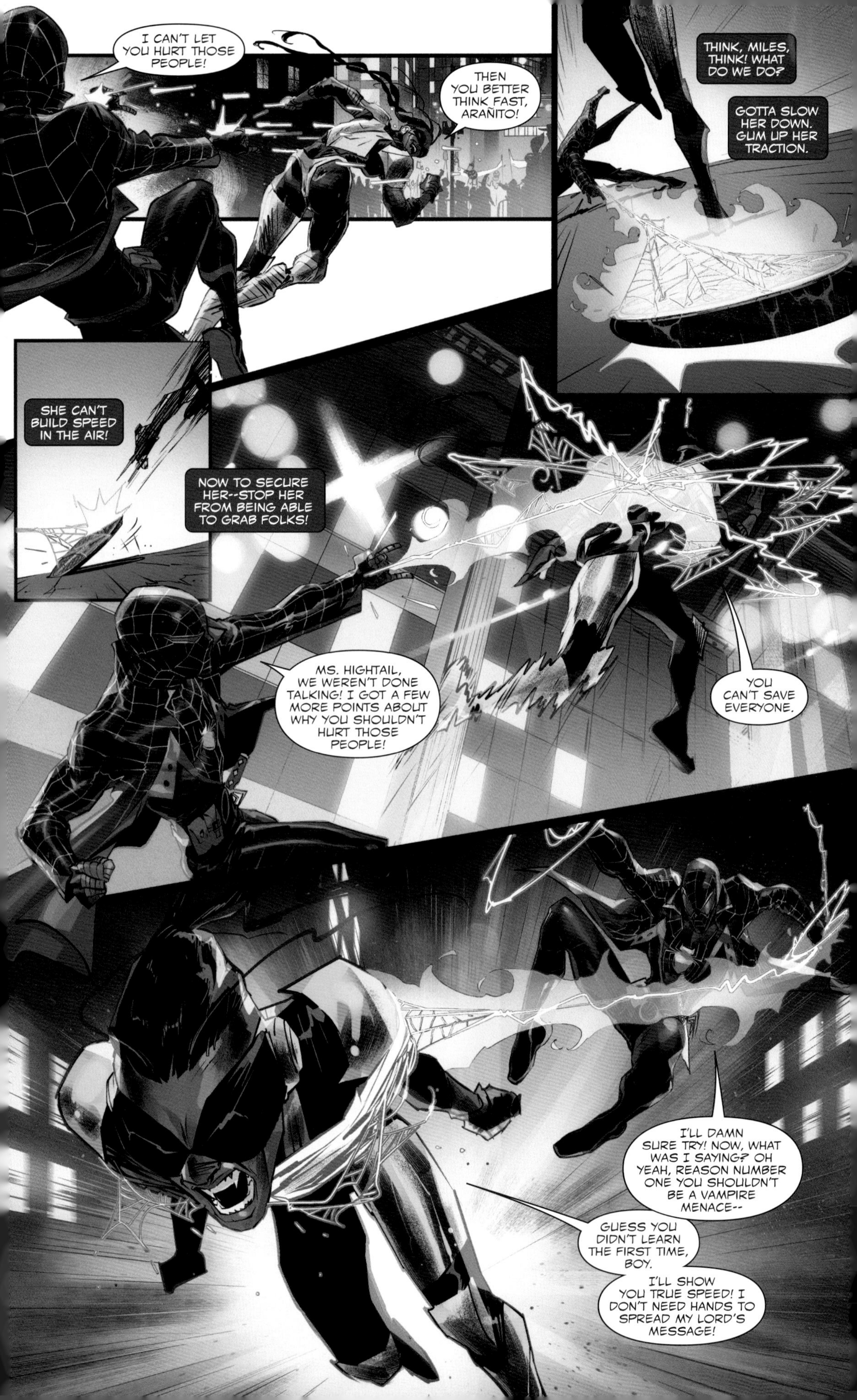
I CAN'T LET YOU HURT THOSE PEOPLE!
THEN YOU BETTER THINK FAST, ARAÑITO!
THINK, MILES, THINK! WHAT DO WE DO?
GOTTA SLOW HER DOWN. GUM UP HER TRACTION.
SHE CAN'T BUILD SPEED IN THE AIR!
NOW TO SECURE HER--STOP HER FROM BEING ABLE TO GRAB FOLKS!
MS. HIGHTAIL, WE WEREN'T DONE TALKING! I GOT A FEW MORE POINTS ABOUT WHY YOU SHOULDN'T HURT THOSE PEOPLE!
YOU CAN'T SAVE EVERYONE.
I'LL DAMN SURE TRY! NOW, WHAT WAS I SAYING? OH YEAH, REASON NUMBER ONE YOU SHOULDN'T BE A VAMPIRE MENACE--
GUESS YOU DIDN'T LEARN THE FIRST TIME, BOY.
I'LL SHOW YOU TRUE SPEED! I DON'T NEED HANDS TO SPREAD MY LORD'S MESSAGE!

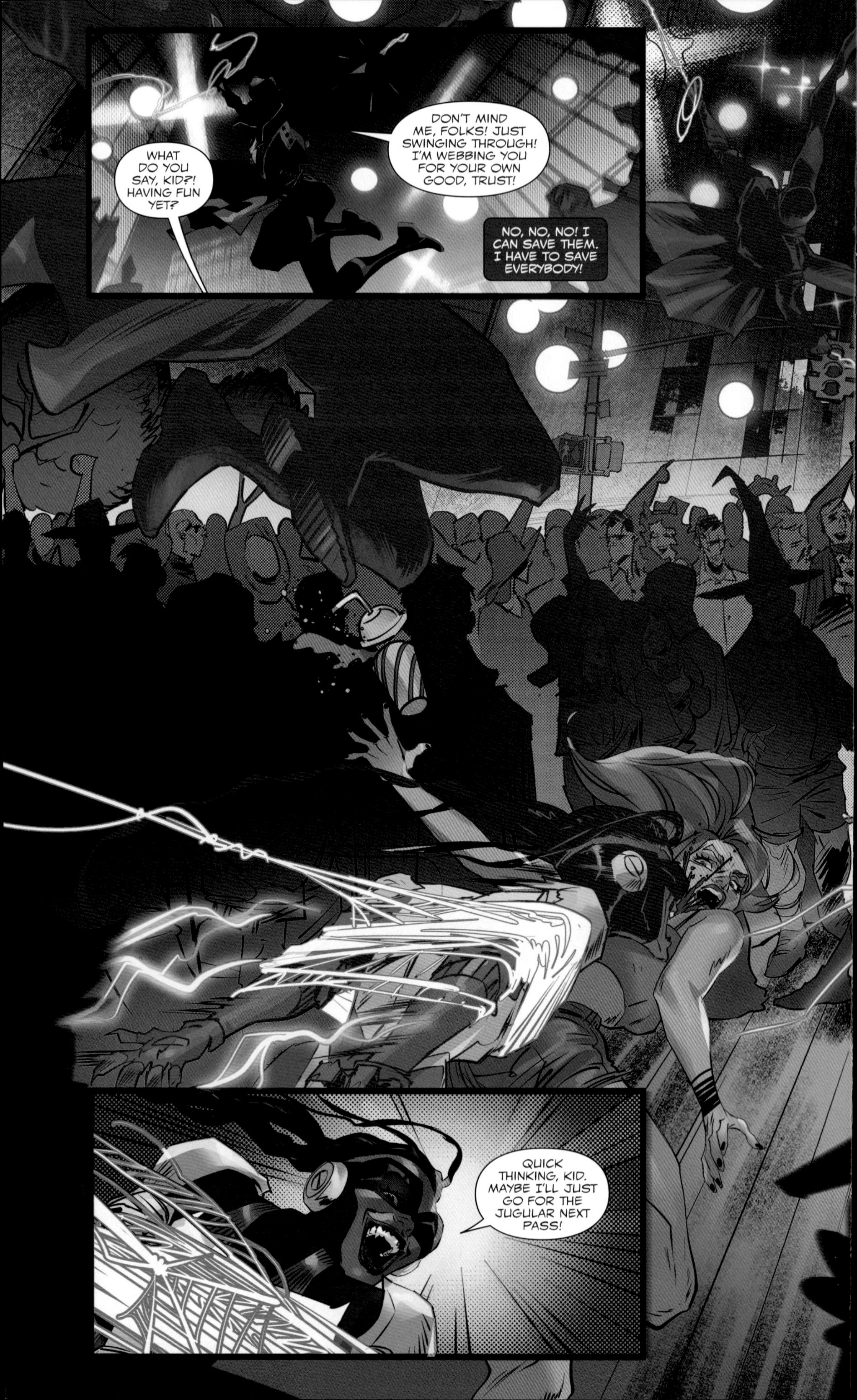
WHAT DO YOU SAY, KID?! HAVING FUN YET?
DON'T MIND ME, FOLKS! JUST SWINGING THROUGH! I'M WEBBING YOU FOR YOUR OWN GOOD, TRUST!
NO, NO, NO! I CAN SAVE THEM. I HAVE TO SAVE EVERYBODY!
QUICK THINKING, KID. MAYBE I'LL JUST GO FOR THE JUGULAR NEXT PASS!

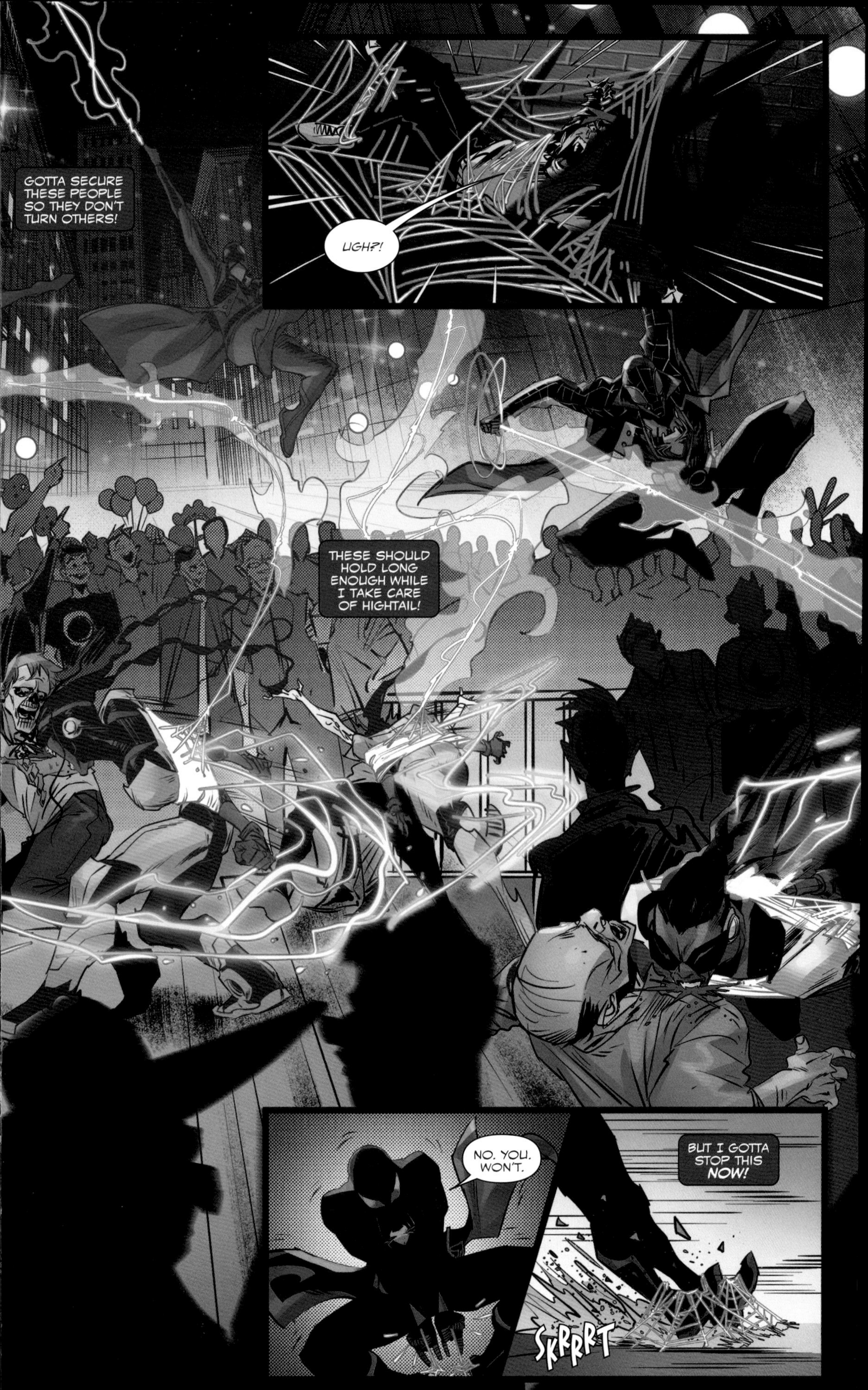
GOTTA SECURE THESE PEOPLE SO THEY DON'T TURN OTHERS!
UGH?!
THESE SHOULD HOLD LONG ENOUGH WHILE I TAKE CARE OF HIGHTAIL!
NO. YOU. WON'T.
BUT I GOTTA STOP THIS NOW!
SKRRRT

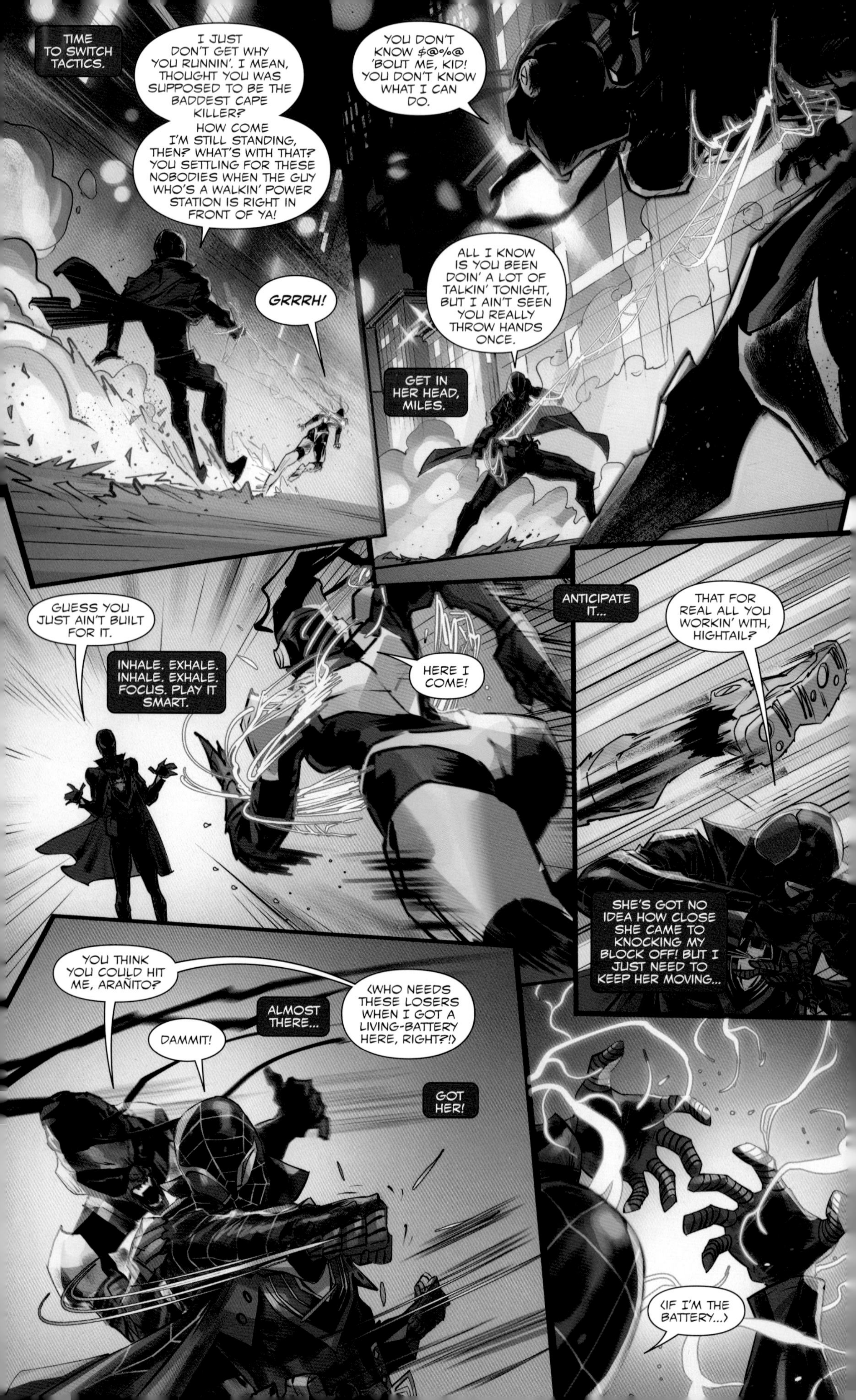
TIME TO SWITCH TACTICS.
I JUST DON'T GET WHY YOU RUNNIN'. I MEAN, THOUGHT YOU WAS SUPPOSED TO BE THE BADDEST CAPE KILLER?
HOW COME I'M STILL STANDING, THEN? WHAT'S WITH THAT? YOU SETTLING FOR THESE NOBODIES WHEN THE GUY WHO'S A WALKIN' POWER STATION IS RIGHT IN FRONT OF YA!
GRRRH!
YOU DON'T KNOW $@%@ 'BOUT ME, KID! YOU DON'T KNOW WHAT I CAN DO.
ALL I KNOW IS YOU BEEN DOIN' A LOT OF TALKIN' TONIGHT, BUT I AIN'T SEEN YOU REALLY THROW HANDS ONCE.
GET IN HER HEAD, MILES.
GUESS YOU JUST AIN'T BUILT FOR IT.
INHALE. EXHALE. INHALE. EXHALE. FOCUS. PLAY IT SMART.
HERE I COME!
ANTICIPATE IT...
THAT FOR REAL ALL YOU WORKIN' WITH, HIGHTAIL?
SHE'S GOT NO IDEA HOW CLOSE SHE CAME TO KNOCKING MY BLOCK OFF! BUT I JUST NEED TO KEEP HER MOVING...
YOU THINK YOU COULD HIT ME, ARAÑITO?
<WHO NEEDS THESE LOSERS WHEN I GOT A LIVING-BATTERY HERE, RIGHT?!>
ALMOST THERE...
DAMMIT!
GOT HER!
<IF I'M THE BATTERY...>

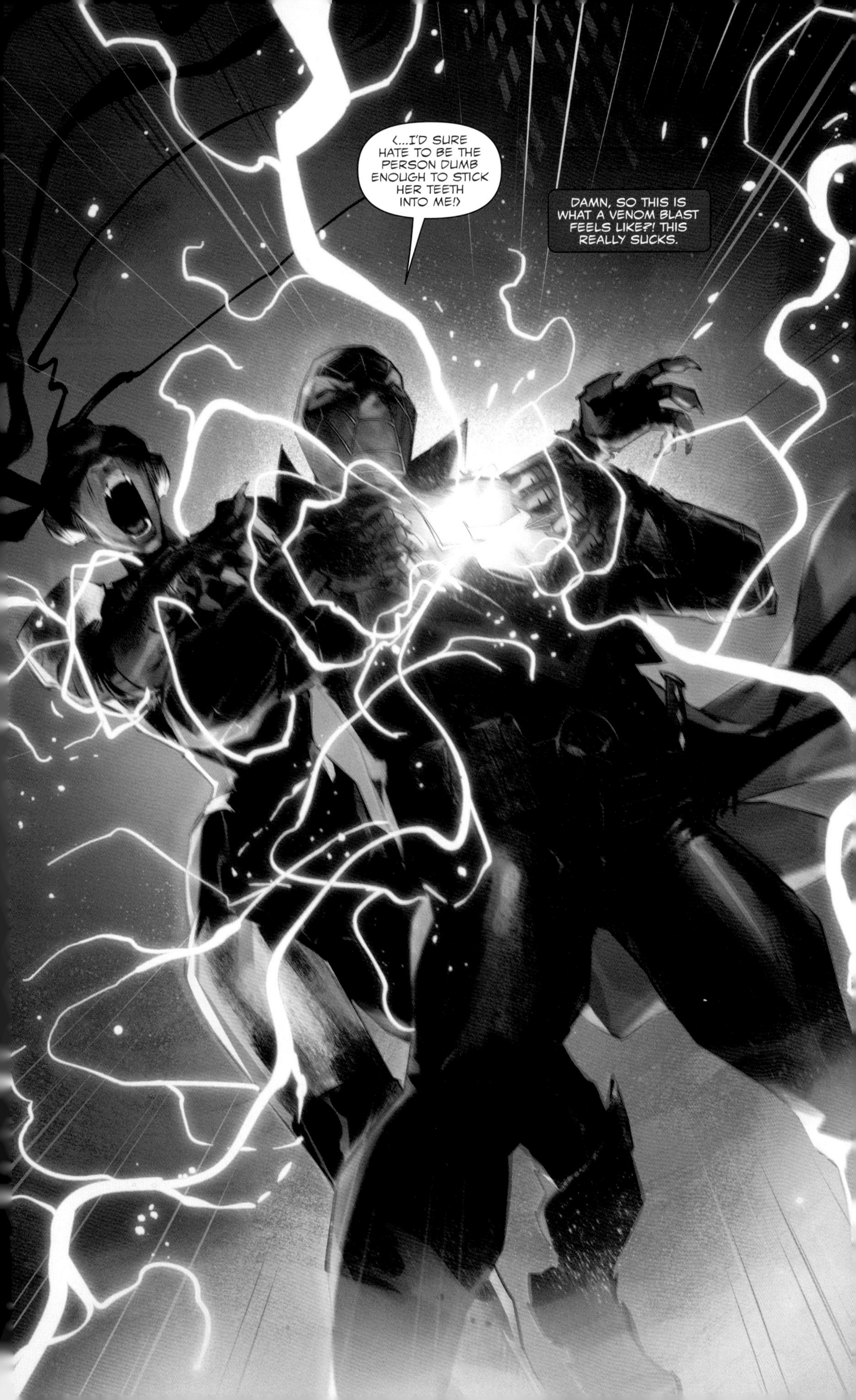
<...I'D SURE HATE TO BE THE PERSON DUMB ENOUGH TO STICK HER TEETH INTO ME!>
DAMN, SO THIS IS WHAT A VENOM BLAST FEELS LIKE?! THIS REALLY SUCKS.

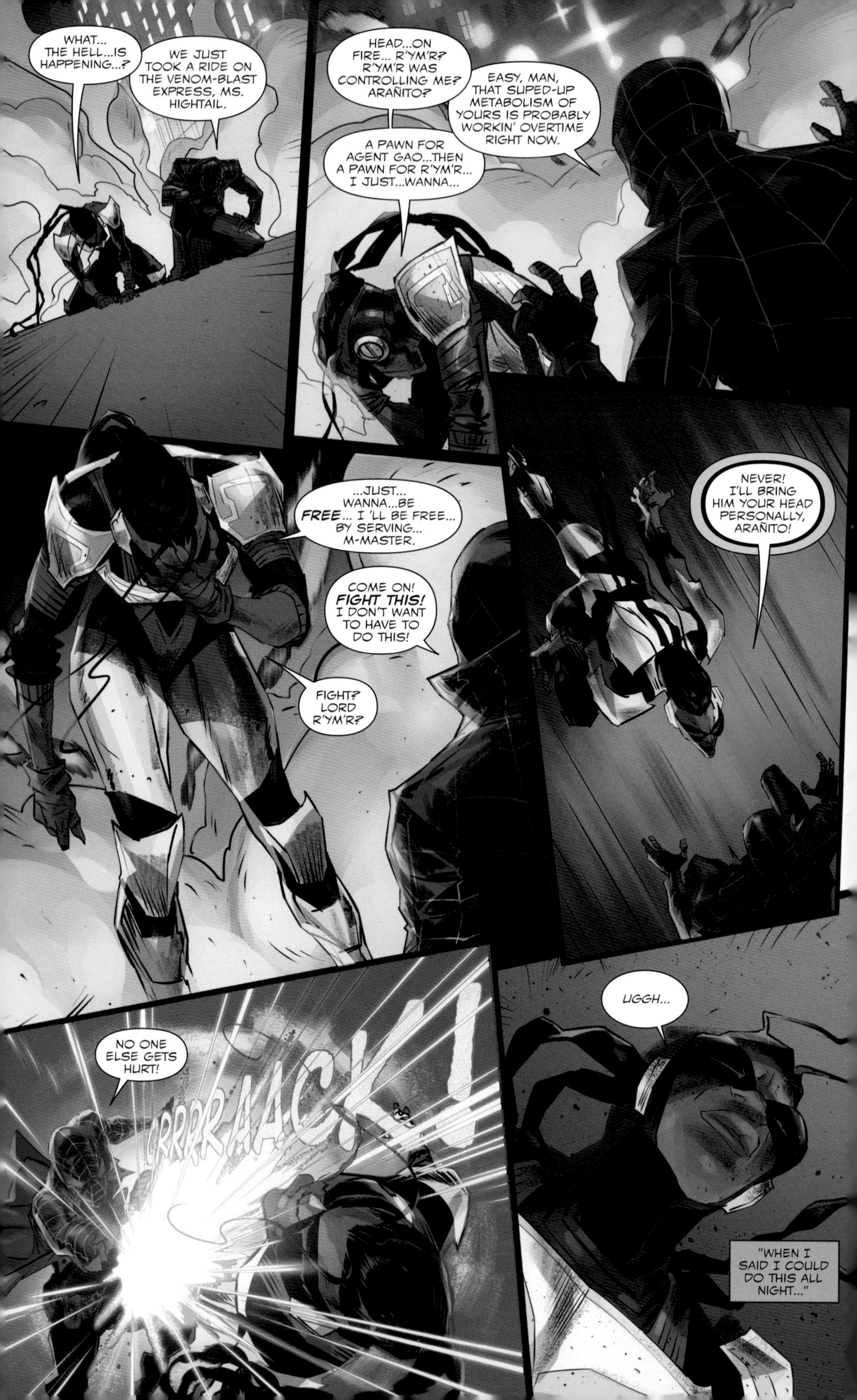
WHAT... THE HELL...IS HAPPENING...?
WE JUST TOOK A RIDE ON THE VENOM-BLAST EXPRESS, MS. HIGHTAIL.
HEAD...ON FIRE... R'YM'R? R'YM'R WAS CONTROLLING ME? ARAÑITO?
A PAWN FOR AGENT GAO...THEN A PAWN FOR R'YM'R... I JUST...WANNA...
EASY, MAN, THAT SUPED-UP METABOLISM OF YOURS IS PROBABLY WORKIN' OVERTIME RIGHT NOW.
...JUST... WANNA...BE FREE... I'LL BE FREE... BY SERVING... M-MASTER.
COME ON! FIGHT THIS! I DON'T WANT TO HAVE TO DO THIS!
FIGHT? LORD R'YM'R?
NEVER! I'LL BRING HIM YOUR HEAD PERSONALLY, ARAÑITO!
NO ONE ELSE GETS HURT!
CRRRRAACK!
UGGH...
"WHEN I SAID I COULD DO THIS ALL NIGHT..."

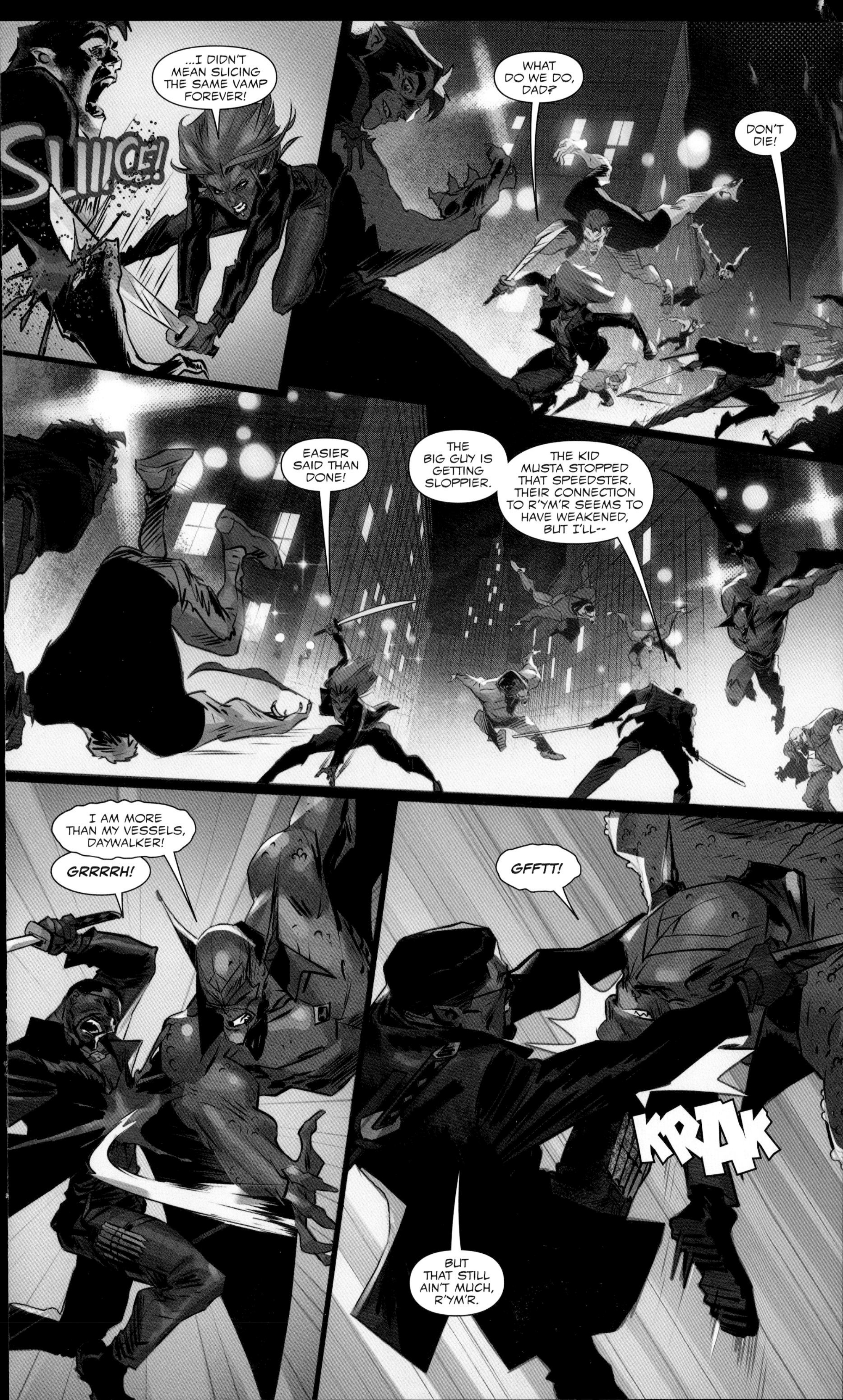
...I DIDN'T MEAN SLICING THE SAME VAMP FOREVER!
SLIIICE!
WHAT DO WE DO, DAD?
DON'T DIE!
EASIER SAID THAN DONE!
THE BIG GUY IS GETTING SLOPPIER.
THE KID MUSTA STOPPED THAT SPEEDSTER. THEIR CONNECTION TO R'YM'R SEEMS TO HAVE WEAKENED, BUT I'LL--
I AM MORE THAN MY VESSELS, DAYWALKER!
GRRRRH!
GFFTT!
KRAK
BUT THAT STILL AIN'T MUCH, R'YM'R.

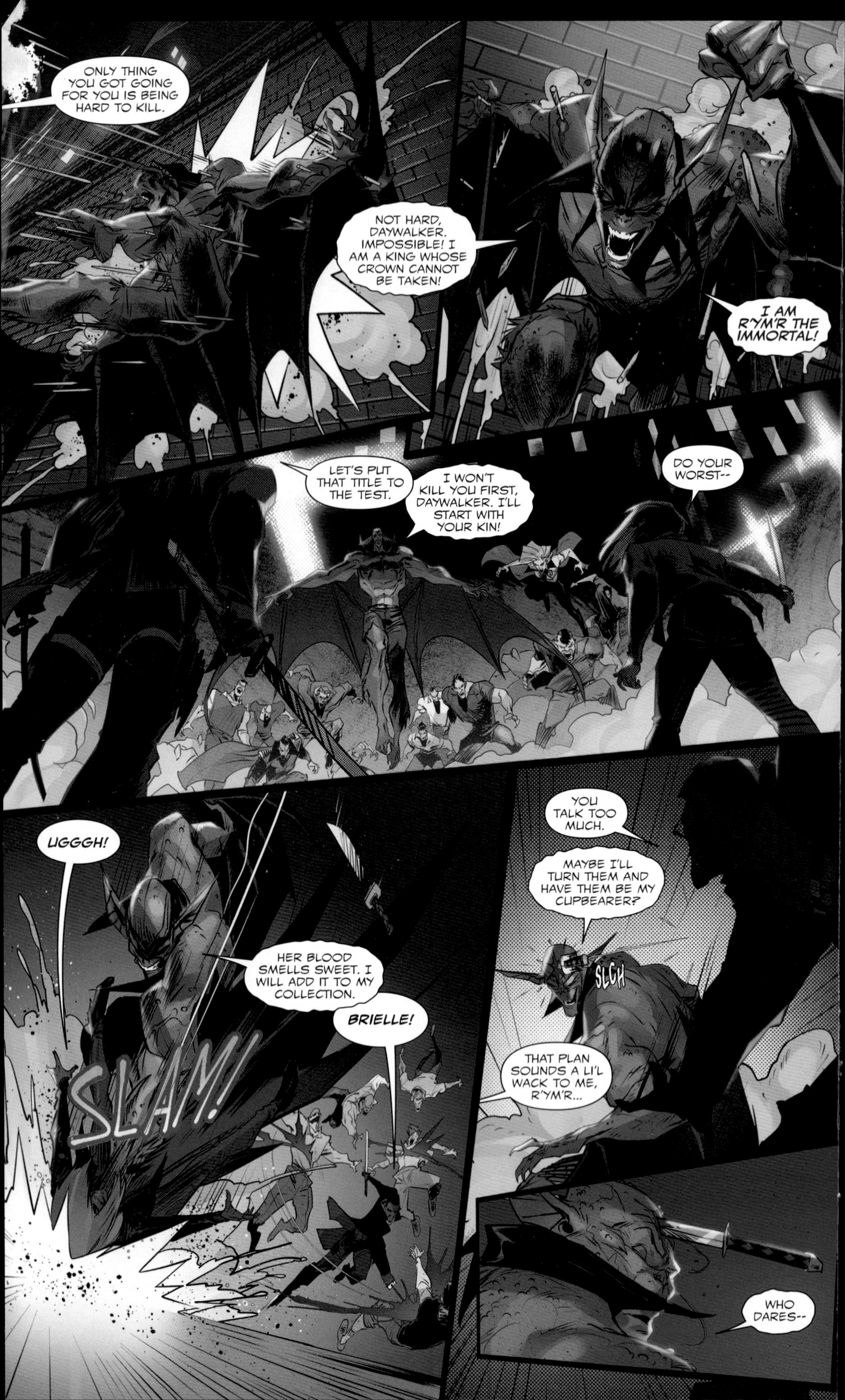
ONLY THING YOU GOT GOING FOR YOU IS BEING HARD TO KILL.
NOT HARD, DAYWALKER. IMPOSSIBLE! I AM A KING WHOSE CROWN CANNOT BE TAKEN!
I AM R'YM'R THE IMMORTAL!
LET'S PUT THAT TITLE TO THE TEST.
I WON'T KILL YOU FIRST, DAYWALKER. I'LL START WITH YOUR KIN!
DO YOUR WORST--
UGGGH!
HER BLOOD SMELLS SWEET. I WILL ADD IT TO MY COLLECTION.
BRIELLE!
SLAM!
YOU TALK TOO MUCH.
MAYBE I'LL TURN THEM AND HAVE THEM BE MY CUPBEARER?
SLCH
THAT PLAN SOUNDS A LI'L WACK TO ME, R'YM'R...
WHO DARES--

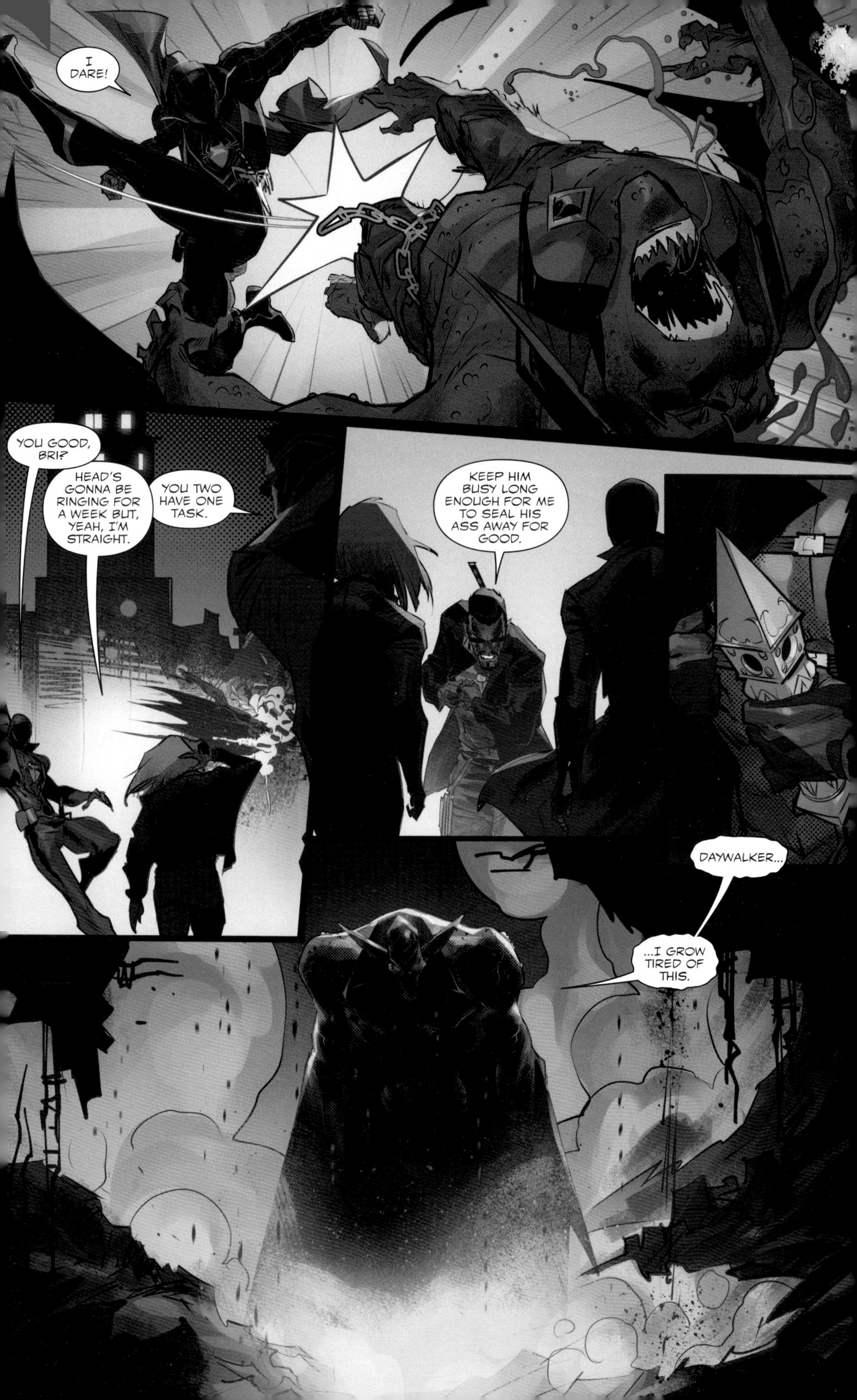
I DARE!
YOU GOOD, BRI?
HEAD'S GONNA BE RINGING FOR A WEEK BUT, YEAH, I'M STRAIGHT.
YOU TWO HAVE ONE TASK.
KEEP HIM BUSY LONG ENOUGH FOR ME TO SEAL HIS ASS AWAY FOR GOOD.
DAYWALKER...
...I GROW TIRED OF THIS.

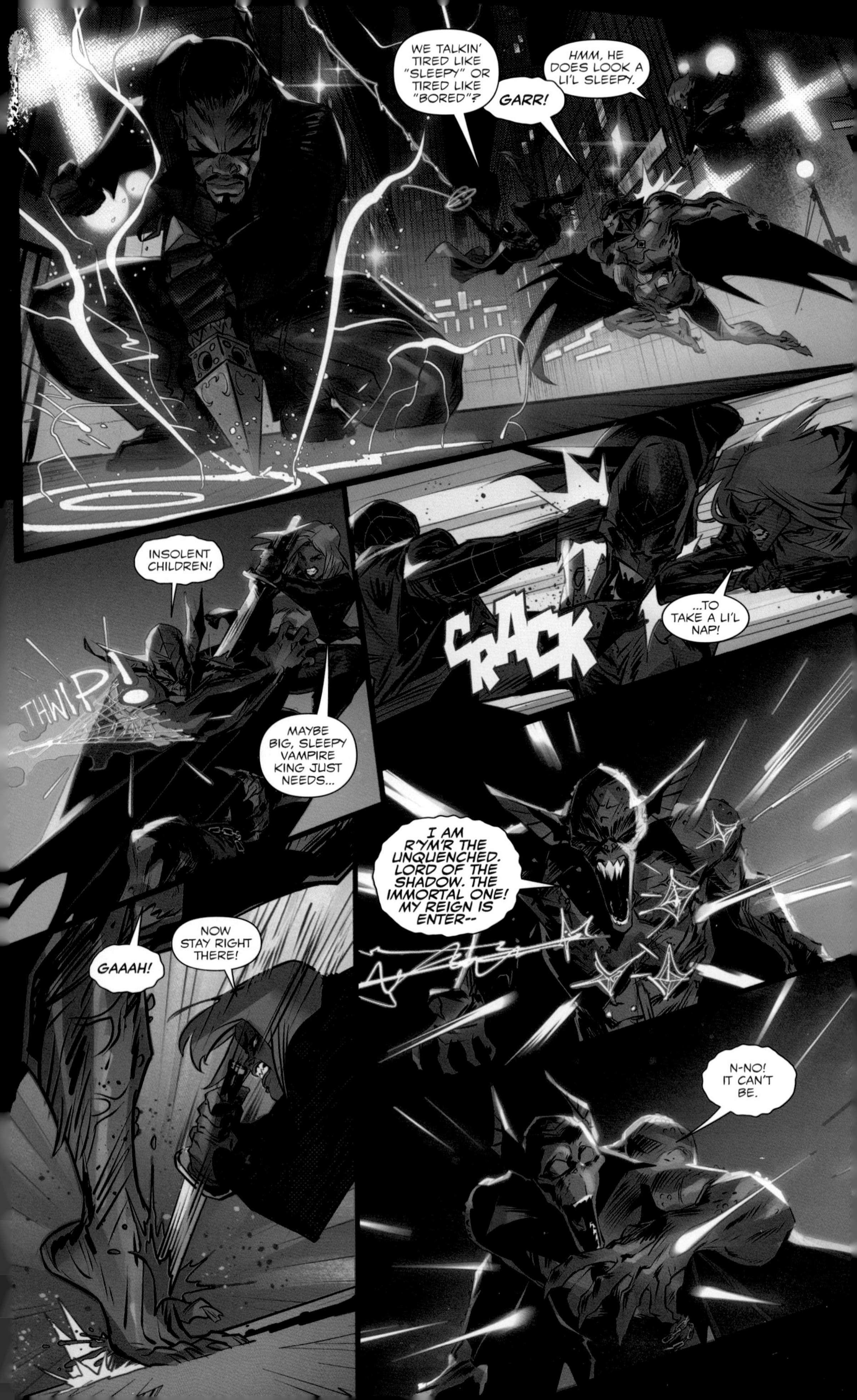
WE TALKIN' TIRED LIKE "SLEEPY" OR TIRED LIKE "BORED"?
GARR!
HMM, HE DOES LOOK A LI'L SLEEPY.
INSOLENT CHILDREN!
THWIP
MAYBE BIG, SLEEPY VAMPIRE KING JUST NEEDS...
CRACK
...TO TAKE A LI'L NAP!
GAAAH!
NOW STAY RIGHT THERE!
I AM RYM'R THE UNQUENCHED. LORD OF THE SHADOW. THE IMMORTAL ONE! MY REIGN IS ENTER--
N-NO! IT CAN'T BE.

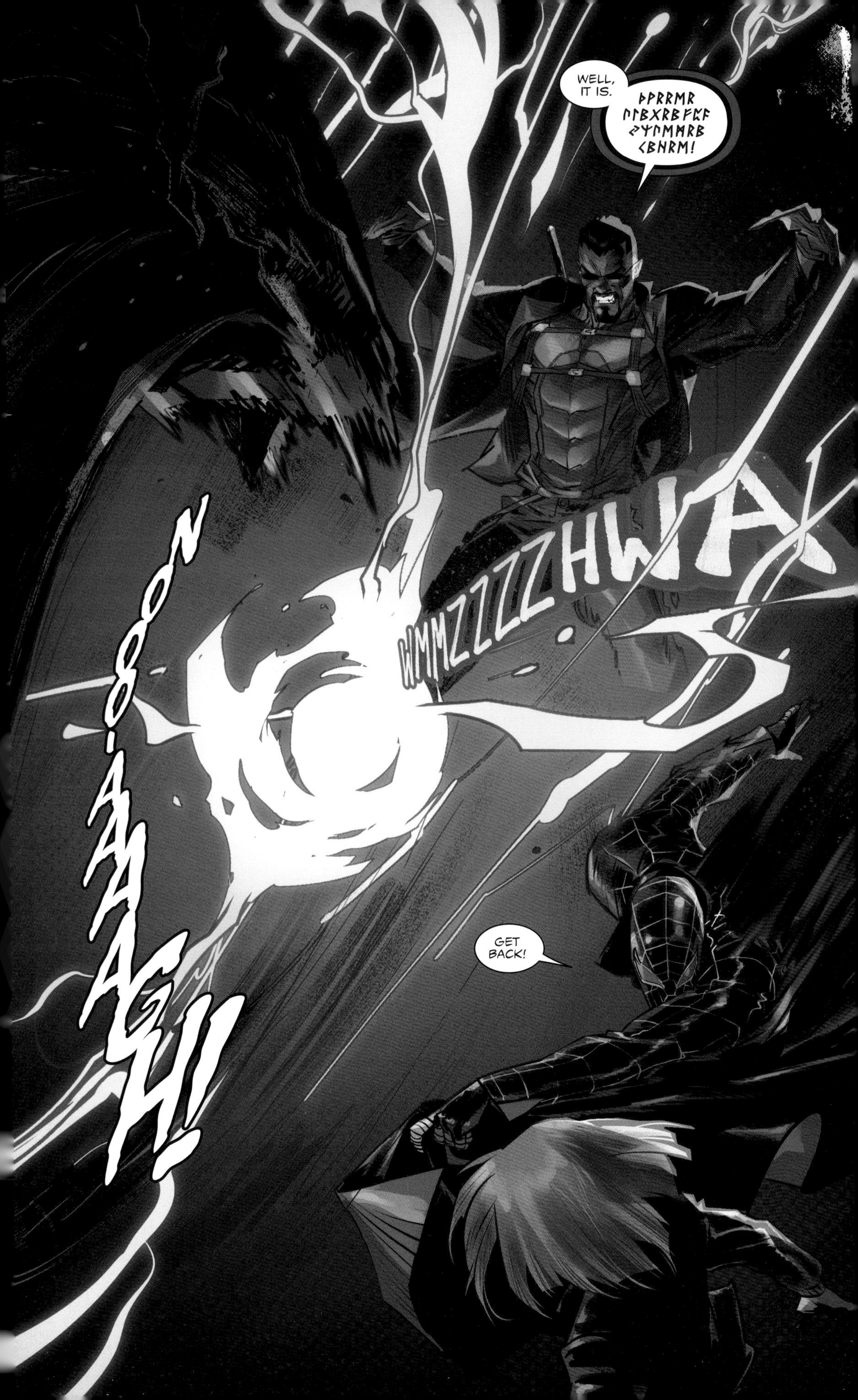
WELL, IT IS.
WMMZZZZZHWA
NOOO-AAAAGH!
GET BACK!

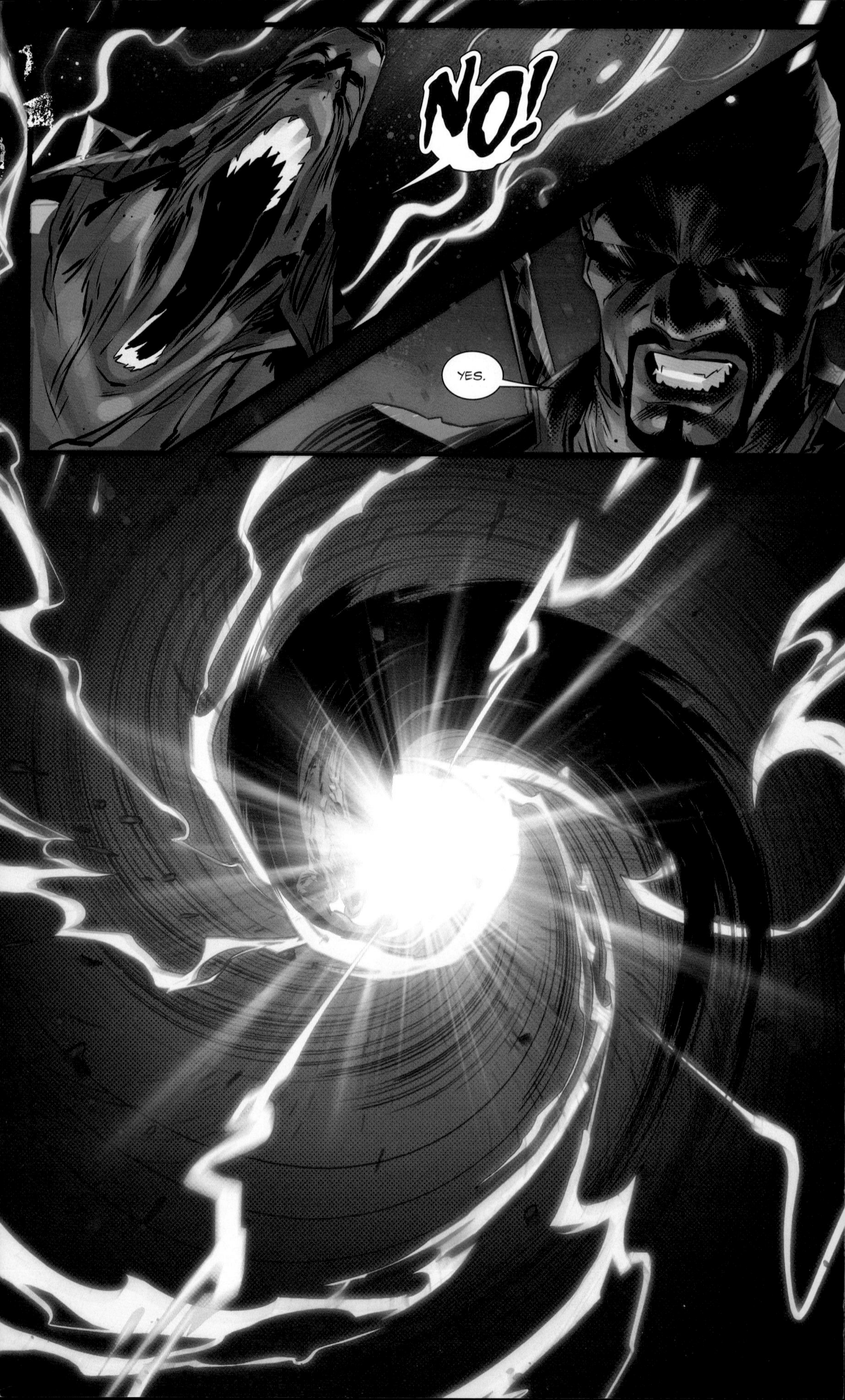
NO!
YES.

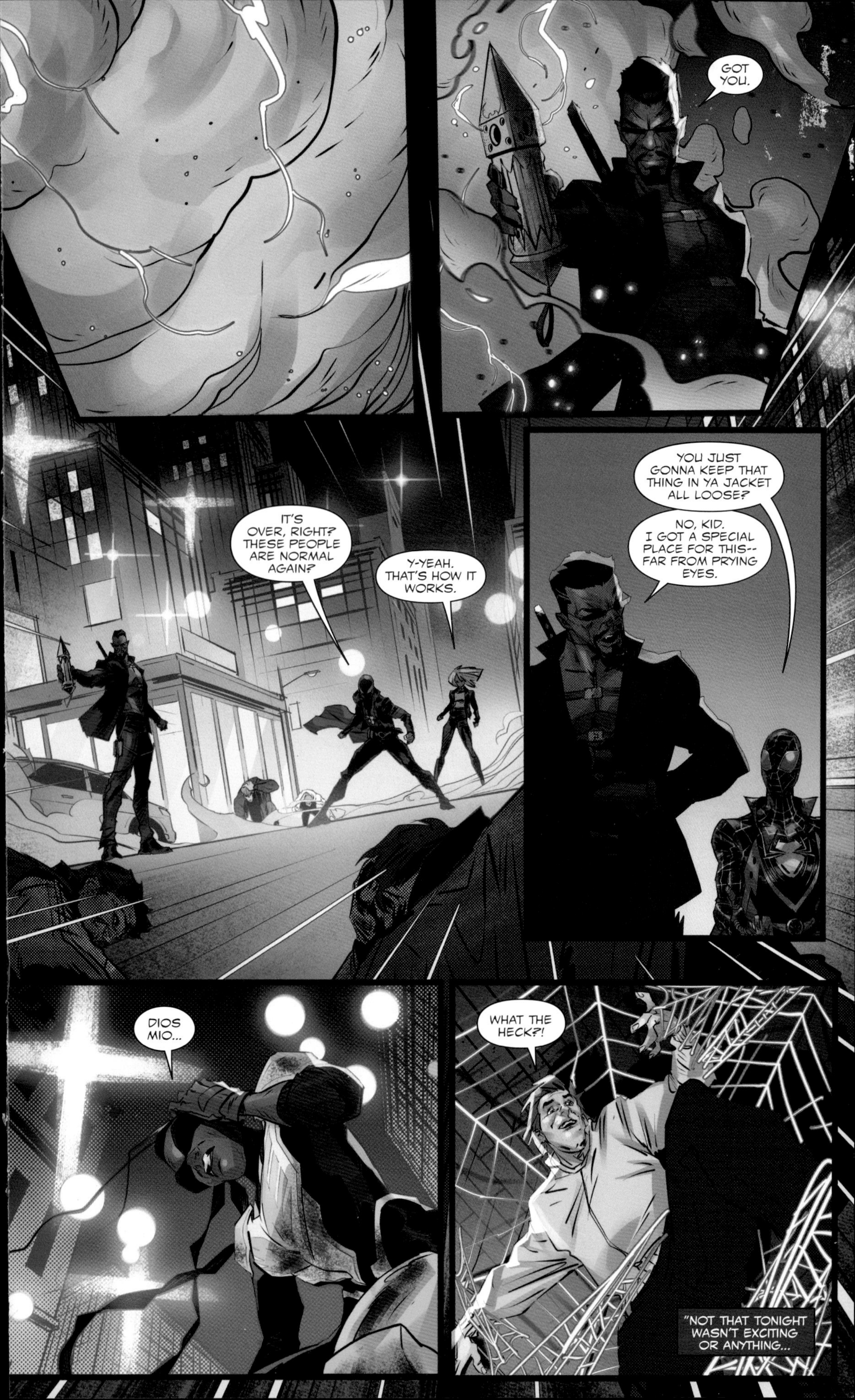
GOT YOU.
IT'S OVER, RIGHT? THESE PEOPLE ARE NORMAL AGAIN?
Y-YEAH. THAT'S HOW IT WORKS.
YOU JUST GONNA KEEP THAT THING IN YA JACKET ALL LOOSE?
NO, KID. I GOT A SPECIAL PLACE FOR THIS-- FAR FROM PRYING EYES.
DIOS MIO...
WHAT THE HECK?!
"NOT THAT TONIGHT WASN'T EXCITING OR ANYTHING...

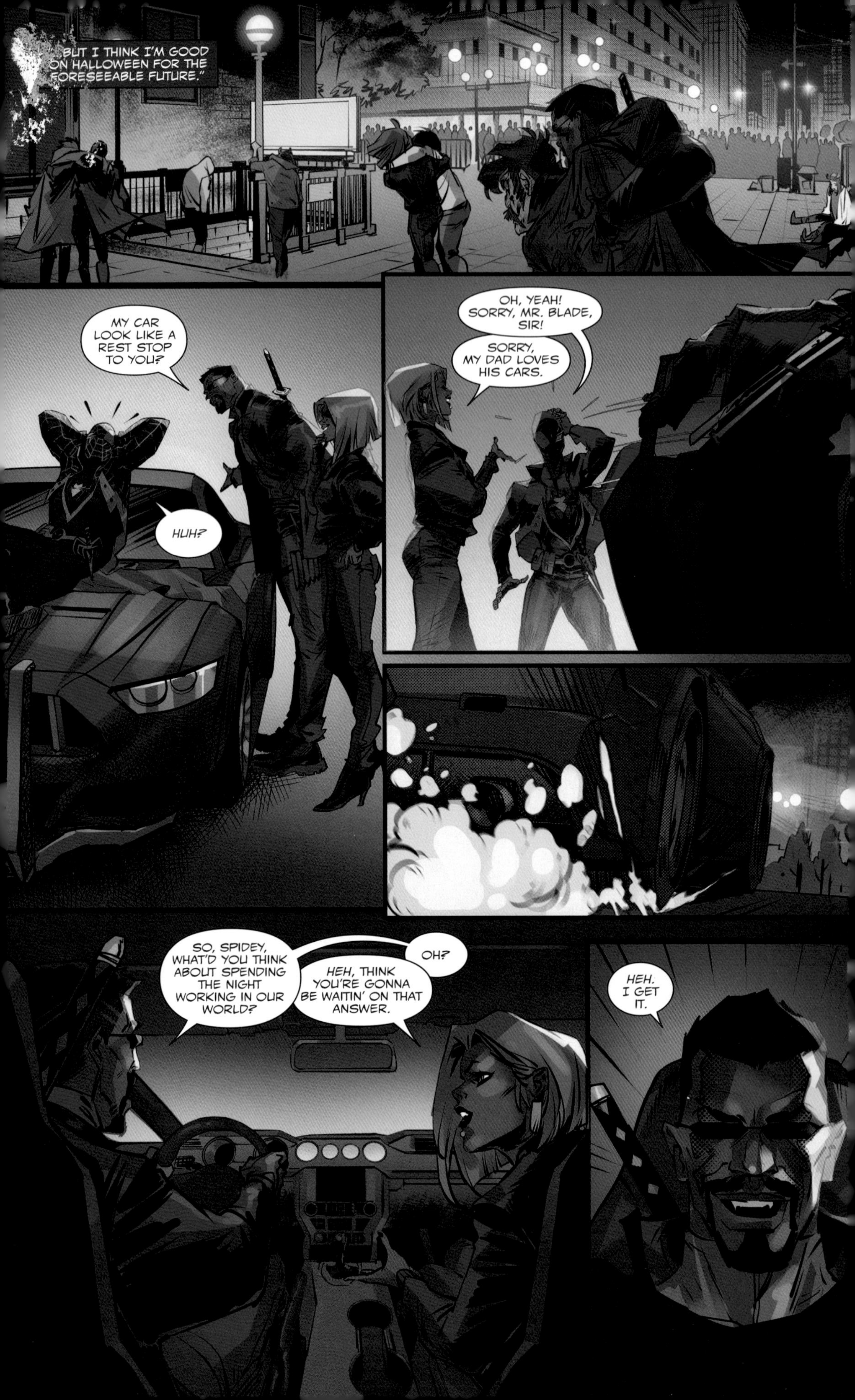
"...BUT I THINK I'M GOOD ON HALLOWEEN FOR THE FORESEEABLE FUTURE."
MY CAR LOOK LIKE A REST STOP TO YOU?
HUH?
OH, YEAH! SORRY, MR. BLADE, SIR!
SORRY, MY DAD LOVES HIS CARS.
SO, SPIDEY, WHAT'D YOU THINK ABOUT SPENDING THE NIGHT WORKING IN OUR WORLD?
OH?
HEH, THINK YOU'RE GONNA BE WAITIN' ON THAT ANSWER.
HEH. I GET IT.

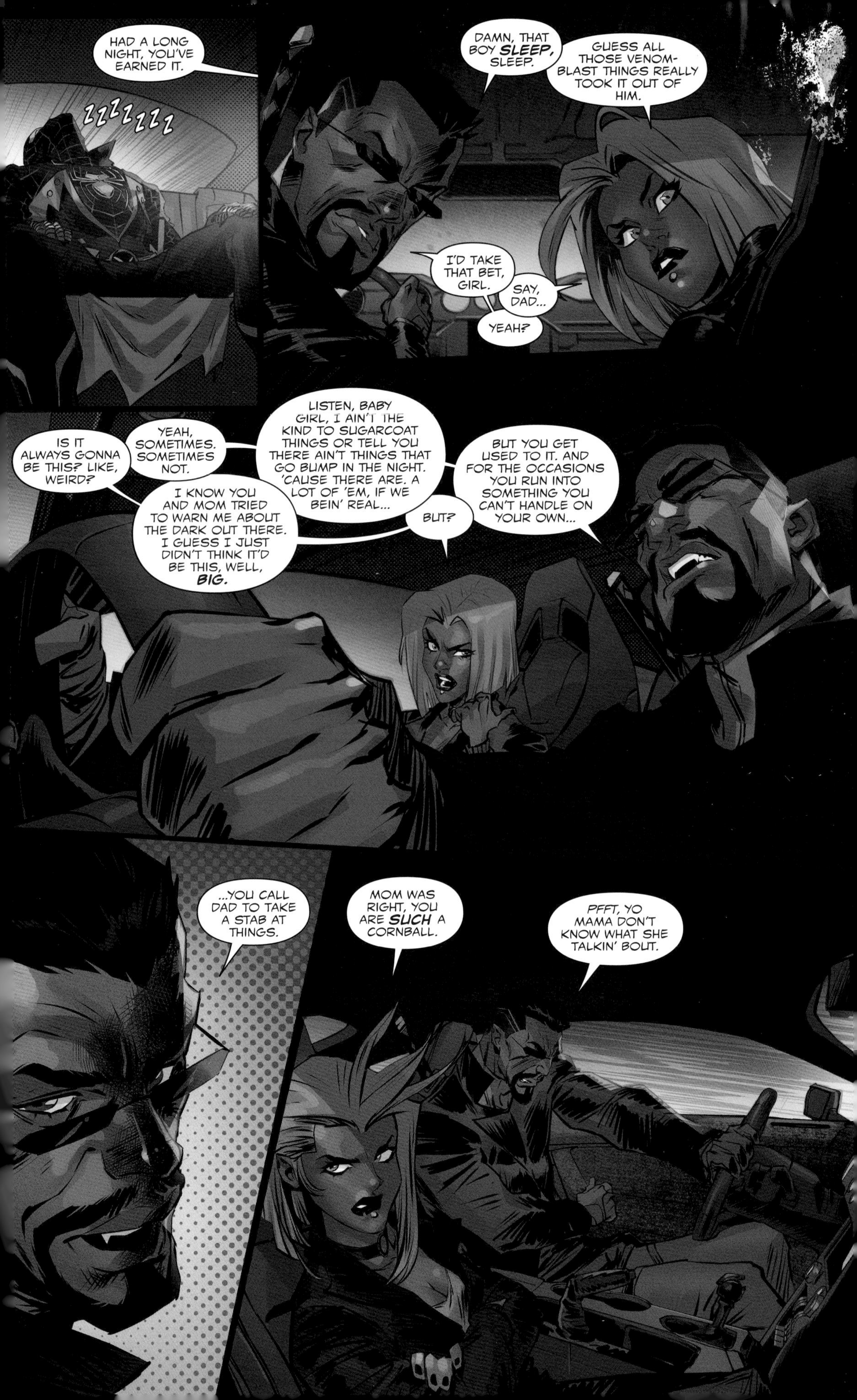
HAD A LONG NIGHT, YOU'VE EARNED IT.
ZZZZZZZ
DAMN, THAT BOY SLEEP, SLEEP.
GUESS ALL THOSE VENOM-BLAST THINGS REALLY TOOK IT OUT OF HIM.
I'D TAKE THAT BET, GIRL.
SAY, DAD...
YEAH?
IS IT ALWAYS GONNA BE THIS? LIKE, WEIRD?
YEAH, SOMETIMES. SOMETIMES NOT.
I KNOW YOU AND MOM TRIED TO WARN ME ABOUT THE DARK OUT THERE. I GUESS I JUST DIDN'T THINK IT'D BE THIS, WELL, BIG.
LISTEN, BABY GIRL, I AIN'T THE KIND TO SUGARCOAT THINGS OR TELL YOU THERE AIN'T THINGS THAT GO BUMP IN THE NIGHT. 'CAUSE THERE ARE. A LOT OF 'EM, IF WE BEIN' REAL...
BUT?
BUT YOU GET USED TO IT. AND FOR THE OCCASIONS YOU RUN INTO SOMETHING YOU CAN'T HANDLE ON YOUR OWN...
...YOU CALL DAD TO TAKE A STAB AT THINGS.
MOM WAS RIGHT, YOU ARE SUCH A CORNBALL.
PFFT, YO MAMA DON'T KNOW WHAT SHE TALKIN' BOUT.

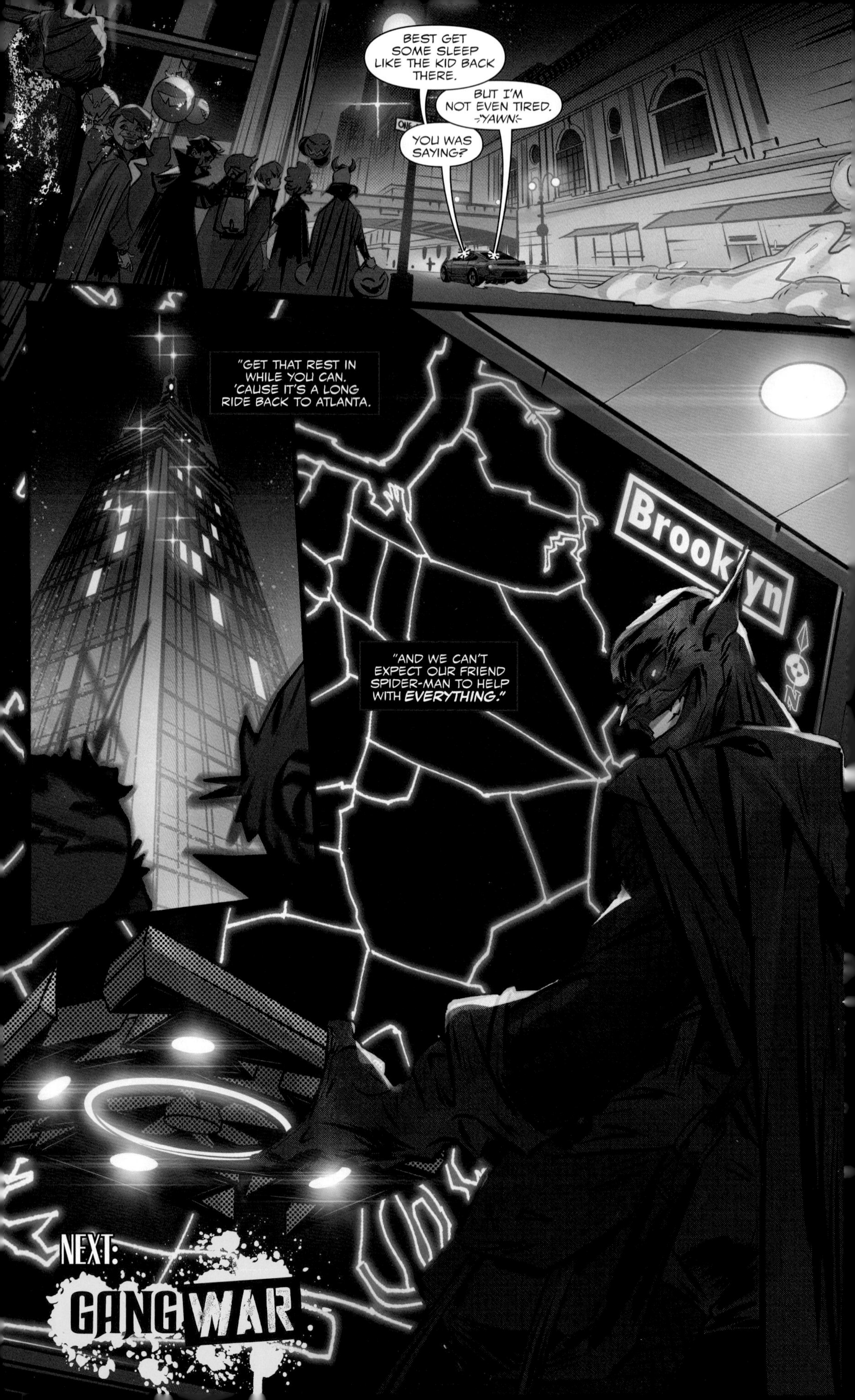
BEST GET SOME SLEEP LIKE THE KID BACK THERE.
BUT I'M NOT EVEN TIRED. -YAWN-
YOU WAS SAYING?
"GET THAT REST IN WHILE YOU CAN. 'CAUSE IT'S A LONG RIDE BACK TO ATLANTA.
Brooklyn
"AND WE CAN'T EXPECT OUR FRIEND SPIDER-MAN TO HELP WITH *EVERYTHING*."
NEXT:
GANG WAR

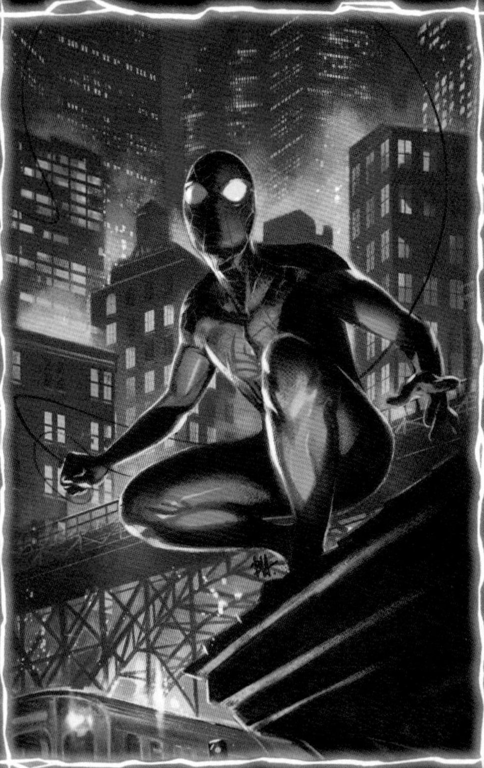

#11 VARIANT BY
BEN HARVEY

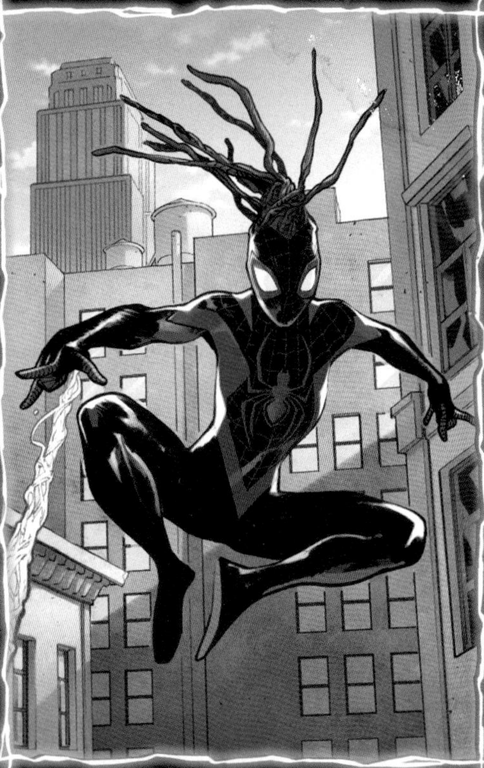

#11 NEW CHAMPIONS VARIANT BY
SARA PICHELLI & FRANK WILLIAM

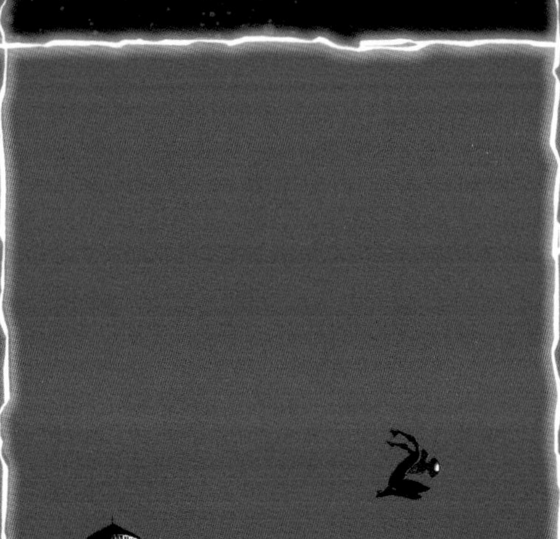

#12 VARIANT BY
DAVID BALDEÓN

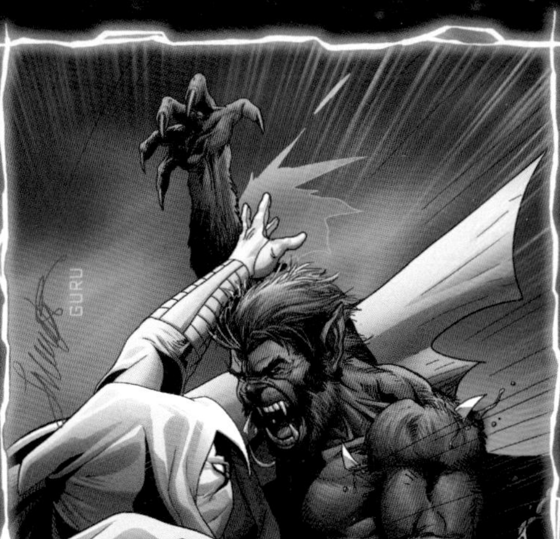

#12 KNIGHT'S END VARIANT BY
SALVADOR LARROCA & GURU e-FX

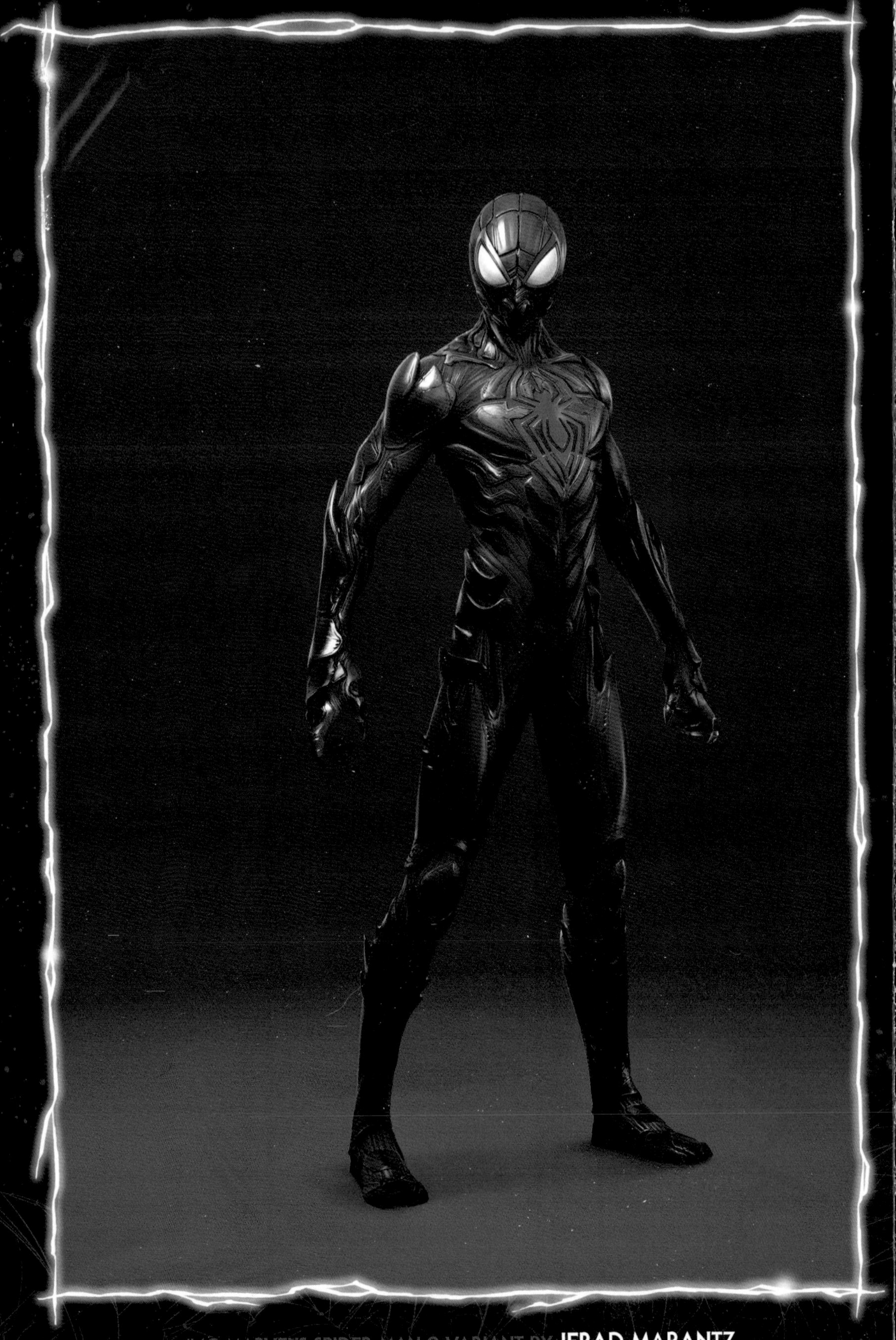

#12 MARVEL'S SPIDER-MAN 2 VARIANT BY **JERAD MARANTZ**